AUTHORITY

EVERY HUMAN'S JOURNEY FROM SLAVE TO FREE

DAVE YAUK

Copyright © 2020 by Garden City Productions and Publications

All rights reserved. No part of this book may be reproduced in any form or by any electronic or mechanical means, including information storage and retrieval systems, without written permission from the author, except for the use of brief quotations in a book review.

Produced in the United States of America

Second Edition Print, 2020

www.gardencityproject.com

ISBN: 978-0-9994673-6-7

For all of those who long for a perfect freedom!

CHAPTER TITLES

Introduction

Act 1 | Scene 1 *Prepared for War*
    Act 1 | Scene 2 *The Diorama and a Promise*
    Act 1 | Scene 3 *The Holy Priesthood*
    Act 1 | Scene 4 *A Servant Leadership*
    Act 1 | Scene 5-6 *The Leper and the Nazarite Comparison*
    Act 1 | Scene 7 *The Glory Equation*
    Act 1 | Scene 8 *7 Lampstands*
    Act 1 | Scene 9 *The Passover Meal*
    Act 1 | Scene 10 *A Wee bit o' Celo'bration*

Act 2 | Scene 1 *Complaints Arise*
    Act 2 | Scene 2 *Leadership Accused*
    Act 2 | Scene 3 *Prayer*
    Act 2 | Scene 4 *The People Rebel*
    Act 2 | Scene 5 *A Pleasing Aroma to the Lord*
    Act 2 | Scene 6 *Korah's Rebellion*
    Act 2 | Scene 7 *The Budded Staff*
    Act 2 | Scene 8 *The Levites*

Act 2 | Scene 9 *A Hatred for the Unclean and Anything Dead*

Act 3 | Scene 1 *Baby Steps*
    Act 3 | Scene 2 *The Enemy*
    Act 3 | Scene 3 *Sex*
    Act 3 | Scene 4 *Progress*
    Act 3 | Scene 5 *Submission*
    Act 3 | Scene 6 *Rhythms*
    Act 3 | Scene 7 *Commitment*
    Act 3 | Scene 8 *Vengeance*
    Act 3 | Scene 9 *Belief*
    Act 3 | Scene 10 *Stages of a Slave*

Act 4 | Scene 1 *There But Not Yet, The Promised Land*

INTRODUCTION

400 years of slavery! Four hundred years of pain, pillaging, and pilfering! Four hundred years of doubt and insecurity securing itself in the very souls of a people that had altogether become convinced that there would never be any hope. Four hundred years of cries that had seemingly gone unheard; prayers that had seemingly been left unanswered, and wounds that had seemingly been left opened to salty bitterness, with little expectation of healing. Four hundred years of a people whose children, lineage, legacy, and dignity continued to rise and fall at the hands of belligerent and belittling taskmasters. Four hundred years of compromise, sin, suffering, and darkness. Four hundred years of broken hearts, defeat, and failure. Four hundred years of bondage!

This is the story of Israel. This is the true story of a people that spent four hundred years enslaved under the pagan nation and leadership of Egyptian rule. Though the Israelite's exile to the land of Egypt was allowed by the hand and authority of God, the hands of the enemy, through the Pharaoh and leaders in Egypt, had anything but the best intent for God's people. They capitalized on God's permission in allowing the people of Israel to be in their care, and they saw it as an opportunity to demoralize and imprison God's people in misery.

To comprehend with our meek and feeble imaginations what life must have fully been like for Israel is truly impossible. It is most likely intolerable for us to fully embrace what kind of mentality must have developed in the people of Israel as their God, whom they at one time believed to be good, had subjected them, sentenced them, and seemingly planned for them such dire and complete humiliation and suffering. Though it is clear that there were those that remained faithful and feared the Lord (Ex. 1:20), one can only speculate as to the effects that such an endeavor had on this people as a whole. Having one's freedom stripped produces a variety of dilemmas, and though some Israelites remained faithful to the Lord, there were others who clearly would have wrestled and struggled with the most unbearable issues.

The people of Israel had endured four hundred years of atrocious slavery at the hands of this Egyptian machine. Most of the Jewish people that had come to live in this land had come to settle there for the sole purpose of having provisions and food for their families in a time of famine. They had first arrived in Egypt seeking help and aid, and Godly men like Joseph exercised Godly leadership and influence over them in order to help the people to receive what they needed to live and prosper. Over the years, the generosity, wealth, and provision of Egypt, in providing for the outcast and downtrodden, turned toward vicious control. Egyptian rule and the Israelite people suffered the death of men such as Joseph, which gave concession to the rise of other leaders of more reviled and evil intent.

Israel now suffered wholeheartedly under the dominant hand of psychopath slave owners, collectively known as the Pharaohs. When Israel came to the very brink of their four-hundred-year enslavement, the current Pharaoh, carrying the current title, took the vision of his reign to a new and vicious height. Having a very clear and defined vision for building a kingdom and a dictatorship that would bear witness to his power and name, he also maintained a deadly fear of the multiplying Israelite nation. His plan in solving his fear and in dealing with the growing numbers in Israel was to build his kingdom and do it on the backs of God's people. With a heavy hand, he transformed the land from a place of provision into a place of poverty. He rejected the God of the Bible and erected altars to other gods around the land. He became so delusional with false worship and power that he even viewed himself as a god. Because of his ever-increasing deceptive self-assessment of himself, he attempted to subject all the people in the land to his authority and power. Due to the prevalence of his pride—as was birthed in selfish-ambition, deceit, evil and darkness—Pharaoh allowed nothing but hurt to come into the lives of those under his leadership.

What emerged out of Pharaoh's self-delusion was a flavored brand of evolutionary natural selection and survival-of-the-fittest mentality. His superiority complex caused him to view everyone opposed to him as inferior, which led to his harsh treatment of God's people. God's family was a threat to him because they acknowledged YAHWEH as the only name above all names. They carried with them the belief that God is One, and this belief excluded and disqualified Pharaoh's claims of being a deity. The spiritual and historical mindset of the Israelites threatened Pharaoh's view of himself and it stood in the way of him creating the kingdom that he desired. Rather than deal with Israel, out of a most certain hidden and secret fear of them and their God, he enslaved them to try and keep them under his control.

The control and abuse of the office of authority left Egypt's culture waste deep in drunken delusion, greed, and false hopes of grandeur. Egyptian authoritarian cruelty was total. The Israelites had been poked, prodded, broken, stabbed, belittled, devalued, and stripped of all their physical, mental, emotional, spiritual, and social dignity. Physically they were overworked. Their bodies were broken and battered during the day and their health deteriorated from long hours in the sun. Though suffering from lack of sleep and hostile work conditions the Israelites were also punished by the Egyptian's manipulative and non-sustaining care. Through their stomachs, God's people were controlled by Egyptian deception. The government provided them food that satisfied to some degree, in order to keep them somewhat quiet in the face of all the ill treatment. Each day brought with it the continued lash of the whip upon their backs, which scarred their skin and their souls. The physical pressure of such torture reached far into the fabric of who they had been and who they were becoming as people.

One can only imagine how this constant torment must cause one mentally to begin to think like a slave. A four-hundred-year period in bondage is enough to cause any well-meaning people group to lose hope. The Israelites apparently lost the ability to see into and embrace a better vision for the future, and they got paralyzed in the moment. They had to survive. Consumed with managing pain and suffering, the struggle caused them to lose perspective on anything else; the constancy of such abuse forces a people to accept enslavement in order to bear it. Their slow-forming delusions of identity began to develop so deeply that they, like other humans throughout history, began to settle into the culture of being slaves.

In this type of environment it would be easy for anyone to become comfortable in it, compromised in it, and completely ignorant of something better. The manipulative banquets and table-scrap-provisions may have at the time become enough to satisfy their dashed and weak desires to some degree, while all the while they allowed for the enslaving manual labor to form and solidify insecurities. If one were to have interviewed them in order to ascertain their view of themselves during this point in time—their identity—one might expect them to say, "I'm a slave."

Can you imagine how emotionally they must have checked out? They had to detach from the torturous mistreatment and hardship or it would have become too unbearable. To entertain any delusion of happiness would only lead to disappointment, so accepting the depression was most likely the norm. In slavery of this extent victims allow suicidal fate to set in. Deep inside, the depression suppresses a person, but outwardly their discontent creases itself harshly into their weather-torn skins. One can only imagine how an emotional callousness would then cause them to interact in their communities and homes in the very same way they are treated in the workplace; men struggling in their homes not to become like beaten doormats after a day of humiliation, or violently angry toward their family in retaliation and bitterness toward the authoritative abusers that had lashed them throughout the day. Women in response might have been left to stand up or back down. Home life would have been difficult to manage as the temptation would always lurk in every shadow in order to entice the people into chauvinistic domestic violence and feminist belittling and control in the wake of passivity and/or aggressive pain. Not to mention that the children became students of this and were inadvertently being trained by what they must have seen; this ill-treatment leading to the creation of a replica generation of passivity and hostility.

Socially, slavery leads to prolific problems. It infiltrates the very depths of societal interaction. A culture of isolation, distrust, alienation, insecurity and skepticism forms. The people of Israel, though hanging on to faith by a thread, must have found it hard not to embrace a cancerous attitude toward everyone and everything—believing everyone to be as hateful as the Egyptians; ultimately causing them to isolate themselves into their own pack and tribe. It's easy to imagine people struggling not to become too individualistic, independent, and anarchistic—socially putting on the face, but inwardly marching to the beat of their own drummer. This dog-eat-dog-fight for survival environment forms a culture of indifference toward one another. People embrace an "I don't care" perspective toward the needs of others, for though they dwell together, it's easy to look out for one's own interests and the interests of only one's own. When it comes down to what needs to be done for the good of the whole, it's easy in this circumstance to embrace a "use or be used" worldview, in that they use everyone for the purposes they need in order to achieve and accomplish what they want and desire for themselves.

If something was needed of them, they had nothing left to give—they were spent. Everything had been stolen from them. The ramifications of this are astronomical. People became objects, stepping stones, and vessels on which to outlet aggression. People were used as tools for momentary pleasure and lust in order to provide a false sense of escape from the state of unrest. Sexual perversion undoubtedly would have run rampant as people sought to medicate their pain; using each other up without regard to the pain it caused. Deceit, manipulation and lying form the undercurrent of the culture as people are forced to protect what is left to them from the authorities.

It's difficult for a slavery mentality not to grow as a people are spiritually mutilated and destroyed by their leaders, and by their own internal struggles to deal with such circumstances. The individualistic and rebellious hatred for authority undoubtedly takes shape in one's heart due to mistreatment by the governing leaders; and the vilest part of all of a growing disdain for leadership is that it ultimately gets projected onto the Master and Lord God Himself.

Though God had always clearly communicated His love to Israel, and had remained loyal to His people by following through perfectly in keeping His promises, His covenants, and His plans, the people who had heard about this good, benevolent, slow to anger, and abounding in love God, began in the circumstances of the current situation to embrace skewed biases of God's intentions. It's clear that the situation became too much to bear and a very prevalent slave mind-set indeed set in. People began to embrace other gods. In their minds, no longer could YAHWEH, the one true God of heaven and earth, be trusted. The people now needed a lord, a master, and someone to lead them. God supposedly had not done it, Egypt had not done it, so following themselves was the only option they had. They needed a sense of safety, protection, rest, and escape and they began scraping around for anything they could find that provided them with a false sense of security. Sadly, in calling into question the entire ethic of heaven, their flimsy hands began grasping for all the wrong things, and they began to fall prey to pluralistic spiritual worship of the Egyptian culture.

In the Egyptian system of worship there were over 80 gods in circulation, including Pharaoh himself. In Exodus 7:14-8:32 it is clear that not only had the Egyptians fallen prey to grasping at these functional, fictitious, nonexistent illusions called "gods," but Israel had as well. From the Egyptian buffet of gods, the people cherry picked from the pantheon of lies—the gods that in their minds best fit their reality and biases—using their own authority and know-how to do so. Their slave mentality produced in them a propensity toward the snares and traps of false belief.

Their society was a version of post-modernity at its finest; everyone fighting for themselves with no regard to others. Everyone believing as they want with no true consideration given to how their beliefs actually affected other people. Israel here is not only enslaved as a tribe, but they individually are enslaved in solitary confinement and aloneness within and around themselves.

And the Lord of Heaven and Earth, the Majestic Almighty, the True God, the God ever present; All-Powerful, All-knowing, and All-Encompassing rose up in His might as a violent storm against the prison system that enslaved His people. He had observed and allowed their suffering to go on for a time, but He had waited long enough for the people to reach their breaking point. A young and forming slave mentality is not solely what rouses God's passionate attention in Exodus, but when the people's fragility caused them to reach to take hold of false gods and false hopes, God's initiative sprung into action.

God waited until depravity reached its peak in idol worship, so that at the proper time He could reveal the height of His ecstasy, joy, and freeing glory. In delivering them, they saw the far-reaches and depths of the goodness that the one true God indeed possesses—the goodness that the Israelite people had indeed forgotten.

God, like a warrior, sounded His call of Deliverance through His messengers, Moses and Aaron, and spoke loudly to them through ten pronounced calls. He said through them to Pharaoh, "Let my people go!" With every command, God exerted His true and only authority over Pharaoh. Pharaoh then began a battle against authority all his own. Pharaoh responded in delusion, believing that somehow he controlled this God YAHWEH. Pharaoh thought he could tame this God. Pharaoh himself was a slave to his belief that somehow he could be a better path to freedom for the earth than the God of Heaven and Earth.

Pharaoh responded to God's advances in absolute stupidity and pride by saying "NO!" He would not let God's people go—or so he believed he had the authority to make this decision. In the wake of Pharaoh's petty tantrum, God began to show forth His work. God was not about to merely come after Pharaoh and only free His people, but God had bigger business to attend to first. He systematically needed to demolish every false hope to which His people had anchored their faith and trust.

One by one God attacked the false premises of the Egyptian land. He attacked their "authorities" and false "masters" that both His people and Egypt embraced. Pharaoh's denouncements and tantrums toward God's commands brought about God's wrath accompanied by ensuing plagues; every plague an act of war against the gods of Egypt.

Against *Osir* the major god of the Nile (the Nile known as his bloodstream), *Hapi* the spirit of the Nile, and *Khnum* the guardian of the Nile, God attacked and turned the Nile to blood, demonstrating His real power over the fake illusion of these make-believe deities. Against *Heqet* the frog goddess who bore the image of a frog and *Hapi* who related to fertility, he cursed the earth with a plague of frogs. He dealt with *Geb, Osir,* and "god of the earth" *Aker,* by sifting up the sand and dust of the land by conjuring up a sand storm that turned into a swarm of lice. *Uatchit,* the fly god of Egypt, goes down in the fight with the plague of flies; *Ptah, Hathor, Mnev, Amnon*—gods associated with bulls and cows—He directly assaults in diseased cattle, and *Sekhmet, Serap and Imhotep*—gods associated with Epidemics and healing, were exposed when the people contract un-healable boils on their bodies. *Nut, Seth and Shu* were believed to be lords over the sky, the land, and the atmosphere and they were attacked in hail. *Serapia* as a protector from locusts was routed by God's plague of grass hopper swarms. *Re, Aten, Atum, Horus and Thoth,* the supposed gods of the moon and sun were attacked in the plague of darkness. Finally Pharaoh's pride, in thinking himself to be god, was attacked in his lineage in the 10th and final plague when God killed Pharaoh's firstborn son—the heir to Pharaoh's make-believe "god-hood" and throne.

God systematically attacked every false god. He destroyed every raised bottle, every karmic idea, every new age crystal, every poisonous substance, every bad theology, every false hope, every comfortable addiction and entitlement, every false belief and educational idea, and He completely took apart the false construct of the entire nation of Egypt, both slave and king.

Freedom! When the construct came down in Egypt, a broken and grieving father, Pharaoh, muttered through his quivering lips, "Go!" In a shear moment of utter dismay, he finally admitted his weakness, and the facade of Egypt's power was exposed for the mirage that it was. In the wake of the onslaught, God, through Moses, led His people in victory out of Egypt across the Red Sea toward the Promised Land and the promised rest that He'd prepared for them.

Their journey out of Egypt did not go off without a hitch however, for we know that Pharaoh had a final lapse of pride, and once again came after the people of Israel only to be consumed by the waves of God's wrath; as the Red Sea parted for God's people but collapsed upon the ensuing Egyptian army. The final breath of victory came in a slow release, but God's people were free!

Though the tyrannical mastery of their false system of leadership and belief were demolished and laid to waste, these people who were now free in reality, still did not think free! This jumbled mess of people had been enslaved for 400 years!! The baggage and the pain that they carried were still fresh in their worldviews, and their wounds were still gaping open. God's people were tender and broken. Perhaps they were more broken than ever before. Not only had they been enslaved, but now this God of Heaven and Earth, whom they had once trusted, had now just assaulted all their comfort, false hopes, and make-believe idols. A dichotomy of fear and joy must have pervaded their souls.

God's act of love in stripping Israel of all that was familiar to them felt like love but also like hate. His discipline and freedom sometimes are unrecognizable and painful. His plan and intentions toward His people in Exodus were still concealed from them in their minds at this point, and their distrust of all things, including God Himself, remained fully intact.

This God was not only getting them out of prison but now claimed to be the sole and only authority over them. In their minds, His Lordship and leadership over them was nothing but a fictitious non-reality. It was only a far-distant memory. They had no real grid for it, not to mention the fact that anything that smelled of "authority" to the people of Israel just wreaked with the flavor of a task master and slave owner.

Israel's expectations of this God were the same as the expectations they had had of Pharaoh. They had known Pharaoh and only his style of oppression for 400 years, and now they projected this same reality in how they believed God would now take care of them. Though their hesitations are understandable and even warranted, their thinking needs transforming. This is what the book of Numbers is about!

The Book of Numbers in the Bible chronicles the aftermath of all that had just taken place in Egypt. It documents His freeing of the Israelite people in their journey toward the Promised Land. As the book of Exodus details the inner workings of God's actual deliverance from Egyptian bondage, the book of Numbers continues the story on as it records what came next. The book of Numbers takes us on a journey and allows us to see into how God redeems His people out of slavery and out of a slave-like mindset in order to train them to know, love, and follow Him. The process for Israel was slow, and the process for every other people group is slow also.

This book will endeavor to retell the story of Israel's journey as they came out of slavery and into freedom. In this fashion, the book of Numbers becomes a deeply profound book to which we can relate. We will be able to see ourselves in it, and recognize how we too have been enslaved by our own biases and beliefs. We too have become resistant to authority because of those that have so hurtfully mastered and ruled over us. We have become battered and bruised by the imperfect idols and affections that we have worshipped. We are forced to deal with what we hold in our hands.

God's storyline for His people's journey toward freedom, and the outline for this book, comes to us from the biblical book of Numbers in which is contained a three Act drama. In Numbers chapters 1–10 we will see the result of God's education and reorientation of the people as they learn His culture, commands, and law at Mount Sinai and in the aftermath of Israel's Exodus. This is Act 1. In Act 2 of the story, Numbers chapters 11–20, we will see Israel's response to God's Lordship and leadership as all their pain and past pretenses toward God bubble to the surface in rebellion and scenes of upheaval, doubt, complaint, and disillusionment. Finally, in Act 3, Numbers chapter 21–36, God benevolently leads His people to the edge of His Promised Land in spite of Israel's failed attempts to turn back, lose heart, or flat out give up.

The book of Numbers gives an honest account of how humanity learns to relate to God. In coming out from underneath what had mastered and lorded over Israel, they came into and underneath the hands of a new leader—YAHWEH. Numbers tells the story of how a broken people leaves an enslaved state of mind—in full rejection of any kind of authority—and undergoes the process of coming under the Lordship of Christ. In a word, this book, just like the book of Numbers, is all about this one idea, *Authority*. Though the God of the Bible is a good and gracious King, Israel's past pain and hurt under the reign of other false masters, fathers, and leaders had left them distrustful. In their distrust and hurt, they projected their view of false "lords" onto the real King of Kings and Lord of lords. This people of anarchy, insecurity, and resistance did not see God's rule and command over them as a freeing, safe, and empowering thing, but they related to it as they had related to Pharaoh. As a result, as we will see in the book of Numbers, every command that comes from God's mouth will ignite anger, passivity, rebuke, and bitter noise in the soul of God's people. Their training under the parenting method and fatherhood of Pharaoh taught and shaped them to respond this way, and a full-regiment of Deliverance is the only remedy.

Themes and Big Ideas...

This book will trace the step-by-step journey of God's people as God's hand guides them through the rehabilitative process toward not merely living free as a human might define it, but in revealing how a human learns to think and "actually" live free in the way God defines it. This book suggests that for God's people to break free from slavery, they need to embrace the Lord's authority. This statement seems to be a bit of an oxymoron at first glance.

This book intends to slowly unravel this idea as seen in the unfolding dialogue between God and His children in the book of Numbers. This book is simply going to record the dialogue going on in God's story in order to mine out insights for us that we can apply to our own journey. As we the readers gaze into the story, we will embrace the full depth of God's Lordship as it unveils itself, and we will most likely see a bit of ourselves in the moments it records. To frame our reading and study of this book, it proves beneficial first, to note some predominant themes that weave their way through the book of Numbers from start to finish. These themes are going to occur frequently throughout the book of Numbers, and we need to know what we're looking for:

Authority & Leadership...

A predominant and overarching theme through the book of Numbers is the Lordship and Leadership of God as He leads His people in and through His people. God's decrees and commands lay the foundation of this book as God is going to tell His people how to act and what to do the entire way. Depending on whether the people listen to God or not will determine their experience, as we will observe in the narrative. We'll observe in Israel how hard it is for the chained human will to surrender and submit to God's ways, and we'll be dumbfounded as we ponder why this is so. It clearly emerges in the story that even though Israel is resistant to God's authority and shelter throughout the narrative, God's authority in the book of Numbers clearly represents *safety* to His people. God's perfect decree is the only thing that is certain to bring perfect rest. God trains His people throughout the journey to see that being under the hand of any other imperfect and false "god" only produces imperfect and empty happiness. There is more that God wants for His people. God wants His people to have His joy. God's authority therefore is something that is safe and is to be desired, not rejected.

Not only are we going to get a glimpse into the authority of God as He leads His people, but we are going to observe how God's human vessels interact with Him along the way. The predominant problem we'll see in Israel is not only their venomous rejection of God's authority, but how it outlets itself in their treatment of Moses and Aaron—their earthly "human" leaders. Though the main human leading characters of the storyline are Moses and Aaron, it is God's decree, commands, and direction that will be breathing through them the entire way. Through these characters we will see the invisible God as He relates to real human flesh and through human flesh. The response of the people to God's ways and to the authority He puts in place in Moses and Aaron is colorful and dynamically emotional. Everything about this book relates to real life, real struggle, and the real issues that a real God has in leading and governing a real and rebellious people into real rest.

Journey & Story...

The context of this book is a *journey*. The reader will notice that Numbers is written in historical story form. This book, *Authority: The Human Journey | From Slave to Free*, is also written in a journey-like fashion. It is framed by the outline of Numbers itself and unfolds tidbits of experience in Israel's sojourn as they experienced it. From beginning to end, this treatise gives us a snapshot into the real timeline of how God transforms and interacts with His people. His movements are anything but instant and impulsive. God patiently, compassionately, and in a calculated way, designs the journey of Israel down to the last mark. Every moment in this book is to be read with great anticipation, for each moment unearths a different set of lessons that progressively nurtures and shepherds the hearts of God's people into learning to trust, obey, and honor God. The journey is not pretty, it feels more like surgery, but through it, the people emerge in greater health, and God's beauty emerges all the more.

Type & Redemption...

This idea of *typology* is a theological idea that emerges often in Numbers. Within the timeline of the Old Testament, typology is predominant in how events, people, and places point to and foreshadow the coming of Christ. All of these types—or foreshadowings of Christ—serve as *sign posts* in our journey. A signpost is not the destination itself, but it points to the destination's reality. Every moment in this book is going to point to the reality of Christ and His redemption of His people through the gospel. The characters, structures, places, designs, and focal points of the story are going to serve as hidden treasure chests all throughout the book of Numbers in order to remind us about the Messiah, the true treasure Himself; who undoubtedly led Israel through every step of their journey.

The reverse is also true. In looking at the Old Testament we can see things in *antitype* form—things that are antagonistic toward the character and plan of God. These events, people, or things present the opposing realities of evil and darkness, which are in opposition to God. All of these signposts are going to inform our view of how God awakens His people from a dead slumber. He not only takes His people on a trip, but in it He teaches them that their redemption and freedom is unlocked in every encounter along the way.

Prayer...

In almost every chapter, and over 88 times in the book of Numbers, we observe an interchange between God and His people through a prayerful conversation. The Lord speaks, and the people listen; the people speak, and God listens and responds accordingly. This is the rhythm of prayer. The theme of prayer in the book of Numbers is a hidden and often overlooked gem of this regularly avoided book of the Old Testament. In taking time to make mention of its role within the story of God's people coming under His Lordship again, we catch real glimpses into the nature of prayer itself. Prayer is not presented in this book as something formal, regulated, overdone, or underused. Prayer is seen as ordinary. Prayer is seen as something that should invade the daily space of our minute-by-minute lives. It cannot be overused, but it can be maligned in turning it into something that it is not. Faith and guidance under our Lord's authority will ultimately rise and fall depending upon whether we learn this artful language of heaven—prayer.

You...

This story, although it is not your story, is certainly going to mimic your story. There are real people in this book who are following a real God. This is as real to you as you are to yourself. I would invite you to enter the Numbers painting and allow it to absorb you into its swells. Read it as if you were one of the characters within its bounds. It will expose you, it will enrich you, and it will envelop you into a rapturous experience of faith. The people of Israel will serve as a mirror to your soul. In looking at them you'll see yourself. Your deep-seated rejection of authority in various areas has led you to slave-like-thinking and a profound lack of *safety* and *protection*. You may be enslaved right now in the most profound sense, in that you are living every day without Jesus and His salvation. You may be, on the other hand, walking with the Lord, but you are journeying into a greater experience of freedom with Him. You might also be freshly on the other side of something God has already delivered you from recently, and may view the journey through Numbers as a chance to reminisce about what God has just done with you. I can tell you one thing, no matter where you are, if you're not dead and in heaven with Jesus, then there is more work to be done. If you let God's authority operate on your enslaved and worn out mindset, and repent of your deepest rebellions toward Him, He'll begin to open up real freedoms to you as He draws you lovingly out from underneath what masters you, and into the shade of His protective care.

The Journey Begins

Come with me. Like Israel, stand on the banks of the Red Sea as you watch your task masters and Egyptian overlords sink into the deep in the wake of God's all-consuming victory. Rejoice in the victory that is found only in God's deliverance by the power of His victory over the enemy and over your sin and slavery. Celebrate with all those around you and relish the fact that your freedom is <u>complete</u>. But now, let's turn our attention to the journey, and admit that though our slavery is over and our freedom is complete, we still think like slaves in many ways. Let this journey teach us not only how to be free, but how to live free—under the beautiful authority of God.

PART I
ACT 1

PART 1

ACT 1

1

SCENE 1

PREPARED FOR WAR

To set the stage for Numbers, we must mention briefly what transpired directly after Israel left Egypt. In leaving the land of Egypt, God immediately made known His leadership over and in front of His people. The Bible tells us in Exodus 13:17-22 that God led the people by day in a cloud and surrounded them in a pillar of fire by night. The authority of the Lord, like a nursing mother in tender embrace, surrounded this company of people in loving power, protection, and provision.

They needed this assurance. One can only imagine what would have been in the people's minds as they left Egypt. First of all, picture the multitude. For example, just two years later, at the beginning of Numbers, the company of men who are listed in Numbers 1 with the ability to fight are alone 603,550. Numbering the women and children would prove to put the number of such a group well over 2 million people at the very least. Though at the time of the exodus this number was less intimidating to a slight degree, a group of this size must have traveled around dumbfounded, delivered, and delighted in what had just happened. Nonetheless this new reality must have felt surreal and overwhelming. It would make sense that the reality of all of what had happened would come screaming to a halt in one loud resounding question; "What are we going to do now?"

The nights were fast and immediate, and they needed shelter, they needed food, and they needed direction. They needed guidance and provisions for an inevitably long and strenuous journey toward wherever it was they thought they were headed. Soon the questions came pouring in. The doubts came flooding in. Two million people who had known nothing but slavery were now looking around and wondering "what are we going to do with all these people?" There was no longer a government in place, there were no laws, and seemingly, though these people were following God's pillar of fire in the sky, they must have still been wondering how this was all going to hold together. Out of Egypt came all of these people following in Moses' train; a people who had, for the longest time, fallen prey to self-protection and survival. They were following God, but still looking out for themselves.

Because God as a good Shepherd is always fully aware of His people's pain and perspective, God quickly dealt directly with many of the questions arising in their minds. In real and tangible ways, beginning with their miraculous deliverance from the bondage of slavery, God begins the journey of building Israel's faith in Him. His intention was to continue this restoration process in addressing some of His people's fast approaching and anticipated stressors.

First, by way of a pastoral and pictorial parable, God led His people to a stream of bitter water, which He intended to be a proper place in which to speak with His people. As the people came to the water and found it to be bitter, He explained the stream's meaning and how it represented the bitterness they harbored for all that had happened to them in Egypt. God assured them that He knew of their hurt and that He was committed to their healing. Through a miracle, God made the spring sweet before their eyes in order to communicate to them that He was going to get rid of their bitterness, and in Exodus 15:26 He voiced His promise to them as they surrounded the freshly healed water: "If you will diligently listen to the voice of the Lord your God, and do that which is right in His eyes, and give ear to

His commandments and keep all His statutes, I will put none of the diseases on you that I put on the Egyptians, for I am the Lord, your healer."

Shortly after this, God again and again proved His loving loyalty to His children. He did so by giving them miraculous food from heaven to eat called manna (Ex. 16), He provided them water from a rock (Ex.17:1-7), and He even fought for and amongst them against the Amalekites, which is the first hostile tribe they encountered on their way out of Egypt. The Lord solved any issues the people had with proper management, governance, and oversight when He organized them for civil, social and financial accountability (Ex. 18), and in a protective miracle from God's hand—when Israel was once again pursued by Pharaoh who had bitterly changed his mind about Israel—God completed His people's deliverance.

As Pharaoh rushed Israel and pinned them against the Red Sea waters, God raised up a great tempest swell to part the Red Sea and lead His people to safety. God purged the earth of Pharaoh's pride when Pharaoh and his pursuant army drowned as the Red Sea waves came crashing in on their heads. In Exodus 14:30-31 it says that this final act of God birthed in the people of Israel a genuine heart response. They "saw the Egyptians dead on the seashore. Israel saw the great power that the Lord used against the Egyptians, so the people feared the Lord, and they believed in the Lord and in His servant Moses." The people's trust and affections had been won over afresh by the hand of God's power and might.

Their traverse continued to the base of Mount Sinai where in Exodus 20-24 we are given the account of how God visited His people through Moses at the location of a mysterious mountain. The people camped at the base of this mountain and began the process of complete restoration. Even though Israel had come a long way since their deliverance a short time ago, their faith was still new and based off a set of experiences they had had during their salvation event. It is only fair to say that much of their ideology and theology was still grounded in the false duplicitous foundation that they had embraced while living in Egypt. God fully knew that their faith was not yet grounded in the truth. He had to move them to a place of believing and trusting in who He was and is, rather than only trusting in the miracles that He had performed.

God wanted Israel here, to know His thoughts, know His ways, and know the culture of His love. As He gathered them at the base of Mt. Sinai, it was there that He spoke into Israel's calloused, syncretistic, pluralistic, and idolatrous mindset to reiterate and communicate to them the law of His love through the 10 Commandments.

The revealing of God's law produced a diverse response in the Israelites. Their time at the base of Mt. Sinai revealed a great amount of truth from the heart of God to His people, but it also surfaced an idolatrous, immoral, and a still rebellious response that sprung from the still immature and broken hearts of the people. The season spent at the base of Mt. Sinai was crucial. God spent time exposing His people to His ethic and teaching them His ways and revealing how much their thinking had been swayed and perverted during their 400-year enslavement. God's law only seemed to amplify their slave mentality and unveil it. Rather than responding to the Lord in love, they had lost the ability to feel any sort of bond or love toward an authority. As a result, they reverted back to old patterns of religious ritual, rule-keeping, and works-based worship.

Against the backdrop of the Exodus the book of Numbers is framed. After the Mt. Sinai law was read, sent out, and implemented in decree, God began to prepare His people to move out of the wilderness of Sinai and on into the Promised Land. What had happened amongst God's people in totality up until this point was God's Deliverance and God's instruction of them. He had gathered Israel completely under His wing, and He had fully instructed her in the ways in which she should depend on Him, organize under Him, and believe in Him. But Israel's understanding of the full breadth of all that had happened, and their application of the ramifications of all that they had been taught, remained to be seen.

The journey toward the Promised Land would be to unearth the very real and broken foundations that still lay hidden in Israel's thinking.

We now arrive in our context in Numbers 1 as God once again numbered His people before ordering them to get up and move out from the base of Mt. Sinai. Although this is not the first numbering of the people, the reason for this second numbering was to ready God's people to remove themselves from the Sinai wilderness and begin their treacherous journey toward the Promised Land. God makes no apologies in what He does in this numbering, nor does He keep secret what is about to happen to Israel in their journey. God began in setting the people's expectations rightly for their journey, in that He began ordering them for war.

In Numbers 1:1-16 God speaks to Moses and tells him to take a census of the people. The purpose of this numbering was to assemble all the fathers, the clan leaders, and the heads of families together to record the amount of men that were among them that were capable to lead and capable to fight. This allocation was necessary, but most importantly it was ordered by the foresight of the Lord.

The first instance of prayer in the book of Numbers shows up right in Numbers 1:1. God "speaks" to Moses and orders the census. God meets Moses in the temple on a specific day, in a specific place, and at specific time to interact with His child Moses. Moses positions himself before the Lord by obediently giving his schedule and time to the interaction, and out of a relationship between God, Moses arrives at the specifics that are pertinent for the next phase of Israel's journey. The authority of God therefore drives this census. Moses' leadership comes through prayer, Moses' influence to speak to God's people is birthed in prayer, and the protection the people experience under Moses' care comes as a result of Moses submitting all of his will to the Lord. Moses seeks not to serve himself in his prayers, nor to call down a laundry list of happiness for himself, but his purpose in prayer is to seek the Lord's heart for the good of God's people. In this first instance God leads this newly saved tribe toward His will and course of action under the protection and guidance of Godly leadership and spirited prayer. This is

God's plan to prepare His people for war, both then and on into today.

Israel in this context is most certainly about to enter a war. Though their limited vantage point cannot see the obstacles ahead of them, they are about to traipse through the desert, and they need to trust the Lord's authority to see for them what they cannot see. Prayer connects them to this foresight and secures their hope in things they cannot yet see. The elements shine down upon them, the ensuing tribes are not about to welcome them, and the greatest struggle and hardship they are about to encounter is about to swell up from within their own ranks. The reality is that their journey will be a fight and a battle. The reality of war is as present then as it is now. This context of their war results from the same tainted root of sin that caused their slavery in Egypt.

The world is saturated with the consequence of sin and unfaithfulness. The world's kingdom is in colliding opposition to the Kingdom of God and it results in manifested tension. Israel came under the grip of Egypt by tapping into a dependence upon the world, and their trek out of slavery, bondage, and sin, brought its own set of consequences. With Israel having been enslaved in Egypt for so many years, it allowed foreign nations to occupy the land that was meant for them; their absence, in places where they should have been in the first place, welcomed in disorder, chaos, and ungodliness.

Israel, about to walk through the hostile countryside that they themselves had taken part in forming, was a place created not by their *presence* but by their *absence*. Their reclaiming of the Promised Land required a journey back through the enemy-ridden road that they had allowed. This journey was going to be a journey of repentance. It was not going to be easy. Sin and destruction's pull had lain waste to what God intended, and was about to reveal to Israel its challenges.

God is with them in this war, nonetheless. God is leading them and taking care of them through and in their frailty, like He always has. The act of His numbering here in Chapter 1 of Numbers is not solely about war, but it is first and foremost about the faithfulness of

God. God is most certainly readying them, but most importantly He is reminding them. In the numbering of the tribes, God retells His story of covenant to His people as far back as the promises He had made to their forefathers.

As he numbers Reuben, Levi, Judah, Issachar, Zebulun, and Dinah, it becomes apparent that God had remained faithful to His love for their mother, Leah. Leah was the woman that Jacob had married inadvertently and unknowingly through the trickery of his father-in-law Laban (Genesis 24:29-60). Jacob never intended to marry Leah because she was unbecoming and ugly compared to her sister Rachel. However, here we see that Leah's lineage in Reuben, Levi, Judah, and Simeon produces a rich harvest which results in the formation of the largest tribes. Not only had God remained faithful even through the seemingly humble beginnings of Leah's offspring, but many of the tribes remained in existence due to God's provision and multiplication of them even amidst and through their immorality, multiple marriages, adultery, and unfaithfulness, and in spite of their trickery and deceit.

Even after seemingly detrimental mistakes had seemed to foreshadow a destructive end for Israel, God had proven His care for them, and His care continues here in Numbers. Israel had lost the Promised Land from the historical choices they had made. They had failed, and they were weak, but God still remained steady. God's care for them is based on a covenant He had made with them. God's numbering here reminds them more profoundly of His fight on their behalf through all their years of their disobedience, as much as it now prepares them for the war they are about to fight. God's faithfulness had not dwindled, and His promise to Abraham to make him a great nation still proves fruitful. Even though it seems that the sins of Israel had constantly diverted their attention through all kinds of distractions, God's work in them never faltered.

Israel's numbering bears witness to the faithfulness of God and it clearly also anchored Israel's hope once again in the promises of God that remained still intact in spite of them. This ordering sobered them and readied them to the very real reality of what their sowing had reaped. God, in exposing His faithfulness to Israel, as juxtaposed against the backdrop of the war entrenched country of their journey, calls for their dependence upon Him. God not only readies them for the reality of all they are about to drudge their way through in order to get back to where they were in the first place, but He secures them within His hand to steady them securely in His peace.

In ordering the multitude here in Numbers Chapter 1, God provides a sense of safety through the method by which he organizes the people. He began ordering the people into families (heads of the home), He then moved to clans (extended family), then into forming tribes (clusters of families), and then in Chapter 2, God orders the people into standards (networks of tribes) around the tent of the meeting. The approach and process of such a numbering was intentional. Its process was done in order to communicate purpose to the people even through the actual numbers themselves.

In beginning with the heads of the households, the men, the God of Heaven reestablished the protection of the home. Similar to their great grandpa Adam, Israel had seen a legacy of permissive fathers go before them. The fathers had grown insecure and/or belligerent in their treatment of their families as a result of what was done to them each day at the hands of the Egyptian whip. God's plan was to structure the family again—to restore the hearts of the fathers back to their children and their spouses. Since the Garden of Eden, which began with a man protecting and expanding the Garden and with the creation of a beautiful wife to help in the task, God's foundational image had always found its origin and best expression in the home. To reassemble a people that would bear His image, God first needed to restore the ethic of the Garden by reforming the family.

It's interesting that in Numbers 1:47-54 there appears to be a Garden overtone developed as a sub-plot to God's reordering of the family. If we are not careful we might miss it. Amidst all the numbering for war, God picks out the tribe of the Levites to be set apart for service to the temple and to the protection of God's worship and Holy Dwelling. This setting apart of the Levites is held in conjunction with God's numbering for war. Not only had the sinful fall of man affected the family unit, and caused the breakdown in order, but the day Adam fell in the Garden, along with his decision, also came humanity's fall from the presence of God. The office and mantle of leadership that God had given Adam—the place of father/husband and as priestly overseer—needed to be restored and made intact once again. God's restoration needed to come into both spheres again.

Two sides of leadership needed restored. The fathers and warriors, who were to battle with the sword and shovel (protection and provision), needed a restoration to courage, and the priests needed to stand in the gap for the people as in a bloody war because a battle for safety was about to rage—they were to sacrifice animals on the people's behalf as a sign of forgiveness to God's people. The animal symbolically stood in the place of a people as a sign of God's restored presence. The sacrifice was to bear their penalty of death as a result of their disobedience. All the while, the sacrifice was to ensure that God's forgiveness would still be made available to them, even as the wrath they deserved would be delivered upon the animal to satisfy God's justice.

The context of war in the streets, home, and religious life resulted from the withdrawal of God's connected presence. The separation that caused an apparent divide between sacred and secular needed to be destroyed. All of life needed to be lived for God's glory and unto and under God's Lordship. In the community of Israel, God's ultimate plan was to restore the division between the trenches and the temple, the street and the Holy, the church and the culture. The people needed redemption through the presence of God and in His delivering power. God is committed to both.

Extending out from the nucleus of a family-like center, a true community formed, as clusters of extended families grew for the purpose of greater support and connection. This ultimately resulted in the formation of tribes. Over all of this were the heads of the home, the leaders of the family, and the head of the tribes. Men were assigned leadership of their fives their tens and their hundreds as originally inspired by Jethro's advice to Moses in Exodus 18.

The origin for this ordering, we must remember, came through God's direct command to Moses. Therefore, there is a fundamental purpose that God has in communicating to His people through this process. In the numbers themselves, He reminds them of His faithfulness and authority over them. In numbering them in the way He does —in regard to family—He reminds them of their faithful responsibility toward each other. This disconnected and disheveled tribe was to see themselves as family. They were to commune once again, be together once again, and look out for each other once again. These Israelites had forsaken their authority to serve each other because they had lost their submission to the authority of the Lord.

The breakdown of male headship and leadership as exemplified even in the Egyptian system of government led to danger, unrest, abuse, neglect, torment, uncertainty, disbelief, and hardened hearts. God here restores His leadership back to the people through the twelve elders of the Israelite tribes under the oversight of Moses.

It is important to realize what God is doing in Israel. In preparing them for the task of war, He robs them out of their individualism and false belief that isolates them like sheep among wolves. He retrains them through His law and Word, and He assembles them into a family of families again to receive the shelter and safety they need as they step out together into a hostile environment.

Slavery drives wedges between people. It alienates father and mothers from each other and from their children, and it possibly even goes so far as to tear biological families apart as slavery brings death, deportation, and the disarray of the home environment. Orphans and widows abound, and a nagging feeling of fear resides still as a burning ember.

God systematically continues to attack this slave mindset as He carefully and slowly unravels Israel's past. This tribe is like a newborn and battered infant and it needs parents. Though the victory of coming out from underneath the weight of a sinful, dark and deep oppression through the waters of God's salvation and deliverance is fresh in their minds, their growth, formation, and betterment is ensured only within the confines of a safe community. This community will assure some measure of effectiveness as they continue on in the journey. This community-life is to fasten them to the support, to the hope, and to the storyline of God's faithfulness; a storyline that they undoubtedly need to cling to through the bumps and doubts that are fast approaching.

2

SCENE 2

THE DIORAMA AND A PROMISE

After ordering the people into families, clans, and differing tribes, the task then became to organize the camping arrangements so that everyone had a space and area to call their own as they lived, served, and traveled together. In Numbers Chapter 2 God turns His attention away from the small family units and toward the bigger family dynamic of the whole nation. God not only attempts to build a family in and through Israel, He establishes a culture of redemption.

In Numbers Chapter 2:1 we again see the authoritative voice of God speaking to Moses and commanding him to put the people in *standards* for camping purposes. Standards were not the tribes themselves, but a group of tribes clustered together. The purpose for ordering these tribes into the giant sub-groups was for land purposes, civility purposes, but more greatly to exemplify the ultimate purpose God had in His work in and through Israel. God proceeded to order these tribes into their different groups around the tent of meeting that housed His presence; which was placed in the center of the encampments. In 2:1-8 God orders Judah, Issachar, and Zebulon around the East Side. In 2:10-17 he arranges Reuben, Simeon, and Gad along the South Side; in 2:18-24 He orders Ephraim, Manasseh, and Benjamin along the South Side, and finally in 2:25-33 He orders Dan, Asher, and Naphtali around the West Side.

It is as if in the specific ordering God tries to set up something more than a mere arrangement of people and parts. It is almost as if God creates something, molds something, or even models something of Himself and His story into the fabric and DNA of this setup. In order to see what lies under the surface of Numbers Chapter 2, we need a tangible example that might frame for us the intent of this passage.

A great example that will set the stage for what is going to emerge as we mine out what is here in these verses is to consider the concept and process of how one creates what is known as a *diorama*. Dioramas are those little crafty shoebox displays that kids create in 1st grade that are assembled for the purpose of resembling and pointing to something greater. The child takes a shoe box and fills it will figurines, sand, rocks, sticks, and leaves, all pinned against a blue background, and this craft is to look like and represent what things must have been like in cavemen days. Another child dresses their diorama in tumbleweeds and cowboy hats to look like the 'ole west, and yet another child makes a colorful display of coral, fake fish, and cut out paper water bubbles to create the illusion of the ocean floor.

The dioramas are insignificant in what they are in and of themselves, but they point to something real—they tell a story. This is how it is in God's diorama in Numbers Chapter 2. His encampment is created with the intention to order and organize the people in a manner that points to something greater and more real—God's story. In order to discover the full intention of God in this chapter, we have to do a bit of mining into the actual names of each tribe. The titles of the collective tribes themselves are important, and they tell a story that alludes to the greater promises of God.

First God begins with the East Side of this little arts and crafts show as He starts placement with the tribe of Judah—which means "praise," Issachar—which means "to bear a burden," and Zebulon which means "dwelling place." These names are pronounced and purposeful in their meaning, and in order for us to understand in detail what God is doing through the meaning of these tribes and their names, it is most important that we first understand in Scripture what the East represents. Laying this foundation will help us to understand the rest of this chapter in its meaning.

In Scripture the East is a significant coordinate. A foundational element that helps us to understand the meaning of this placement comes to us first in the Garden in Genesis 1-3. The Garden itself was placed *East* of Eden. This Garden, provided to Adam and Eve by God, was a place to experience His power, His presence, and His leadership. Most importantly, this place in the Garden was where Adam and Eve particularly encountered and experienced in depth the *glory* of God. In the Hebrew, this word glory comes from the word *kabod* which implies a weighty presence. This weighty presence is known throughout Scripture as the *Shekinah* glory (that which dwells).

Moments of Shekinah glory in the context of the storyline in Numbers are seen in the pillar of fire and cloud by day in the Exodus (Ex. 13:20, 21), as well as in the consuming cloud and thundering light around the top of Mount Sinai when Moses received the law (Ex. 24:16). Though this shaking presence of God was powerfully "awe" full to the sinful and broken people of Israel—for they had become so far removed and defiled in their once prolific purity before God— this *kabod* and *Shekinah* presence for Adam and Eve was *home*. The glory of the Lord was a perfect tent of dwelling, and a satisfaction to Adam and Eve. Amidst this tent they experienced joy and power, and they were tantalized by the weighty and intoxicating presence of the Triune God. The idea of this glory as being a home, a shelter, a protection, a shade, and a banner of love that swayed over the Garden as Adam and Eve as they dwelled in security, should captivate our thinking as we delve into the ideas contained within Numbers Chapter 2.

When Adam and Eve forsook their place in the Garden in rebellion against God, the glory of God had been lost to them. Colossians 3:23 says, "for all have sinned and fallen short of the *glory* of God." This place of *home* became the most significant thing that Adam and Eve lost. They had lost a sense of protection, power, provision and priesthood that had been theirs within the Garden's confines. As a result, they were issued a punishment, in that a Cherubim was placed and stationed on the East side of the Garden to protect it and ensure that nothing imperfect ever entered its safety—this included all of humanity. This is what has produced to this day a sense of loss in the souls of every human. On down the line, and further into the Old Testament, this loss of *home* is often dramatized in the priests throwing down the burnt offerings to the east side of the altar, which conjures up the image of what is gone, what has died, and what has been given up on account of sin. Due to the increase in sinful worship and human imperfection, in Ezekiel 8-11, the systematic loss of God's presence even from the temple is described. As a result of perverted idol worship that had come into Solomon's Temple in that time, the glory of the Lord slowly left the temple and again alienated people from God's most intimate presence just as had happened in the Garden of Eden.

The East is a powerful symbol throughout Scripture, and now that we understand it briefly, let's return to the names in God's *diorama*. The encampment on the East Side of the Tent of Meeting bore witness to far more than an organizational structure. It bore witness to the praise (Judah), the rest (Issachar), and the dwelling place of God (Zebulun). This side of the tent of meeting was to proclaim and remind the people of the rest and glory that existed in God—a *home* for His people. The reason that God built this into His little drama of history is in order to create a culture within Israel. God wanted His ethic and dynamic of *kabod* glory to work into the very ethos and fabric of Israel's life and tapestry. He wanted everything people do to point to His glory; to seek after His glory, and to aim at His rest and victory.

This is not the current feel within the culture of Israel, as seen exemplified in the names of the tribes that are ordered next—the tribes dwelling along the South Side of the Temple. Along the South Side of the temple dwelt the offspring of Leah. Reuben's name means to "see my affliction," Simeon's name means to "hear my affliction," and Gad's name means "troop and invader." This is a far different cry than that of the hope-filled meaning of the East Side Gate. Whereas *glory* and *Shekinah* can also refer to a dazzling beauty, the lineage of Leah's heritage in her boys Reuben, Simeon, and Gad, is based in drab ugliness. Leah had been known as the black sheep and the ugly duckling in her community. Her life symbolizes rejection and turmoil. Her life symbolizes tarnished bronze and a wounded life. Her life points to the state of all of humanity in light of God's *glory*. Whereas the East Gate exemplifies God's reminder and cry for *home*, the South Gate is humanities reminder of the *affliction* of their *homelessness* in the tide that flows out from sin and disobedience. The South Gate sums up all of human history; standing as a sign post within the culture of Israel's encampment, causing them to remember and reflect upon the slavery that resulted from forsaking God's home.

This story of glory and sin, as juxtaposed together, is indeed not the end, nor the point of God's intended pictorial diorama. In setting it up, He most assuredly wanted to paint a picture for Israel about what they had lost, and He most certainly wanted them to be aware of their current state. However, His plan reaches far deeper for them. In Numbers 2:18-24, God placed three more tribes around the Western edge: Ephraim—which means "fruitful increase," Manasseh—which means "forgetfulness and forgiveness," and Benjamin—which means "son of my right hand."

God's covenant made to Abraham is still in effect, and His plan to multiply His people had never vanquished. Though God's people had left their home and were now enduring all its darkening effects, God is on the move. This pursuant God pursues His lost and disheveled prostitute—like a woman wasted and used up within the world's system. The West Gate is included to proclaim that such a promise still existed. Benjamin, also included, though the smallest tribe, means "son of my right hand." In Scripture, the right hand is the hand of power. God's goal in forgiving His people here is not solely to raise Israel out of the fire and rescue her, but to purify her and raise her up in her weakness to be used in great strength and power. Her pain is to become her praise.

In Numbers 2:25-33 God's glorious image is summated with His conclusion to this little diorama. With the name Dan—meaning "judge," Asher—meaning "happy" and Naphtali meaning "wrestling," located at the North side, a circle of redemption and promise is enclosed within the encampment of Israel and within Israel's history. God's goal and ultimate end is to rule in favor of His people's betterment. His finale to this storyline is to sing a song of exuberant joy—joy based in the fact that this human war and wrestling would one day completely cease. God plans to transcend the plight of Israel's journey. He plans to move beyond their ever-present danger and desperation to place them upon His wings in order to soar like an eagle to His heavenly rest. The trajectory and movement around the encampment proceeds from a *home lost* because of *sin embraced* on into a *brokenness that's forgiven* or *a restoration that heals*. Pay attention to the order.

This *diorama* points to something greater, a greater truth not only contained here but elsewhere. This encampment alludes to God's plan not only for Israel, but points down the road further into Israel's history in the restoration of Jerusalem, and into the Kingdom of God itself. It points first and foremost to a restored Jerusalem, and ultimately to a restored *all* in the person of Jesus Christ. To gain a picture of such a concept, let's look briefly out into Israel's future into what they cannot see. Let's begin by examining the rebuilding of the city of Jerusalem and its wall in the time of Nehemiah. In Fig. 2.1 we can observe some similarities to that of the encampment in how the enclosure is laid out, but we can also observe some profound differences that are informative in helping us to know how to understand Numbers 2 as it fits into the grand narrative of Scripture.

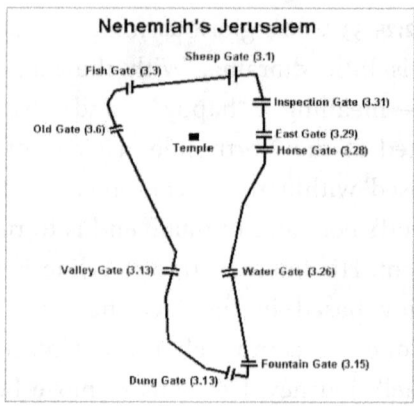

Fig. 2.1

Though the Nehemiaic wall structure is more of a "blown up" view of the encampment that we see in Numbers Chapter 2, it profoundly expresses a truth that needs to be known. In Numbers 2, God's order of operations in describing the encampment begins with the East, moves to the South, then to the West and finally to the North. The progression moves from *home, to sin, to forgiveness, to restoration.* In setting things up this way, God reminds Israel of their roots. He preaches to them regarding how they lost sight of glory in their affliction. He speaks life over them. The encampment itself contains His promise to still pursue them and bring them joy. This is where God meets Israel. Fresh in their affliction, He speaks to them tenderly.

In the record of Nehemiah's construction project however, the order of operations proceeds symbolically in the opposite direction, as we'll see—*restoration, forgiveness, sin* and *home.* Whereas the Numbers grouping begins in the East and ends in the North, Nehemiah's vision starts in the North and ends in the East—a broader picture of what is to come in Christ.

On the North side of the encampment, where God's joy, judgment, and cessation of wrestling and struggle had been, there now is present in Nehemiah's Jerusalem-layout a Sheep and Fish Gate. Where there had been on the West of the encampment the legacy of multiplication, forgiveness and increase, there is now along the Jerusalem wall the Old and the Valley Gate. On down around the Southern end of the Nehemaic structure, in the place of the affliction, there is now the Dung and Fountain Gate. Working up along the East where there once was joy, glory, and home, is now different gates and entrances known as the Water, Horse, East, and Inspection Gate.

The opposite trajectory of movement around the gated wall of Nehemiah, when compared to the encampment in Numbers, shows how the two of them interplay with one another. Whereas the encampment in Numbers proclaims what God is doing with Israel, Nehemiah's work became a *type* that foreshadows what God was going to do with all of humanity.

In the New Testament, Jesus enters into humanity in order to explain and make known what had been hidden to some degree in the Old Testament. When Jesus began His ministry, He looked for His *sheep* (John. 10:1-21) and called *fishers of men* (Mt. 4:19). Jesus began His journey to the cross by calling people to follow after Him, He Himself being the *restoration of humanity*, claiming that He is the rest to their wrestling, (Mt. 11:28) the joy to their sorrow, (Heb. 1:9) and the justification and Judge which leads to righteousness (Rom. 5:1). The North wall in Nehemiah's work contains overtones of the Exodus, but is much more profound. Whereas the order in the book of Numbers points to what Israel had lost (*home*) and would eventually regain (*joy in Jesus*), Nehemiah's work starts with what is gained in Jesus (*restoration*) and what we will leave behind (*the coil of this world when we join Jesus in His forever kingdom—Home*).

To further our understanding, on down the West side of Nehemiah's wall is a series of entrances and gates called the Valley gate and the Old Gate. Similarly, as the first step for Israel in their journey of redemption was to enter the wilderness of Sinai and come to the mountain to be retrained in how to think correctly, the Old Gate paints much the same picture. Like Jeremiah beckons in 6:16, "stand by the ways and see and ask for the *ancient* paths, where the good way is and walk in it, and you will find rest for your souls," the first step proceeding from Jesus' calling of His sheep, and telling them of His truth, is His effort to lead them through the valley to unearth their false foundations, to retrain them in new ways, and to fully complete His forgiveness in them. God *catechizes* and retrains His people first. Just like in Numbers, this process leads to a "South end," where the Dung Gate and place of "dumping affliction" resides. Where the valley is long and drawn out to defrag a broken people of their worldly mentality, the distance between the Dung Gate and the next gate, the Fountain Gate, are far closer in proximity; whereas the Dung is a place of exposure, it is quickly washed away by the fountain of mercy.

On up into the East side, whereas the Israelites waited for the Promised Land, now in Jesus one waits for the eternal kingdom. While waiting, God sanctifies and prepares His people through His Word (Water Gate: Eph. 5:26) and in a symbol of war He is to come back on a horse to Deliver us at the Horse Gate (Rev. 19:11); only then to deliver His people once again to His Garden and Kingdom *home* in the sky at the East Gate (Ps. 24:7)—judging unbelievers to torment, and believers in order to give them their rewards (Mt. 25:31-34).

The Old Testament trajectory, as seen in the Numbers diorama is that everything started with God (*home*). Our separation in sin followed (*law*), then forgiveness was temporarily provided in the priesthood and sacrificial system—all the while awaiting a coming KING of Joy. The story of history has moved from *home*, to *sin*, to *forgiveness*, and now toward *restoration*. The New Testament portrayal in the Nehemiaic work is that the King finds us (*North*), the High Priest forgives us (*West*), the Law and sin are fulfilled by His grace (*South*), and now we await our eternal home that is coming with Jesus (*East*—Ex. 43:2-4—beginning at *restoration of humanity in Jesus, moving to forgiveness, moving to a doing away with sin, and ultimately to leading us back home*).

What this teaches us in our interpretation of what's happening in Numbers 2 is that God's journey had just begun with His people as they left Egypt and slavery. He rescued them from slavery, numbered them for war, but here in Numbers 2, God equips those within the camp around the tent of meeting with a purpose. Their purpose is central, in that they are being remade into the image of God and to be examples and "tellers" of the redemption story of God to the rest of the world. The very message that God wants them to tell is hidden even within their encampment structure itself. This process of redemption is not a onetime occurrence, but a daily deliverance. God's authority has everything to do with ordering this encampment in the way that He did, for He did not merely mean to rescue a people out of slavery, but He wanted to place them on line with His purpose in using them to bring His redemption story to all those still locked in bondage.

3

SCENE 3

THE HOLY PRIESTHOOD

The encampment was set, and the construct was laid out in such a way that the culture of Israel was to be lived within and shaped by the idea of redemption. The story of God ordered the lives of His people, and the familial communities were the contexts in which the people shared life together. Every day as people walked around, experienced life, and spent time with each other, the culture that God created was one that continually preached to them and spoke of His grand reversal. The structure not only formed the people around land occupancy, but it spoke to and taught them in regard to their purpose in history—and in regard to God's purpose for, in, and through them.

In Numbers chapter 3 God explores a different form of *diorama*. This next representation exists to set forth an even more specific display of His authority in Israel. First, it is as if in Chapter 2 the lens of His camera zooms out to catch the broad vision of His plan through the encampment, and in chapter three, His lens zooms in to focus upon a particular tribe—the Levites. The Levites became explicit representatives of His plan for *Holiness* amongst His people. The encampment communicated God's heart for the *collective* redemption of His people, but His focus upon the Levites highlights His desire for *individual* holiness within His people. In Numbers Chapter 3:1-4 God zooms in on the children of Aaron as if to address the set-apart tribe of the Levites. To understand in brief the tribe of Levi, as to their origins, we must recall the 10th plague of God upon Pharaoh as God took the life of Pharaoh's first-born son.

On that fatal night, the first-born son of every family was taken except for those who chose to trust in God's provision in the sacrificed lamb. God provided Israel a way of escape and justice through the blood of this lamb. If they smeared the lamb's blood on the doorpost, it was to be a sign to the angel of death to pass over their home in order to spare their children. In the thick of that night, the boys who were spared due to the faith of their parents were named as the tribe of Levi. This redeemed group of men was to serve solely and wholly in the temple of the Lord as pure intercessors in worship that would stand between a Holy God and a sinful people. Aaron himself was the High Priest in this order of Levitical heritage, and in chapter 3:1-4 God particularly documents the names of his family line; Nadab the firstborn, Abihu, Eleazar, and Ithamar. They were the helpers, successors, and aids to priestly work. Their calling is of the greatest priority and significance, so much so that God reminds us of Nadab and Abihu's horrific death in Leviticus 10:1 when they disobediently offer fire not authorized or commanded before the Lord.

This priesthood were to be men that exemplified the holiness of God in their complete and utter surrender to the authority of God. They were not to test the Lord in anything, but simply to be wholeheartedly devoted to acting on every word that proceeded from His mouth. They were set apart to reveal God's nature and to "approach the throne of grace with confidence" on behalf of God's people. These men were also to pay due attention to Aaron, their leader, and to seek only to provide for his needs as he served the people. They existed to watch after his affairs, steward God's commands as they passed to them from Aaron, and they were to be diligent to serve unto the glory of the Lord.

In chapter 3:21-26, subsequent men like Gershon were assigned even wider duties within the tribe to guard the tabernacle, the tent and covering, the screen for entrance, the hangings, the screen around the altar, the cords, and the servicing. In 3:27, Kohath was tasked to help with the ark, the table, the lamp stand, the altars, and all services. Finally in 3:33, Merari was placed in charge of the actual structural care and transportation of the tent of meeting; its frames, bars, pillars, bases, accessories, pillars and bases, pegs and cords. Everyone had a calling within the temple of God and God assigned them each tasks as He saw fit.

The way in which all of this design was assimilated into Israel's culture came through the Lord's decree. The Lord once again "spoke to Moses saying..." The firm and steadfast relationship forged between Moses and God birthed every step and every new endeavor for Israel. There was nothing done by Moses here with any intentionality outside of God's own design or specific vision. Moses wholeheartedly committed to the vision that God intended to communicate, and his commitment to God held secure through prayer.

Prayer is the divine hook-up between heaven and earth and it enables the dialogue of heaven to infect the reality of the world. God is Israel's lifeline and Moses' leadership is built on dependence to the Lord. This surrender is important, for it built trust and rapport among the people as they followed Moses and Aaron as God's representatives. All the people had known in Egypt was the selfish ambition and drive of a self-worshipping narcissistic man in the person of Pharaoh, and ever so slowly their hearts and minds were placed at ease under the rest, authority, and provision of their leadership and the Lord's guidance. The leaders were different in their love. Additively, the culture of redemption was preaching daily the hope of God rather than despair, and the hearts of Israel as a result continued to rehabilitate under the shadow of God's wing.

Continuing in dealing with the role of the priest in Israel, their role went beyond the simple day-to-day logistics of taking care of

God's house within the temple of meeting. The example of the priesthood went far beyond just that of mere grunt labor. The priests, like the encampment, were to be walking illustrations meant to display God's glory and intended purpose for humanity. We will detail their life and holiness in a moment, but let's first amplify our understanding of God's intentions here by making mention of the way they dressed.

In Figure 3.1 we see the colorful display of the priestly garb. Its detail and design points to something far greater than a simple earthly service. It provides yet another *diorama* that God uses to remind and recapture His people's imaginations and purpose.

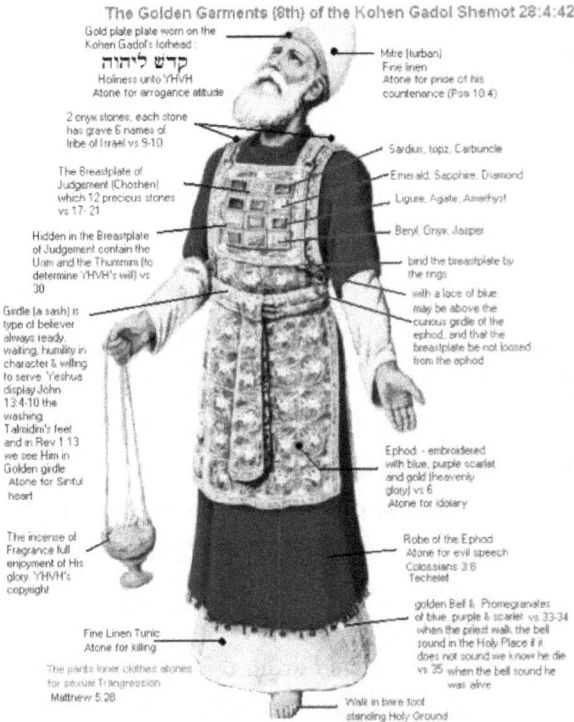

Fig. 3.1[1]

The high priestly vestments are representative of the whole people of Israel and are designed by God's decree to Moses in Exodus 36:12, 14, 28, 33, 36, and 38. Two onyx stones were attached to the shoulder straps of the priest, on which were recorded the names of the 12 tribes of Israel—six names on each stone. These stones in conjunction with the 12 stones upon the priest's breastplate are to symbolize God's remembrance of Israel and His covenant to them (Ex. 28:12, 21, and 29). God placed the stones on the priest's shoulders and on their chest to represent power and authority, but also to allude to the love that God held for Israel in His truest heart. Within this breastplate, and closest to the priests heart lay the Urim and the Thummim (meaning "lights" and "perfections"). This oracle-like aspect to the breastplate provided the priest the ability to gain heavenly answers to important questions. The placement of the Thummim upon the central part of the priest—over his heart—represents closely the placement of the Tent of Meeting in the center of the Israelite encampment. It represents that the true source of guidance: light and perfection is to be sought in and desired from God alone.

The priestly garments also speak of great purity. Each piece of clothing represents a particular purity that is needed in order to completely cover and atone for the whole of the human race. The tunic covering the priest's body was to atone for killing, the pants covering their legs was to atone for sexual transgressions, the turban was to atone for pride, the belt which wound around the heart was to atone for the improper thoughts of the heart, the breastplate protected against judgment, the ephod from idolatry, the robe from evil speech, and the crown from arrogance. The priest, who served at the tent of meeting and walked around amongst the people each day to fulfill their required services, was a walking representation of God's love for Israel—a reminder of His constant spirit of forgiveness and grace toward them.

Even further, the priest's dress represents a microscopic view of the entire heavens. The backdrop of the blue robe set in place the scenery of the blue ocean, on which is laid what Philo believed to be the twelve jewels which not only symbolizes Israel, but the twelve constellations in the night sky which hung over God's creation. Over the sea is laid the ephod, which symbolizes the land in the creation account, in which the 12 stones represent the central Garden that was placed in Eden. The stones not only point to God's people and their place in the present, but it also anchors them in their purpose of the past. Their purpose was once to dwell in the Garden within the perfect light of the Urim and Thummim of God's guidance and presence.

The Garden atmosphere, a reality at the Genesis of creation, is here still the goal to God's unfolding story. Adam, in the Garden, had been a priest in service to God. The garden was his temple, and there Adam daily was to serve before the Lord in providing leadership, stewardship, protection, and daily expansion of God's kingdom. As the garden was placed "in Eden," the breastplate represented a garden placed strategically in a man's chest. Upon the head of the priest was a turban, which represents the holy city of God in Eden where God ruled and reigned over creation in holiness and light.

Each day, God's moving *priestly-dioramas* walked around the encampment and told the story of something greater. Everything they were pointed to the authority of God in creation, in holiness, and in and amongst the nation of Israel. The priests, as they went into and out of the tent of meeting, and observed all that they were instructed, told this story.

Like the priestly vestments, the tent of meeting, which ultimately grew into a designed temple, was also designed to demonstrate God's story of reversal. As shown in figure 3.2, in the same way that the priestly garment contained a tri-part form in water, land, and heaven for purposeful reasons, so did the temple. The outer court symbolizes the visible earth (both land and sea, the place where humans lived); the holy place primarily represents the visible heavens (though there was also garden symbolism); and the holy of holies stands for the invisible heavenly dimension of the cosmos where God dwells.

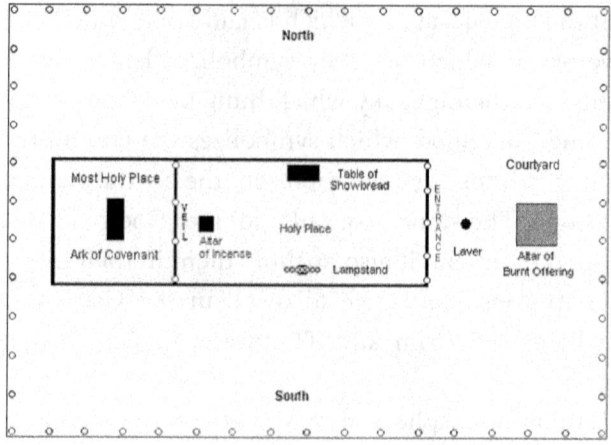

Fig. 3.2[2]

The Tent of Meeting in Numbers is cruder and more primitive than the Temple that would ultimately take its place, but its framework is the same. Much like the priestly garments, the structure of God's house pointed to a reality that is designed into the fabric of Creation. The outer courts contained the altar for burning sacrifices and the laver and washing basin in which people washed as a symbol of purity and forgiveness before the Lord. The sacrifices upon the altar—identified as the mountain of God (Ex 20:24-25)—represent the death that comes into creation through the sinful choices of humanity, and in artful expression, the life of an animal was to be taken each day in place of the people—dying on their behalf. The people were to wash in a basin, known as the "sea"—alluding to creation—which looked like a water lily and was surrounded by images of oxen (2 Chr. 4:2-5).

The priest on behalf of the people entered the inner courts which would have looked and felt like a Garden. Surrounded by tree embroidery and rich color, the priest stood beneath a "canopy," a lofty house (1 Kngs. 8:13), and within a wide open room that felt like the Garden sky. This implies that the Garden was conceived of as a holy temple. In the corner stood the lampstand fashioned in the form of a tree on which shined seven lamps—associated with the seven light-sources visible to the naked eye (5 planets, sun and moon)—and the presence of light that is likened to the stars and angelic throng in the heavens. In this space, the priest prayed, enjoyed the Shewbread or bread of God's presence, and ministered before the Lord on behalf of God's people. The symbolism of Adam's rule and reign is strongly typified here, and his priestly role is revealed to be the true and holy purpose of humanity since the beginning.

Everything in the rhythm of Israel moves from the outside in. Everything outside God's house ultimately moves closer and closer into the destination place of the Holiest of Holies. God's Holiest place, in which was housed the ark of the covenant, which contained the ten commandments, the budded priestly staff, and the manna representing God's provision, was veiled by a curtain and was sealed off from the people. This system of order was in place to direct people in how they were to approach God's throne room.

However, though the rhythm of Israel's system moves from the *outside in*, it was to serve only as a reminder of creation's original purpose in moving from the *inside out*. Adam, in the Garden, began in the proverbial "presence of God" as He served in perfection, under the priesthood, and within the provision of God. His mission was to move from and within God's presence out of the safety of the *inner* Garden into the barren wilderness of the *outer* underdeveloped wilderness. His mission was to expand God's kingdom throughout the earth, and the temple served as a symbol of this perfect design of God in creation.

This typological design analyzed here arrives at its paramount conclusion in the person of Jesus, who completes the intended mission and purpose of the priesthood of Adam, when He came from God's presence to take on human likeness. He crossed Eden's (heavens) borders and stepped down into the inner courts of Creation as a man. While on earth, He perfectly served as a priest, He was and is the bread of life, and He upheld perfectly the law of love as found in the Torah and in particular the 10 commandments themselves. His mission was to tear the veil between the Holy of Holies and remove His presence from a structure and place it back into its intended place; within the priest's heart (the human chest). In 1 Peter 2:9, the Scriptures call all people who contain the Urim and Thummim of God's spirit in their heart by name as a "chosen people, a royal priesthood, and a holy nation."

This was the intended plan from the beginning; that the people of God would carry His authority and priestly office throughout the earth. It was and is intended that God's people take His presence, while enjoying His Garden rest, to the greater and underdeveloped "outer" courts of the world and all its nations.

In light of all this, the particular design of the priestly office points toward something much greater than itself. God's orchestration of such an office is to demonstrate before the eyes of His people all that they had lost, and all that they were meant to regain. Israel's slavery mentality introduced even more shame into how they related to the presence of God. Their slavery-like sin isolated them in the outer courts, away from God's presence. It trained them how they were to view themselves and their purpose upon the earth. They became too easily pleased and satisfied with what appears most "free" to them, and little did they know that in living out from underneath God's plan of redemption, they were most bound. God's giant drama and artful painting, done on the garb of the priests, and held within the structural design of the tent of meeting, was to give them great hope and promise of a true freedom. The priesthood is the image of holiness and liberation. They are to be an illustration and depiction to all of humanity of a holy picture of the authority of God.

Numbers 3:40-45 then tells us that the lives of the Levites were to be taken in full service to God on behalf of the people. It also tells us that their cattle were to be taken in place of the people's cattle. Therefore, the Levitical tribe and people group were targeted and cherry picked by God for a life of sacrifice. Everything they did was on behalf of the people and for the people. Their life was spent waist deep in the blood and stench of dying animals. Their life was spent listening to the groans of God's people and standing in their place within the inner court and making known those requests to God. No regard was paid to their desires in this matter, nor was there any regard paid for the hardship that this would cause to their life. The priests did not get to enjoy the pleasures of the world. The priests were not able to give way to their own entitlement and desires. God had picked their road for them and they were to obediently follow it.

This was not a bondage to them, but a life-giving and deep breath of fresh air. The life of serving God and serving others is set in contrast against the backdrop of the slave-like mind-set of Israel's human thinking. Being linked and obedient to a real GOD does not appeal to a slave who has only known abuse at the hands of an overlord and who reeks with a stench of bondage. In God's eyes and by His command, the unshackled nature of the priesthood exemplifies a life of service that is secure within and underneath His perfect oversight and good command.

This is why the New Testament makes no apologies in exalting Jesus' authority as the High Priest over and above every believer who carries the Spirit in their heart and serves on earth as a little priest. Jesus stands in heaven as Priest. His life, His riches, and He Himself, as the firstborn, are taken on our behalf. His life is bound to the Father in utter surrender. All of His choices are an example to God's people. He spends all of His time serving and interceding for His people on behalf of their groaning in the wake of their sinful tidal wave.

His desires are His Father's desires and the circumstances and pain He encountered on earth are for the purpose of procuring a much greater pleasure for all of humanity. His authority is found in His freeing allegiance to the Father. His ability to do all that the Father instructs is what makes Him the greatest picture of victory. He does not experience any more mistreatment or unjust ill-will within Himself, nor does He fear or relinquish to the control of frustration, bitterness, or un-forgiveness. He is completely and utterly released and emancipated from the threat of anything that can possibly befall Him. He is the most secure, the most safe, and the most conscience of all the power of which He possesses. In other words, being High Priest makes Jesus the most FREE, and His call to us to be His priesthood is a call to freedom under His authority.

4

SCENE 4

A SERVANT LEADERSHIP

God slowly rehabilitated His family. He led them out of Egypt through the gentle and relational guidance of His voice. He delivered them from the hands of their abusers, and organized them into a unified culture once again. Through the model of the encampment, through creative and tangible artistry, and through the organizing of the priesthood, God preached vision to this newfound assembly. He made His intentions known to them through His plan of redemption and reversal. God guided His people, loved His people, and saved His people.

Something further is still at stake, nevertheless. To lead His people, He would have to once again regain their trust in the fullest sense. Though God instructed His people and spoke through Moses to lead them, their hearts were still fragile, and one can sense in the beginning of Numbers that a tender care is used in how God conducts the first stages of His plan. Their hearts had become calloused, and their ears had grown hardened to the commands and tactics of their Egyptian predecessors. To the wounds of their hearts, God now applied a soothing and healing salve of gentility, compassion, and great mercy. A detrimental mindset had formed in the people of Israel in how they had been trained to respond to leadership and authority, as well as in how they knew to be in authority themselves. God treads gingerly as He addresses this mind-set step by step.

In Egypt, the rhythm of relationship that formed between the Egyptians and the people of Israel was a dance between *acts of control* and *responses of cowardice*. Egypt, being the formidable power, exercised their authority with great dominance, aggression, and abuse. Their leadership did not provoke a loving bond between themselves and those they were leading. The goal of their leadership was to get things done, and do it in the way that most pleased them. Because of this, the Israelite people became pawns in the game of them establishing their own vision and agenda. Being used in this way makes them tentative and distrustful of God.

They as a people maintained that there is only one response to such control, and that is passive cowardice. They had been stripped of the right to maintain a position of disagreement or refusal to their attackers. They did what they were told, knowing that most of what was asked of them was only going to lead to more heartache. Due to this, their desire to serve those in leadership over them had waned and had altogether disappeared. Their initiative and desire had been ripped from them. Their dignity had been left in shambles, and in turn formed how they lived out their own lives.

This interaction between control and cowardice made them a problem to themselves within their own homes and communities. Their broken spirit either fashioned them into dead weight within their families—doing nothing at all—or their response to their control had led them to control what still remained available to them. Because of this, the same control and cowardice patterns in Egypt had crafted their relationships and formed how leaders interacted with followers amidst the tribe of Israel.

This rhythm that had formed had to be unlearned. This rhythm that had been modeled had to be reformed and repackaged in such a way as to communicate a different system and model for governance. God knew, in His infinite wisdom, that to instantly task His people with assignments would most likely only lead to resistance. For God to have His people listen to Him, as He moved them toward the mentality of working with Him and for Him in His mission, He would first have to undo slowly what had been formed in His people. In order to establish a new culture, a new ethic, and new philosophy of relationship between those in authority and those following authority, God began to assign roles to segments of the Levitical tribes.

We must pay attention not merely to what He assigns them to do, but the culture He is trying to create within His leadership structure.

In Numbers 4, God again speaks to Moses and Aaron regarding a section of the Levite tribe known as the Kohathites. In Numbers 4:19b God directs that every man from of Kohathite descent was to be "appointed a task and to a burden." At the command of the Lord we are told in 4:49 that "according to the commandment of the Lord through Moses, they were listed, each one with his task of serving or carrying. Thus they were listed by him, as the Lord commanded Moses."

In verse 1-15 it tells us that Kohath's task within the temple was to take care of the most holy things. Whether setting up camp, or breaking down to leave, God instructed that the veil, the ark, the bread of presence, the utensils, the bread, the lampstand, and all vessels for service within temple were to be put away correctly and specifically and covered with the skins of sea cows. Aaron's son Eleazar was also given a job in that He was in charge of the incense, the oil, and the grain offerings, as well as carrying the curtains and the covering to the tent of meeting, along with the screen over the entrance (vv. 21-28). Eleazar was given the generous responsibility of overseeing everything in regard to how the transport of God's tent was handled.

Finally, Merari was charged to carry the tent frames, bars, pillars, and bases; along with the pegs, cords, and all the accessories. Everyone, through Moses and Aaron, were ordered to do a work and a service in the Temple at the command of the Lord.

What is important to note from the start is not so much the specifics of what is to be carried, but the nature by which they are assigned. God's system of authority here is not one of control or of cowardice, but one of service. Everyone within God's system has a role and function; not only before God, but unto one another. Though each person's role carries with it a different set of responsibilities and items for transport, each job was essential enough for God to include it in the Bible. Everyone had their responsibility and was *in authority* in regard to some aspect of the transport, and in another respect everyone was *under authority* in that the Kohathites, Gershonites, and Meraritites served under the direct oversight of Eleazar; while Eleazar served under the direct oversight of Aaron. Aaron is one who is also overseen by Moses, who is himself taking his commands from God.

There is a clear chain of command extended down from God into the ranks of the Levitical tribe, and this system not only models God's structure of leadership but also teaches His people His ethic. His ethic is service. Everyone in the different tribes had a job, both big and small, and everyone contributed to the greater good of advancing and protecting God's Holy purpose.

This culture differs from that of the dynamic in Egypt in that in God's culture, a humble, loving, benevolent master is now at the helm commanding the work. In His goodness, He is unable to holster any false ambition, delusion, or prideful arrogance. The system created under God deems it right that security is to come to all those within the ranks. This ethic also ensures that no job is taken lightly, nor is it looked down upon as any less—and vice versa. Gershon took one of the smaller roles while Eleazar had a greater mantle of oversight, but both served the same King. Their response is not out of fear and terror of the Lord, as had been the construct of intimidation in Egypt, but their hearts are being trained to respond generously to the accountability of a kind and gracious God.

In working *under* authority, both in relationship to God and each other, and in taking responsibility *in* authority over what God had entrusted them to steward, they are rightly able to work *alongside* each other in the process. Each stage of *authority* serves the purpose to teach and train the people's heart to un-learn what has been observed and implanted in them in slavery. Not only do the Levites unlearn this mode of thinking, but the people of Israel play spectator to the Levite's daily service. The Levites are like a live drama of God's kingdom as displayed before His people. Their service became a tangible way for God to paint what life in His kingdom is like.

Being *under* authority had now become something that represents clear and concise vision and direction, as well as results in the purification of God's people in His protection of what was sacred and Holy. Every command that God gives brings with it a seriousness of responsibility, but in every step of the way He makes it clear that His intention is in an effort to preserve His image of Holiness amongst His people. In asking the people to be under authority, God sets a standard of holiness and legacy to be passed down from generation to generation.

For example, the Kohathites (vv. 17-20) handled the most holy things, such as the ark, and they did so even under David and Hezekiah's rule. The wide breadth of time in this area of service needed a structure of accountability to ensure that the integrity of such an office continued. This is why in vs. 19 of Numbers chapter 4, God says that if the Kohathites were to wane in their care of the Holy things, they must be "thusly dealt with."

This "dealing with," was done in order to keep the line of holiness sketched clearly. It is God's plan for leadership to protect His image in and amongst the people. It is His plan to help His people through loving them and, when called for, in executing extreme correction and discipline when His house is profaned. Without such a system in place, people might venture into areas of lesser satisfaction and even death without even knowing where the line of destruction is drawn. If a root of rejection towards authority is allowed to enter at any point, the people might fall prey to letting something else or someone else rule over them in dealing "thusly with them." This allows for another round of slavery to enter at the hands of a new taskmaster, and ultimately winds up imprisoning an entire nation all over again.

Particularly, in this passage, the possibility of this nation reverting back to its old ways is still a great risk. In verse 21-49 it can be observed that many of the men in service were between the ages of

30-50. These were younger men who needed guidance and oversight. Their youthfulness, though filled with zeal, needed understanding and discipleship in order to learn and grow. The structure of God in how He organizes His family ensures that the younger and immature servants in God's economy are watched over, protected, and educated lovingly and intentionally as family.

The leadership, like an umbrella, provides the shade, as the younger ones are allowed and enabled to grow up into trees with strong roots. Another element is also crucial in order to ensure apt formation. Those under authority are still given jobs, tasks, and ownership in the economy of Israel as God continued with them through the journey. This ownership is also to ensure that the younger generation of priests remains responsive and obedient to the commands of the Lord. The most important thing for the culture of Israel is that the subsequent generations are trained to serve as their forefathers.

These younger men in the temple were examples to those in the culture of Israel as a whole. They served as a constant and daily reminder to the men of the nations that this is what real authority looks like. As they submitted to authority and to the command given from the Lord, and as they took ownership to steward what God entrusted to them as they diligently watched over the equipment of the tent of meeting, those looking on also followed suit. God began His restorative work in His chosen tribe with the work intended to spread into the ethos of the entire encampment.

This redemptive rhythm presented a due change regarding the ways that Israel had grown accustomed. It truly caught their attention. The priests, who were leading the community in regard to spiritual matters *under* God's authority, and acting upon those commands *in* authority through serving the community in diligence, were showing forth the kingdom of love. Their structure of authority and submission was to cultivate a spirit of brotherly love as they worked *alongside* each other. God created a cathartic workout for their spiritual muscles. In working alongside one another every day He unified them around a mission and a set of principles. The mission crafted them, formed them, and moved them together—forcing them to depend on each other in intertwined harmony.

Symbolically this sweet harmony smells of a sweet fragrance and must have felt as that of a healing oil in the deep open wounds of a beaten up Israel. It is no accident that Eleazar was placed in charge of the entire endeavor of the tent of meeting's transport and care, and that he was also assigned to take care of the oil, the incense, and the grain offering. The oil symbolizes the light that is produced out into a community because of the love and service that is billowing forth. The waft of sweet service smelled of a tantalizing community, as the priests together bore witness to (2 Cor. 2:14-15), imitated (Eph. 5:1-2), gave (Phil. 4:18), and worshipped (John 12:3) adoringly the glory of God. Their work dripped richly over the heads and down the back of the people in the encampment like the oil upon their heads, and ministered to the people's pesky distrust, entitlement, and diseased thinking. And finally, like the grain offering, it pleased the community to observe the result of their hard-earned work in the fields of grain, as it was being put to good use in providing for the men of those in service to the temple.

The ideology and construct of leadership, authority, and what it means to submit oneself underneath something or someone, undergoes a re-tooling and re-formation in the minds of the Israelites. God's vision is like a stone being tossed into the quiet stream of a few delicate souls, causing ripples to begin. These small stones, be they ever so small, are intended to grow into thrashing and raging waves, as the ethos of the temple seeps its way out from the inner courts into every crevice of the newly formed community.

5

SCENE 5-6

THE LEPER AND THE NAZARITE COMPARISON

As the message of God's redemptive story unfolds through the dioramic and dramatic presentation of the encampment, the leadership, the priesthood, and the tent of meeting, the formation of a new community and culture ensues. This culture was altogether different than what had been present in Egypt. The changes in the environment, though welcomed, must have felt like cross-cultural experiences to the Israelites. Their spiritual nervous system had been trained to transmit information in a specific way. They had been trained to relate to life and all of their surroundings as slaves, and now everything around them had changed. No longer was there a fear-and coward-based culture surrounding them, but rather one of love and leadership. No longer was there a feel of *control* in its most evil sense, but there was a peaceful sense of *sovereignty* and direction underneath and within the leading of the Lord.

As the Israelites learned how to eat, sleep, live, and breathe within this new *home* that God provided, it must have felt to them like that of an adopted child coming into something completely unfamiliar. This new environment required a new set of skills in order to relate.

Israel became here like a newly born baby. Like newborns they were to learn language, new movements, rhythms, and the voice of the Lord. They were to learn to respond to the loving tone of their Father in heaven, and it must be well expected that the transition of change was not smooth.

Through the process of change brought about upon Israel in Numbers, it becomes increasingly apparent that the natural inclination of the human heart is to respond to such adjustment in two diverse ways—in *rebellion* or through *religion*. In order to demonstrate what resides at the basest heart-motives of those within the ranks of humanity, God once again devotes time and attention in Numbers 5-6 toward two *dramatized* people groups within Israel itself. He does so in order to give us a living case study of this phenomenon.

In the first couple chapters of Numbers, it is as if God uses a wide-angle lens to survey the entire encampment of Israel in order to broadly assemble everyone into His redemptive story as a "people." Following, the lens of examination increasingly grows smaller as God hones in on the priesthood and the work of the temple to portray what a community kingdom looks like. Now in Chapter 5-6 we arrive at God's narrow lens view into the actual individuals within the community itself. In particular, God zooms in on two types of people that are particularly helpful and instructive to us in our approach to the story of Numbers. He begins in talking about the *Leper* and then He moves to outlining the lifestyle of the *Nazarite*. In the next two scenes we will look at the specifics of each people group, and discuss how they become like miniature *dramatic* figures in God's story in order to point to the deep and real condition of the human heart.

The drama begins in Numbers 5:1-4 when again the Lord speaks to Moses, saying, "'Command the people of Israel that they put out of the camp everyone who is leprous or has a discharge and everyone who is unclean through contact with the dead. You shall put out both male and female, putting them outside the camp, that they may not defile their camp, in the midst of which I dwell.' And the people of Israel did so, and put them outside the camp; as the Lord said to Moses, so the people of Israel did." Again we can observe in the story this dialogue between God and Moses, and we must keep in mind that God is instructing Moses to do all that is contained in the aforementioned verses. Those who are unclean, those with discharge and those who had come in contact with the dead in any fashion were to be cut off from the community of Israel. To us, this may seem unmerciful that God would order and command that certain people be cut off from the culture, but a careful study of the leper reveals a deeper purpose.

Leprosy was a very common condition in the Old Testament, and its prevalence continued even on into the time of Jesus. A leper is someone who cannot heal themselves nor fight off infection. Due to their inability to fight off minor diseases and abnormalities, something as simple as a minor cut or healable staph infection can turn into a deadly ordeal. Not only can a leper not fight disease, but the disease produces two dramatic effects. On one hand, the leprous spread produces numbness within a person's body. As limbs grow increasingly infected, a leper loses sensation, and whole arms, toes and legs can fall off or remain broken; and aside from loss of mobility, the leper may not even feel anything. In the exact opposite way, the cancerous venom can travel pervasively about a person's body in such a way that wreaks painful havoc on everything in its path. The decaying nature of the disease exposes nerves, breaks open sores, and creates painful discharge that seeps out from open cuts and unhealed breaks or wounds.

One can only imagine what kind of physical toll this takes upon a person. It becomes extremely destructive upon the whole of an individual. Not only must we consider how this must have affected the leper physically, we must also consider the toll it took on the social, mental, emotional, and spiritual fabric of the person who incurred the disease.

Anyone with leprosy, per God's orders here in Numbers, was to isolate themselves from the community at large. They would gather into colonies outside the city gates because they were extremely sick, infected, and contagious to anyone outside their group. To touch one of these people would have been to spread the disease like a cancer throughout the encampment.

Their isolation put them only in proximity to those who were also sick. Due to their place outside the city gates they were exposed, cut off, and alienated in a sense from the city's protection, from its governance, and from all that is provided to its people. Because of this, all the amenities that come with being part of a city, a community, a family, and people is hopelessly lost to them—with no cure in sight.

For those with the disease, this isolation developed within its victims a mindset and way of looking at the world. They would become secluded, alone, and cut off from any real help. They would be exposed and unable to defend themselves. Not to mention the fact that if they actually do defend themselves, they risk getting cut, scraped, or injured; which ultimately leads to greater numbness or excruciating pain and/or death for them. In whatever way a person comes to contract the illness, the result and promise is always the same—death. The leprous community here, as we can only imagine, must have been a very tentative, fearful, and reclusive one. They avoided getting bumped or scraped at any turn, and they spent their time in their cut-off communities nursing their wounds; surrounded by the company of those who cannot help them, but can solely and merely hurt with them.

Not only did fear start to cripple them in their approach to each other and to all of life, but it formed in them a view of themselves—an identity.

The leper is defined by their leprosy. If someone were to inquire of them and say for instance, "tell me about yourself…" they would simply reply, "I am a leper." In this one word, they hold all their meaning. It became who they were, are, and ever would become. Their identity became formed not only in their own view of themselves, but they defined themselves by this identity in the eyes of others. If people were to walk by the leper compound, the leper would most likely be carrying with them a bell. If a person were to come too close, a leper would yell out, "Unclean, Unclean!" and would ring the bell violently to warn anyone who may come near and become infected as a result. Every day became a reminder of their shame, their impurity, their guilt, their disease, and their alienation from the community of God.

This kind of infection crushes a person emotionally and spiritually in every way. Not only is the outside of the camp a dark depressed and miserable place, but the state of their soul is a pit of despair, hopelessness, and suicidal thoughts. Every day brought with it the smell and desire for death. These colonies, due to the large numbers of lepers, would smell of an odor and fragrance of decay. They were associated with and they associated themselves with the dead.

This is a very desperate, destitute, and disheveled people and they are a very unhappy lot. Their grief and sorrow multiplies into everything around them. The depth of their grief resembles the state of their body. They would either become *numb* or they became *neurotic*. The weight of the pain was too much for the person to emotionally and spiritually bear, so it pushed them toward one of these two exits. The person who is numb seeks to dull himself or herself to the pain. They force themselves to become accepting of the pain, and possibly even drive themselves to become satisfied in it. So much attention is spent on simply managing the sorrow that this rips their perspective away from anything beautiful or satisfying in the world. Any good news, any hope, anything that pertained to faith, joy, and abundance proves to be a lost message on a leprous person.

In the opposite fashion, those exposed to the elements in extreme sensitivity are like live electrical wires. They are emotionally neurotic and unstable. Their awakened nerves set them on edge. Their triggers come right near the surface, threatening to set a person off in a rage of anger, venom, or hurt at any point in time. When around them, one has to "walk on egg shells." They are the loose cannons that can blow at any moment.

As this community of numb and neurotic people would interact, they would play off each other's fears. They couldn't console each other because the only thing they knew was hurt—they'd never been helped. As their bitterness came out—their depression, their vulgarity, discharge, their death—it continued to create a culture much different from the one God created in His community. A great summation in how this leprous culture differed from the one God was forming in His people is captured in the life of one leper in 2 Kings 5.

His name was Naaman. Naaman was a King, a nobleman, a man of importance, and His name meant "beautiful." This typifies what leprosy actually represented. It was the antitype of God's beauty and love; it was everything unbeautiful. Whereas God's community strove to beautify and redeem His broken people, the leprous culture threatened all that was lovely. Every smell was toxic, every sight was lethal, every touch was deadly, and any hope of survival was trivial. This was a living drama, not only of what a disease can do to the outside, but it was God's statement to the people of what a slave-like-mentality can do to the inside.

The question must be asked here, why did God allow such a thing? Did He allow diseases like this to exist because people are so sinful they need to be punished? That is the belief of many. People even embraced this belief on into the New Testament. But as we see in many cases throughout Jesus' ministry, He often rebuked this assumption and stated that someone's sickness is left purposefully intact in order to magnify God's glory in healing and in sustenance (Jhn. 11:4).

Is leprosy then only to teach about the nature of how diseases like AIDS can infect us and harm us—like some sort of warning and PowerPoint presentation on health? This does not seem likely, as Jesus Himself touched the leper intentionally (Lk. 5:12-15). What seems to be happening here is none of what is aforementioned, but rather it seems that leprosy is allowed here by God to demonstrate in visual and *dramatic* fashion the true reality of sin and the effects that a slavery-like mindset has upon a people.

I believe we derive this intention by simply looking at the continuous flow of thought throughout the rest of Numbers 5. It's interesting that in the next verses in Chapter 5:11-31 the passages delve straight into the erroneousness of the sin of adultery and sexual immorality, and is linked to verses 5:1-4 concerning leprosy, by Numbers 5:5-10, which speaks about confession of sin.

> And the Lord spoke to Moses, saying, 'Speak to the people of Israel, When a man or woman commits any of the sins that people commit by breaking faith with the Lord, and that person realizes his guilt, he shall confess his sin that he has committed. And he shall make full restitution for his wrong, adding a fifth to it and giving it to him to whom he did the wrong. But if the man has no next of kin to whom restitution may be made for the wrong, the restitution for wrong shall go to the Lord for the priest, in addition to the ram of atonement with which atonement is made for him. And every contribution, all the holy donations of the people of Israel, which they bring to the priest, shall be his. Each one shall keep his holy donations: whatever anyone gives to the priest shall be his.'

God's warning against adultery and sexual immorality is very pertinent to our discussion. Adultery, and all sin, destroys the soul and the heart in the same way that leprosy destroys the body. Here in Numbers 5 the description for the act of adultery is given almost three times as many words as that of the description of leprosy. Adultery is not merely a condition, but it is a premeditated act of destruction that is born in the mind and breeds anxiety, worry, regret, shame, and stress in the body. Adultery, is an example of how, like leprosy, sin kills the whole person. It not only involves the body, but the temptation and discharge of it starts in the person's mind. It culminates in refocusing a person's will, emotions, and desires. Adultery, as equated with leprosy, is a gross look into a person's whole being, and is an indicator of one who has chosen a path of wickedness. Here in Numbers 5 God gives some succinct advice and protocol for dealing with the healing of such sin.

In vs. 15 the husband who suspects a wife is to bring up the iniquity in accusation before the whole community and bring it to the priest. In a dramatized fashion, the sin was to be paid for in acts of offering and sacrifice (vs. 15), and in a public display, the women was to let down her hair in front of the people into a bitter and symbolic pool of water. For the women in that culture, the letting down of the hair was a sign of a prostitute, a loose woman, and was a shameful act (vs. 18). She was to wallow in the wake and pool of her bitterness, so much so that her thigh would swell, her womb would fall away, and out of her unclean womanhood she would be unable to procreate as a sign of punishment (vs. 23-28).

But the linking of verses 5-10 to this passage tells us that confession, reconciliation, and restitution for such sin—for such leprosy—is available. Sin, and all that draws a person away out from underneath the protection and shade of a loving God, is to be confessed as the darkness that it is. It steals the heart away from God's bounty, and it robs others of that same authority. It divides relationships and thus confession brings those relationships back together—reconciliation. Not only this, confession, true confession is to be followed by true repentance and restitution. Every sin steals something from God and from another person, and it needs to be paid back five-fold. In Exodus we see that the thief gives back his spoils (Ex. 22:2-3), and that restitution is to be made in the wake of many sins—e.g. assault (Exodus 21:18-19); bodily injury (21:26-27); liability (21:33-36); theft (22:1-4); property damage (22:5-6); irresponsibility (22:7-13); and the loss or damage of borrowed items (22:14-15).

This reminds us of the story of Zaccheus, who as a lording tax collector—an authority of sorts—stole from people, not only in what he took, but in what he failed to give. Every time he gave in to the sin of greed and skimmed off the top of what people were giving him, he deprived others of service and generosity. Every time he spent lavishly, he deprived the widow, the orphan, the fatherless, and the destitute of their nourishment. As he lived in isolation, he deprived others of love and hope, and as he held onto selfishness, he kept from others the true taste of God's forgiveness that is meant to be seen by all. And in Luke 19:9, when Zaccheus saw all the sins of his *commission* (things he did) and *omission* (things he'd failed to do), he tells Jesus that he will repay multiple times all that he had stolen from the people. This is a sign of true repentance and confession. It is a sign of true healing. It is not a sign that Zaccheus had earned his forgiveness, as we know fully that Jesus payment for sin is the ultimate 5-fold repayment of debt, but Zaccheus, in meeting Jesus, simply shows his response to Jesus' grace in desiring to give all he had to give grace to those he had harmed.

Leprosy is a representation to all people of one course of action that can be taken in response to God's leadership. It is a dramatization that can be visually seen, and that points to the results Israel would get if they chose to disobey the Lord's authority. Israel could live outside all of God's ways in sin, but it would only result in premeditated harm toward each other as it would give way to any and every kind of immorality and sin to reveal itself. They could choose to live outside His city, out from underneath His governance, and outside the ranks of His family. They could choose to embrace fear and live only for themselves and think of themselves only as tarnished; only continuing to solidify their thinking that they were "lepers," they were "unclean," and they were slaves. They could continue to buckle under the weight of their emotional distress; they could continue to lash out at each other in sore anguish, or they could continue to slide through life in calloused numbness. The people could spiritually feel all the effects of being under the mastery of anything the world had to offer, or they could remain surrendered to the loving hand of their Father.

Leprosy is a warning, not only to the people of Israel, but to the lepers themselves. Not only this, but it is also a gracious picture that God paints for His people in order to show them what awaits them if they ignore His commands and choose to step out into the street in front of oncoming traffic. It is very clear, that even in the case of Namaan, that everyone is subject to these leprous effects, even a king, but that God is willing and able to heal and restore even those debilitated by the full weight of the disease's effects. It is a dramatic display of all that life has to offer apart from God—it is ugly—but it is a reminder of the power and ability God maintains to restore and make all things beautiful. This tarnished beauty is one road that is left to the Israelites should they fail to submit to the authority and leadership of the Lord. This is one of the only two roads left to them.

In Numbers chapter 6 an altogether different road appears. The consequences of rebellion is implicitly and visually portrayed in the plight of the leper, but what about considering the possible opposite course of action? To consider this, we must reflect on what it was like to be a Nazarite.

The Nazarites were also an odd group. Their name literally means to "separate oneself and consecrate oneself." The Nazarites therefore were an intensely religious people-group that took vows of fervent commitment to the Lord in order to display holiness and deny any attachment to the world. They could be those people particularly set apart and chosen as eminent among the other people, such as Joseph among his brothers in Genesis 49:26. Many well-known people throughout the Bible were Nazarites (e.g. Samuel, Samson, John the Baptist). Their lives are marked by living a lifestyle that is worthy of their calling. Their job as a Nazarite was to reflect and project to the world what it was to model full devotion and holiness to the Lord.

To do this, the Nazarites underwent drastic measures. Some of the tactics included in their regimen was not bathing. They did not eat anything from the vine, nor did they touch or have anything to do with anything dead. They were also to let their hair grow long and un-manicured. As this smelly, unkempt, and peculiar little bunch marched around the Jewish community, their lives must have drawn much attention. Every vow they made was done in order to deprive and pay no mind to the flesh. The entire meaning of their denying anything "physical" was so they could demonstrate the realities of living in perfect communion with God. This was as a crown of glory to them (vs. 13-20).

The Nazarite's vow to the Lord involved many good things and should in no way be misconstrued as a "negative lifestyle." In fact, often times this particular separation from the world and the flesh was often instituted by the Lord. The Lord gave these people to the people of Israel as a gift and a live *dramatization* of the good news of the gospel. On into the New Testament, we see that Jesus Himself was a Nazarite, and through His death and resurrection, anyone who believes in Him is added into the line of the Nazarite. The basic foundation of what it means to be a Nazarite, in being elect and chosen among many (Rom. 9); in being holy, consecrated, and set apart (Eph. 5:3), and in being completely filled with the spirit and not given over to the flesh (Gal. 5:16), is truly what exemplifies the life-giving holiness of God Himself in the life of a believer.

What we must emphasize first is the positive nature of the Nazarite's vow and lifestyle, for it is the lifestyle that every follower of Christ should adopt. Nevertheless, as a warning, we must however take note of something important in vs. 13-19, which says;

> And this is the law for the Nazarite, when the time of his separation has been completed: he shall be brought to the entrance of the tent of meeting, and he shall bring his gift to the Lord, one male lamb a year old without blemish for a burnt offering, and one ewe lamb a year old without blemish as a sin offering, and one ram without blemish as a peace offering, and a basket of unleavened bread, loaves of fine flour mixed with oil, and unleavened wafers smeared with oil, and their grain offering and their drink offerings. And the priest shall bring them before the Lord and offer his sin offering and his burnt offering, and he shall offer the ram as a sacrifice of peace offering to the Lord, with the basket of unleavened bread. The priest shall offer also its grain offering and its drink offering. And the Nazarite shall shave his consecrated head at the entrance of the tent of meeting and shall take the hair from his consecrated head and put it on the fire that is under the sacrifice of the peace offering. And the priest shall take the shoulder of the ram, when it is boiled, and one unleavened loaf out of the basket and one unleavened wafer, and shall put them on the hands of

the Nazarite, after he has shaved the hair of his consecration, and the priest shall wave them for a wave offering before the Lord. They are a holy portion for the priest, together with the breast that is waved and the thigh that is contributed. *And after that the Nazarite may drink wine.*

Picture this. This stinky, unkempt, and disheveled people group, who had been abstaining from all worldly and fleshly amenities, reaches the pinnacle end of their time of fasting. As a Nazarite would then come to offer his "consecration" and holiness to the Lord, he came to the altar in a dramatic display.

We might imagine that his holiness and odd lifestyle may have made him a celebrity of sorts among the people—he was well known. His coming to the altar may have been a celebrated spectacle of exalted holiness amongst the people of Israel. If not this, the Nazarite's humility may have caused him and his walk to the altar to go unnoticed. Whether this person became a spectacle of idol praise and admiration among the people for his religious loyalty, or whether his plight humbly went unnoticed is not what matters. His display of holiness is not what matters. For with him he carried the real spectacle; one lamb and ewe without blemish—a beautiful offering.

We know from the Scriptures that these animals, specifically the Paschal Lamb, are representations of the unblemished man of Jesus Christ, the Messiah. As the Nazarite came bearing oil, which is interpreted in the New Testament as the Holy Spirit, he bore witness to the Holiness of God. Here he would come, an aromatic, earthy, and almost tousled view of man—in his display of consecration and holiness—carrying these beautiful gifts of unblemished goodness and grace—things that probably smell sweet like grain, wafers, and mixed oil. The dichotomy of this drama is meant to convey this attitude; "Do not look at me, for my mere attempt at holiness and living separated from the flesh produces something unpleasing to the eyes and nostrils—it's still not complete. But this entire display means nothing if it is not covered, paid for, and atoned for by the Paschal Lamb (the image of Jesus Christ)."

It was a powerful reminder to the people of God's authority. The nation of Israel could walk away from the Lord's leadership in *rebellion* or they could try and cover their tracks and become super performers in *religion*. However, if the people's hopes were to be anchored in anything else but God, and God's work in them and through them, then both the leper and Nazarite approach would cause them to end up still victims to the mentality of a slave.

A leper knows their hopelessness, as does the Nazarite. God wanted the people here to embrace the fact that they were set apart from sin and its effect, but just as one group can become enslaved in putting their identity in their leprosy, the other group can just as easily fall prey to the same trap in putting their identity in their own display of holiness. Though the Nazarite comes with all they have to the altar—this man of holiness, rightness, goodness, and commitment—God demonstrates that all that man can possibly put their faith in is ultimately good enough only to be burned. This symbolizes and preaches about the meaninglessness of all of it if what is done is not done for the Lord and unto the Lord.

This demonstration of the Nazarite helps bring us to a conclusion. God is trying to communicate something specific to the people. The Nazarite vow of abstinence is not the *end*. Rather the *means* of their lifestyle is to point to the true end of enjoyment in God Himself. A nugget of meaning can be mined from Numbers chapter 6 verse 19 when God instructs, in the aftermath of such a display by the Nazarite, that "the Nazarite may drink wine."

After all that the Nazarite would give up in fasting from the world, and after their fast awakened them to the seriousness of the flesh and of sin (Num. 6:9-12), God reveals the true meaning. Their fast is to awaken their "truest" desires, not kill them. Their fast is to awaken them to God and God's Word (Num. 6:9-12). It is to humble them in dependence and submission upon the Lord (Ps. 35:13, Mt. 6), and it is to purify their body and awaken their voice to the spirit (Is. 58). It is to give them victory over their slave mentality (I Sam. 7:5-11), it is to make them fruitful (Acts 9:9; 2 Cor. 6:5), and it is to soften them to pray and hear answers (1 Sam. 1:7). It is to establish them under God's protection not their own (Ez. 8:21-23), and it is to quicken to think like God in all their decisions (Acts 13:1-4). Their fast is also to dramatize for the people of Israel, and for the world, the path to deliverance (Jonah 3:1-10). It is to model for Israel how to follow God's lead and understand His agenda (2 Chr. 20:2-26). The Nazarite's plight is given to serve God and others (Mt. 6:4), and it is to rescue a nation (Neh. 1:4).

God clearly communicates through the leper and the Nazarite that His desire is not for His people to be enslaved to their unclean sin, nor to their unsatisfied displays of holiness, but whether in their *rebellion* or their *religion*—in their *depravity* or *sufficiency*—they are to find their place in God. They are not to define themselves by their sickness, shame, and slavery, nor are they to try and rescue themselves out of their mindset through self-effort and works righteousness, which causes them to become slaves all the same to their self-made holiness and rightness within themselves. The only true answer to becoming free is not in coming under sin's fake promises and false façade of freedom, or falling prey to religion's promise of leadership and rescue.

Freedom only comes underneath the authority of God. Only in this place can leprosy be healed. Only in this place can one truly enjoy the world in its goodness and *pure* drink without falling victim to its drunken and *profane* lusts. It is imperative that the Israelites take their cues from the Almighty not from any construct of their own devising. This is why Numbers 6 ends with a benediction and closing of sorts. Verses 24-27 puts a bookend on this section to communicate that part of God's purpose, up to this point, as communicated in the leper, the Nazarite, and even through the encampment, the priesthood, and the tent of meeting, are all to answer the same prayer and bring Israel to one united and single blessing; "The Lord bless you and keep you; the Lord make his face to shine upon you and be gracious to you; the Lord lift up his countenance upon you and give you peace."

6

SCENE 7

THE GLORY EQUATION

In Chapter 7 of the book of Numbers comes a turning point for Israel. They are now to act upon and in response to the truths of all that had transpired, and are to obediently submit themselves as a people under God's leadership and rule. In a gigantic display and unified rally, God brings all of His people before the courts of the temple in order to call all the people to follow in the way of the Nazarite. The call is not that everyone must take a vow of fasting, but it is that God's people in some measure should begin to worship in His way around His Holy presence. In 7:1-3 it reads, "On the day when Moses had finished setting up the tabernacle and had anointed and consecrated it with all its furnishings and had anointed and consecrated the altar with all its utensils, the chiefs of Israel, heads of their fathers' houses, who were the chiefs of the tribes, who were over those who were listed, approached and brought their offerings before the Lord." Up until this point the Israelites were spectators to the drama of God's story in salvation as they were delivered up out of Egypt into the hands of freedom. They had enjoyed the work of God in His judgments, in His commands around the base of Mt. Sinai, and in His guidance through leadership and management, but the tent of meeting represents a new era of worship for God's people as God's presence dwells among them.

The leadership, namely Moses, provided Israel with this opportunity because of their obedience to the call of the Lord. Moses' obedience in all things pertaining to God's instruction allowed God's people to arrive to this point. Moses' faithfulness in the smallest things opened up new moments to hear the Lord. What enabled Moses to hear God, receive new insight from Him, and gain new understanding into the next steps of the journey is that Moses did as he was told, one step at a time. Moses must have had his doubts and misgivings along the way. When God calls him to rescue Israel out of the clutches of Egypt, Moses was insecure even in his own ability to speak. No matter how farfetched the commands of the Lord may have seemed to Moses, he followed. Moses followed the task that God had laid out for him. He'd listened to the voice of the Lord and he had remained true to do the entire task that God commanded of him.

In chapter 7:1 we see the painstaking care that Moses takes in this endeavor to offer this opportunity to the people. This day arrived only after Moses had consecrated and anointed all the furnishings, even down to the smallest utensil. Every little detail matters in Moses' care for God's people. Every minute and moment that involves his service is taken seriously, for what is at stake is not merely the good of the people, but the appropriate representation of the glory and wonder of God. As a result of God's goodness in enabling Moses to lead the people to this point, the people now had the opportunity to respond in how they too would follow the Lord.

In Numbers chapter 7:12-88 the people began to follow the leadership's example in seeking the glory of the Lord. Everyone began bringing their offerings, their possessions, and their attention to the tent of meeting. The verses in chapter 7 record the fact that each day another tribe of Israel would bring offerings of animals, grain, shekels, flour, oil, and other gifts to the tent. Everything they would bring in their hands was particularly meaningful to them. The grain that they threshed came from hours of hard work in the fields. The cattle they had raised often represented the wealth and stature of the home, and much of the money and other items brought for offerings caused them to forfeit much of what they possessed. All the time spent building their household, all the talents they invested into their well-being, and all the treasure that they amassed was now brought forth for one primary purpose, the honoring of the Lord.

The tent of meeting was in the center of the camp, and in the narrative, it is now toward the center that everything moves. Everything points to the glory of God. Every minute that God's people spent in the fields points to the glory of God, and every ounce of success that anyone experienced as a result of fertile ground, plentiful cattle, or time spent served to exalt the presence of God in their midst. This rally, this all day festivity of gift giving and sacrifice is a heart training exercise for God's people. Even though Egypt is now a distant memory as the reality of it passes over the last few years, the Israelites still maintain some of their self-centered ideas.

The leadership of Egypt had forced Israel to fight for survival, which caused Israel to hold dearly and strongly to all and anything they could in order to simply survive.

When the hand clutches tightly around everything in hopes that what little it has will not get away, it trains the heart to handle all things in this fashion. In this display in Numbers 7, God lovingly forces the hand of Israel to open and be generous. He calls them to honor His presence, not in tightly cling to the little that they have in fear that they may lose everything, but to give generously to honor the Lord in faith that they might gain everything.

The same reality is at stake for the people of Israel as it is for Moses in his leadership. Every person had to provide an answer to what is called the *glory equation*. God's call upon each man, woman, and child is that they obey Him. In obeying Him they are in some sense forfeiting their own desires.

Their money may be something that they consider to be the only thing they can save. Their food is the only thing that seemingly keeps them alive, and their cattle is the only thing that set them apart, and yet in choosing to forfeit in the little things they gain from these earthly things great reward. They had to make a choice to honor something and someone far greater. The predicament became about *glory*. Whose fame, honor, majesty, recognition, support, allegiance, authority, headship, and name were they ultimately desiring? Would they spend their lives amassing wealth only to exalt themselves, or would they spend the best they had in their time, their talent, and their treasure to serve and glorify the living God in and amongst His people? Whose image did they want people to see, theirs or Gods?

This is the glory equation. It's the equation that all of mankind has to answer. If each person's life is a giant equal sign, the question must be asked "what does a person want their life to add up to?" A person can decide to add in such a way that can fill a bank account, build an empire, fatten their tummy, serve to beautify the flesh, or do the countless things available to them that puts what one possesses or does at the *center*. The tent of meeting, the presence of God, the fame and name of God is the center here in Numbers. It is the center of everything. In all their ways the people would converge upon this presence. They came from whatever point they are at in life, and from wherever placement within the encampment in which they lived to bring their due to the Lord. Some had only to walk a few steps. Some were far off from the tent of meeting and may have had walked miles to get there, for the encampment was so large. Whether their lives were close to the glory, or far from the glory, their choice to choose was all the same.

This choice was not just reserved for Moses and the people but also for the Levites in the temple. In Numbers 7:5 the Levites are told to recognize all these gifts in dedication of the altar: "Accept these from them, that they may be used in the service of the tent of meeting, and give them to the Levites, to each man according to his service." These men were to steward all that was brought before the Lord. It was laid into their hands, and they were to accept it and use it to serve within the temple unto the glory of the Lord. They were not to spend the riches and lavish wealth upon themselves. They were not to eat and grow fat with greed. They were not to run away and start their own encampment with the riches they had pillaged from God's people, but they were to glorify God in their service all the same. Each Levite had this choice in the *glory equation* no matter how sizable their portion to steward.

The text tells us that they were apportioned these gifts from the people in different weights "according to their service." Again, this is an instruction and command given through Moses to the Levites. However, we must ask ourselves how we are to interpret the meaning of this text within the whole of Numbers. Are the Levites to take what is given to them and see it as due payment *for* their service? This is the typical mentality of a *wage earner*. A wage earner gives their service for a paycheck, and they are paid based on their worth. This mentality produces in a person the desire to work harder to earn more worth, and therefore service and work becomes a mantle on which to hang one's identity. Was this God's intention—that the Levites work and get paid *for* their service? It seems that this mentality is dangerously close to the mentality of a slave. A slave thinks this way, for they put themselves underneath the leadership of the "something" that God provides, rather than God Himself, and looks to the *gift* to affirm their dignity and value rather than the *giver*.

Jesus speaks about this in His parable of the talents in Matthew 25:14-30. In the parable, three men receive different measures of talent and finance. Whereas the first two invest and multiply the money in order to honor the giver Himself, the last man buries the money in the ground in fear of losing it. In Matthew 25:24 the man divulges his reasoning for doing so;

> He also who had received the one talent came forward, saying, 'Master, I knew you to be a hard man, reaping where you did not sow, and gathering where you scattered no seed, so I was afraid...'

The desire to self-protect and self-provide is driven here by a fear of the Master Himself. The slave mentality can again be seen. A *wage earner's* trajectory becomes to fight for every nickel, and once it is gained it is deemed best to be used in matters pertaining to "self"— for self improvement, self proving, or self promotion. The motivation for such pursuit is based in a self-protection mechanism and belief that a person is the source of their strongest defense, not God.

It seems that a mentality such as this does not fit the position of the Levites within the temple, and it seems that God does not encourage such a mentality within His people. Remember, the Levites owned nothing, and therefore their overhead was very low. Also we know their history, in that they were spared through the miraculous events in Egypt, and therefore needed no proof of their worth before God because He had already set them apart to serve specifically and beautifully in His service.

To arrive at the correct conclusion, we must consider the source from which the Levitical provisions are coming. It tells us in vs. 11 that as the people in the community received from the Lord, they "turned and made offerings." Everything that the people gave was freely "surrendered" funds. All that was surrendered into the Levite's hands came from a people who were responding to God's leadership in generosity.

We must remember that God is training their hearts not to be motivated by self-protection, but to give generously out of their realization that God is their protection. In giving, the people recognize grace in its smallest form. They are trained to come out from underneath any false sense of security that their "things" provide them in order to trust the Lord.

Everything that came into the Levite's hands to fund their service in the temple was given in grace and in response to the authority and grace of the Lord. The abundance did not come from a people who were working *for* the Lord but from a people who were working *from* Him. Everything that was brought into the temple's courts was provided by the Lord's grace in blessing the people. The people were not so much giving, as they were responding to the Lord's grace. They were stewarding what they were given by giving back what they had received—they *gave* what they *got*. In turn, the Levites did the same. They gave out of what they got. Their service came as a result of *grace giving* and they were not paid here for their services. They served out of the measure of grace God dealt them through the provisions they received within their own areas of responsibility.

Whether the Levitical priest's role and service in the temple included tasks of grandeur or of simplicity, it does not matter; they were to take what "little" or what "much" was given to them and they were to invest it into the service of God. Just as the people of the land had received their paycheck from the land that provided their grain and fed their cattle, the Levites, who owned no land, received their paycheck from the people.

Uniquely and collectively God molds and shapes the people's mindset to see that all that they have comes from Him and is for Him.

Through Moses, through the people, and through the priesthood, God devises a rally to train the people's heart's to serve Him, to serve from Him, and to serve for Him alone. This is the planned trajectory of all that is to be done within God's family. It is all to point to His glory. Anything that man has to bring to the table, whether good or bad, is not sufficient.

It is not like God needs the funds or craves the gifts given by His people as if in some way He is dependent upon them. Hidden even within the tribes themselves is a nugget of truth regarding this.

The 12 tribes, in coming forward offered their gifts, but the number 12 is divisible by the number 6, which is a notorious number used for "man" throughout the Bible. It is 1 number short of 7, which is God's number for perfection which appears in Chapter 8 in Numbers (the next chapter). The division of six is used here to exemplify the nature of man, in that it falls short of God's full expectation of glory even in generosity. Man cannot provide anything to God based on human merit or willing. God Himself provided everything to Israel on the basis of His own merit, grace, and glory. The rally and the offerings are merely a reminder and a curriculum designed particularly and specifically for Israel to learn the motivation of their hearts.

The human heart best serves in an environment where the *glory equation* is solved. When people answer this question correctly —"from whom and for whom are we doing this,"—everything falls into place. God fashioned everything in the Israelite culture around the sole purpose of telling His story—the story of His glory through Redemption. Like a continuous and ever focusing zoom lens, God zooms in once again. In the first part of Numbers, He catches a wide-angle shot of His story through the layout of the encampment, a narrow angle shot through the priesthood and the tent of meeting (the prototype temple), and a small look into the tendencies of His people through the Nazarite and the Leper. Nevertheless, the undercurrent of Numbers 7 deals with the inner lens and view of the human heart itself. In these passages God creates and fashions a framework and culture within the broken tribe of Israel. This is not to be a tribe motivated by their own lusts, their own wants, nor their own desires, but at their basest, most human, and most succinct level, their hearts are to want what is the most complete and satisfying thing to them—the glory, the fame, the reputation, and the image of God.

7

SCENE 8

7 LAMPSTANDS

A dynamic community is forming. A community once filled with a band of slaves and disarrayed in governance, identity, meaning, authority, and purpose, now gather, assemble, and aim toward a destination of legacy and significance. God's story of redemption fastens each man, woman, and child together in family. Everyone begins to think less like slaves, and they begin to think deeper in regard to how they relate and serve unto both God and man.

In the previous scene, the rally toward God's glory took place in order to point the encampment of Israel toward the final exclamation point of their journey. The journey is not about them. The journey is not about providing them with what they want or think they need, it is about God Himself. Numbers 8 arrives at a pinnacle passage that in some way provides a crowning moment for Israel. To understand the depth of what's going on in this chapter we will have to mine down a bit, but underneath the sediment and debris we will once again find that God is making statements and promises that reach far deeper than what first meets the eye.

In Numbers 8:1-4, the text transitions from focusing upon the rally and parade of offerings and captures a conversation once again between the Lord and Moses as the next wave of instruction is transmitted;

> Now the Lord spoke to Moses, saying, 'Speak to Aaron and say to him, When you set up the lamps, the seven lamps shall give light in front of the lampstand.' And Aaron did so: he set up its lamps in front of the lampstand, as the Lord commanded Moses. And this was the workmanship of the lampstand, hammered work of gold. From its base to its flowers, it was hammered work; according to the pattern that the Lord had shown Moses, so he made the lampstand.

A repeated and prominent object emerges in these first few verses. The lampstand in the tent of meeting comes prominently into view. The lampstands were precious in that they are made of hammered and refined gold, symbolizing something of great value. Not only were they priceless, but their significance is beyond measure.

The lampstands provide yet another artistic clue and *type* within the story as they point to something far greater than their mere beauty. To the community of Israel these seven lampstands and their design were given to Moses by God's instruction according to a pattern that He set forth for the shaping of His meeting place. The Israelites knew these beacons of light to have been divinely shaped and crafted by the Lord's decree. At this point in Israel's history the people saw the light on the lampstands and maintained limited reference points by which to link and understand the lampstand's true meaning.

The lampstand itself looked like a flowering tree with seven extending branches that broke off and traveled into 3 arms on each side of the long and central trunk. Exodus 25:31-36 pictures the tree as having "bulbs and flowers," "branches," and "almond blossoms." The lights lit up along the top of the trees branches illuminating the tent of meeting in its darkness, much like the stars in the night sky.

The meaning derived from these lampstands is poignant. Israelite understanding and memory took them immediately back to God's creation within the Garden. These lampstands were the picture of the perfect creation, as Adam and Eve served as (p)riests unto God within the Garden; among the trees and fields, and beneath the calm of the brilliantly illumined starry-night sky. The fact that there are seven of them caused them to think of the seven light-sources that were directly visible to their naked eye in the night sky (five planets, sun, and moon).

However, the limited perspective of Israel only provided them a glimpse into the full-reality of meaning held within these lamps. In the New Testament, Jesus replaced the tent of meeting and temple (Mt. 27:51), as He also replaced Israel who was to be His light to all nations (Is. 42:6), and ultimately became the *place* and the *person* for God's dwelling. He declared Himself to be the "light of the world." (Jhn. 8:12) Rather than remaining veiled and tucked away behind a curtain, Jesus' light shone publicly. In the same way, Jesus also compared His followers during the time of His ministry to this same image of being as like lamps set on a stand. (Mt. 5:14-16) In fact, after His death, resurrection, and ascension, His formation of the "church," which is a "people" in a universal sense that came into His light in obedience to the gospel through placing faith in Christ's work (Eph. 1:22, 23), and in a local and specific sense (place), pointed to the reality of a body of believers who fellowship together in work and worship. God's people are like a beacon of hope to a dark onlooking world. (Rom. 16:16; 2 Cor. 1:1; 1 Cor. 16:10)

Even further in the book of Revelation, we hear John speaking of Jesus walking amidst the seven lampstands which represent God's people and church. (Rev. 1:13-20). We hear of heaven as being lit by the light of the Lamb unto all nations (Rev. 21:23, 34), which is surrounded by a multitude (Rev. 1:20) of His church—the light here is again pointing to all of heaven being filled with His presence.

The *glory equation* that initiated in Chapter 7 is now given a point. Not only are the hearts of the people to specifically seek God's glory in all things, and through all things, but specifically people are to become bearers of light. They are to be filled with the presence of God and are to be sent out on mission to a broken world.

Revelation 1-2 talks about a mystery guest who is present among the lampstands and maintains the mantle of honor. The one who is indeed among the lampstands is Jesus Himself. This is what the lampstands point to and speak about. Their physical appearance emerges here in great significance, but their numerical meaning is equally as important.

In the inner courts there were 7 of these lampstands as contrasted out and against the 12 tribes—a number divisible by 6. To the Israelite mind, they were well acquainted with both letters and numbers, as their numeric system and alphabet were one in the same, and would have had at least an idea of the significance. The very genesis of their history had begun in God with the seven days of creation in the Garden. Combined with the imagery of the inner courts as looking like a Garden, they most certainly recognized the comparison. Any person paying attention understood and remembered the fall of Adam and Eve in the Garden through their disobedience to God's authority, and they most certainly equated the number 6 with the number of man; a number that has been tied to the "mark of Cain" who is the first offspring of Adam. The contrast between the number 7, which means perfect, and the number 6, which alludes to the imperfection of man, flavors the entire scene.

In the Jewish language, letters stood for numbers and vice versa. Therefore, for every word and sentence uttered in the Jewish language, there is always a corresponding sum number that links the letters and words when added together. This is where the number 7 is particularly important for correct understanding, both for the Jewish mindset, as well as all of humanities, even into the New Testament interpretation.

From the onset of Genesis, God and His work in and through His people has been deeply associated with the number 7. Beginning in Genesis 1, God is seen as Creator and Lord (LORD being a division of 7). There is a pronounced link provided between God as Lord and His ability to "speak" from His mouth in a manner that causes creation to come into being. The phrase, "and from God's mouth," appears 70 (7x10) times, which foreshadows how the New Testament also speaks of Jesus—Jesus being the very Word spoken (repeated 7x in John 1).

The word of the Lord in perfection is again linked to His creation of the law and 10 commandments in Exodus (the giving of the law taking place in the 70th chapter of Scripture). God's law is perfect and the Scriptures tell us exactly 14x's (7x2) that He "has written them on our hearts." Unfortunately however, man's imperfection in keeping the law perfectly once again appears at the base of Mt. Sinai as it did in the Garden of Eden, which allows the story of God's ultimate plan of redemption to continue on through our place in Numbers 8—with the lampstand imagery provided, and ultimately into the lineage of Jesus (who is 77th in His family line—7xII).

This Savior, Jesus, the ultimate light of the Garden, is, like Adam, given the title of "Son of Man," which is a phrase used 196 (7x28) times in the AV. The last use of this phrase in the New Testament providentially occurs in Revelation 14:14 which when multiplied equals the same number, 196. During Jesus' ministry He is recorded in John as performing 7 signs which authenticate Him as the Messiah in perfect completion to the Old Testament foreshadowing, which also proves Him to be the perfect "do-over" which undoes all of humanities mistakes.[3] He is recorded at the last supper, the Passover (77 times), as proclaiming His death and resurrection to His disciples as the sign that He is ultimately the deliverer of all men, and is linked to the deliverance that took place in Egypt with the 10 plagues.

And in the following moments, as recorded in all four Gospels, Jesus was in fact hung on a cross to die. Above Him was written this statement; "This is Jesus the King of the Jews, The King of the Jews, This is the King of the Jews, Jesus of Nazareth is the King of the Jews." This inscription contains a total of 28 words (7x4) and remains the same across all 4 gospels. It states unequivocally that Jesus is the light represented in the 7 lampstands. When Pilate was asked to change the words that were written, Pilate responded with a 7-word proclamation: "What I have written I have written" (John 19:22).

As a result of Christ's death and new life, the church was birthed. A new people are revealed, in that all men and women from every tribe and nation can believe in God and come into the kingdom simply by confessing their sins (spoken 7 times). Our hope is in the gospel and good news of all that Christ died for us through faith (49x5), and this comes by way of hearing the message (49=7x7). In the wake of such confession comes forgiveness (42=7x6)—provided by Christ's death and wounds on the cross (35x's=7x5). By this forgiveness and payment we are now reconciled and made right with God (used 7x's). Following this salvation, a new believer in Christ is baptized into the Triune name God (used 77x's), and the person's life is now washed in order that they may forever become a life giving representation of the saving power of God's grace.

Finally, Jesus commissions His followers to spread this same message to others. This commission, the Great Commission, is foreshadowed in the Old Testament, when after the flood of judgment in the days of Noah God repopulated the earth through 70 descendants (7x10—Gen. 10); which continued to preserve Israel's legacy, as they would later experience hardship and come to Egypt seeking food (Gn. 46:27). As we know, this resulted in 400 years of bondage, but out of it came God's deliverance once again when He renumbered His people in Numbers chapter 1 under 70 appointed elders to help Moses in administering the Israelites out of the wilderness and into the Promised Land. The number 7, as shown, not only refers to a Holy God, but to a perfect people that are created in and through God's work of deliverance.

Fast forwarding into the book of Revelation, this story completes itself when we see a perfect God writing 7 letters to 7 Churches who were broken yet hopeful for perfection only through Christ's salvation. Upon those not included in the people of God in Revelation, 7 Seals and Judgments are reserved along with 7 Trumpets and 7 Bowls. The 7 Golden Lampstands reappear again in correlation with the 7 Stars, the 7 Angels, the 7 Spirits of God, and ultimately point to the Lamb with 7 Horns and 7 Eyes who brings down 7 Thunders upon the Fiery Red Dragon with 7 heads and 7 Crowns; ultimately laying waste to the Leopard-Like Beast with 7 heads, the Scarlet-Colored Beast with 7 heads, the 7 Mountains, and the 7 Kings. This is the perfect victory of God.

All this to say, the lampstands add one more flavor to God's artistic journey, in portraying through sign and symbol the true depths of God's purest intentions. The encampment of redemption spirals down into the priesthood and tent of meeting in its focus. The community of Lepers and Nazarites point to and instruct a people to come to the Lord corporately and individually. And ultimately, the Lord to whom they come is the final zoomed-in image of Christ Himself. This is the completion of the glory equation. Not only to see the glory of God, but to see that all God's glory is wrapped up in the man of Jesus Himself.

This explains how the following verses, Numbers 8:5-22, flow forth from verses 1-4. The text drives quickly, speaking about the Levitical priesthood once again. Particularly in verses 16-18 God says,

> For they are wholly given to me from among the people of Israel. Instead of all who open the womb, the *firstborn* of all the people of Israel, I have taken them for myself. For all the *firstborn* among the people of Israel are mine, both of man and of beast. On the day that I struck down all the *firstborn* in the land of Egypt I consecrated them for myself, and I have taken the Levites instead of all the *firstborn* among the people of Israel.

The cause for the apparent and quick focus shift is that the Levites themselves, like the lampstands, are also to point to kingdom reality. The lampstands point to the Garden, but the priesthood points to the role that mankind had lost. Mankind was meant to function in being priests unto God, and in service to God. This was lost in Adam's folly. God drew poignant attention to this fact in repeating heavily the word "first born." To the Jewish mind of that day, they would have known this to resemble Adam's place in the Garden through and before God in daily service and worship. They would have sensed their purpose in this. Their purpose was to regain this, to retain this, and to reclaim this. However, the full revival to re-awaken this is through Jesus Christ Himself;

 He is the image of the invisible God, the *firstborn* of all creation. For by him all things were created, in heaven and on earth, visible and invisible, whether thrones or dominions or rulers or authorities—all things were created through him and for him. And he is before all things, and in him all things hold together. And he is the head of the body, the church. He is the beginning, the *firstborn* from the dead, that in everything he might be preeminent. For in him all the *fullness of God* was pleased to dwell, and through him to reconcile to himself all things, whether on earth or in heaven, making peace by the blood of his cross.

As we traipse through the pages of the New Testament—that which was unknown to the Jews in that time—we see that the New Adam is ultimately the one coming and Promised. "The first man, Adam, became a living being; *but* the last Adam, a life-giving spirit" (1 Cor.15:45). This life giving Spirit, given through Jesus, is the one being expected here, and the Levitical priesthood points to the ultimate ministry of Jesus before the Father in heaven. Here's the main point summed up Hebrews 8:

 We have a High Priest who sat down in the place of honor beside the throne of the majestic God in heaven. There he ministers in the heavenly Tabernacle, the true place of worship that was built by the Lord and not by human hands. And since every high priest is required to offer gifts and sacrifices, our High Priest must make an offering, too. If he were here on earth, he would not even be a priest, since there already are priests who offer the gifts required by the law. They serve in a system of worship that is only a copy, a shadow of the real one in heaven. For when Moses was getting ready to build the Tabernacle, God gave him this warning: 'Be sure that you make everything according to the pattern I have shown you here on the mountain.'

But now Jesus, our High Priest, has been given a ministry that is far superior to the old priesthood, for he is the one who mediates for us a far better covenant with God, based on better promises. If the first covenant had been faultless, there would have been no need for a second covenant to replace it. But when God found fault with the people, he said:

'The day is coming,' says the Lord,
   'when I will make a new covenant
   with the people of Israel and Judah.
   This covenant will not be like the one
   I made with their ancestors
   when I took them by the hand
   and led them out of the land of Egypt.

They did not remain faithful to my covenant, so I turned my back on them,' says the Lord. 'But this is the new covenant I will make with the people of Israel on that day,' says the Lord:

'I will put my laws in their minds,
   and I will write them on their hearts.
   I will be their God,
   and they will be my people.

And they will not need to teach their neighbors, nor will they need to teach their relatives, saying, 'You should know the Lord.' For everyone, from the least to the greatest, will know me already. And I will forgive their wickedness, and I will never again remember their sins.'

When God speaks of a 'new' covenant, it means he has made the first one obsolete. It is now out of date and will soon disappear.

The whole plan of God as observed in the first section of Numbers seems to spiral toward one end—Jesus Christ. Everything points to the Messiah and His work in and amongst a new people that He creates for Himself and for His purposes. To bring people to the point of recognizing their role before the presence of God, God takes a roundabout way in order to make His point. He begins with an encampment and slowly zooms down in ordering a people, which orders their hearts, and directs them solely and only toward the main focus of all things—Jesus. This is the rehabilitation plan that converges and spirals down to the very core of all human existence and meaning. All things in creation are to exalt this one man and one glory. This refocusing is the only thing that can rehabilitate an enslaved heart.

It is curious to see in the remaining journey throughout the book of Numbers, that the spiral then begins to spin outward in the opposite manner. In bringing people in around His presence in heart response, God reconciles the people back to the Garden ethic. The Garden was not a secluded place, however. God tasked Adam to propel the Garden culture back out into the world in order to spread its message and harmony back out into the unformed wilderness.

This was to be the task of Israel as well. Slowly, in the next few chapters, God will prepare His people in their hearts to respond to Him by turning them toward the world in the power of His presence, in order to set out and spread the power and presence in and through them. His presence is to come symbolically from the lamps, into the hearts, into a people, into an encampment and out into an unaware world.

8

SCENE 9

THE PASSOVER MEAL

Before Israel left Sinai and embarked upon the Journey toward the Promised Land, God needed to ensure that the work that had been done up until this point would not be forgotten. He needed to intentionally craft a *rhythm of remembrance* into the fabric of His culture in order to ensure that His story would be recounted, reminisced upon, and would continue to ruminate in the hearts of His people.

God knows the tendencies of humanity. We are prone to forget. Israel was prone to walk back into their old slave-like ways that were all too familiar to them, and a design for remembrance needed to be instated that served as a kind of "seasonal landmark"—revisiting itself on the people strategically in order that they might remain awake to all that He had done, all that He was doing, and all that He was going to do.

Chapter 9 of Numbers describes such a landmark. In Numbers 9:1-14 we find once again the command of God coming from God to Moses:

> And the Lord spoke to Moses in the wilderness of Sinai, in the first month of the second year after they had

come out of the land of Egypt, saying, 'Let the people of Israel keep the Passover at its appointed time. On the fourteenth day of this month, at twilight, you shall keep it at its appointed time; according to all its statutes and all its rules you shall keep it.' So Moses told the people of Israel that they should keep the Passover. And they kept the Passover in the first month, on the fourteenth day of the month, at twilight, in the wilderness of Sinai; according to all that the Lord commanded Moses, so the people of Israel did. And there were certain men who were unclean through touching a dead body, so that they could not keep the Passover on that day, and they came before Moses and Aaron on that day. And those men said to him, 'We are unclean through touching a dead body. Why are we kept from bringing the Lord's offering at its appointed time among the people of Israel?' And Moses said to them, 'Wait, that I may hear what the Lord will command concerning you.'

The Lord spoke to Moses, saying, 'Speak to the people of Israel, saying, If any one of you or of your descendants is unclean through touching a dead body, or is on a long journey, he shall still keep the Passover to the Lord. In the second month on the fourteenth day at twilight they shall keep it. They shall eat it with unleavened bread and bitter herbs. They shall leave none of it until the morning, nor break any of its bones; according to all the statute for the Passover they shall keep it. But if anyone who is clean and is not on a journey fails to keep the Passover, that person shall be cut off from his people because he did not bring the Lord's offering at its appointed time; that man shall bear his sin. And if a stranger sojourns among you and would keep the Passover to the Lord, according to the statute of the Passover and according to its rule, so shall he do. You shall have one statute, both for the sojourner and for the native.'

The people were already well acquainted with all that was included in the Passover. It was a time to remember the dreadfully joyful night of God's deliverance. God had defeated the so called "gods" of the Egyptian people in smiting them through nine horrific plagues of pestilence, until finally, God, at the end of His patience, ignited in anger toward a bitter and rebellious Pharaoh and promised the 10th and final plague—to kill the firstborn male of each family. That night, as the angel of death took the lives of the innocent due to Pharaoh's sinful disobedience, all children living in the homes whose doorposts were smeared with the blood of the Lamb were "passed over." That destructive, erroneous, and momentous night brought the death of "one," however to every home. In the homes of those who were unbelieving, their first born son died. In the homes that honored the Lord, it took the life of a lamb.

That night was to be remembered as both bitter and as sweet, as both a great victory of joy, and as a great defeat of sadness with much mourning—a night of judgment and of blessing. To this day, in celebrating the Passover, Jews enjoy a moment in their *Sedar* meal in which they partake in sweet sugar water as combined with that of bitter herbs and spices. This event is to be remembered in the both/and way that it was experienced. It was a profoundly saddening occurrence but also a completely liberating event all at the same time.

God does not want the people of His flock to forget such a moment in history. As the generations go on, God wants to preserve for His family, in a virtual photo album and time capsule, a moment that is to be instructive to all branches of the human legacy. God wants His people to remember the suffering that came under the hands of all their false masters, the ones that enslaved them. He wants His people to remember their cruel owners so they will not return to them. He also wants them to remember the sweetness of His victory, so as they encounter adversity along the road before them, they will remain firm in faith that His victory will come to them over and over again in the moments that await them in the future.

The Passover as stated in Numbers 9 was for both the native and the sojourner. It was a festival that caused every human being to remember that either "*they* shall bear *their* sin" (vs. 13), and incur all consequences as a result of the lies waiting in the shadows of their slavery, or that in following the Lord, they will receive all the freedom that comes in living in the light of God's sacrifice on their behalf. This feast, and this meal, was to delve into the depths of God's redemption plan and meaning, but it was not only to reach back into the throws of the Egyptian deliverance, but was to help the people of God anchor themselves around a meal that threads the tapestry of His story all the way back into the Garden—a thread that would also continue to weave its way out into the distant future of God's coming kingdom. In an excerpt from *The Tempo of Discipleship*, we are provided with this summation of what the power of this meal would have done, and is still to do for the people of God:

> The meal to some degree would have first connected their thinking to the precise environment of the Garden of Eden. This is where creation started. This is where humanity started. We started in a Garden surrounded by nourishment, supply, and food. God's original plan for the man was that he was to work the garden and eat from it. Being in the garden was a symbol to Adam that God was his source of provision and all his nourishment. The food then was a promise of covenant blessing. It resembled the binding of God to His people for their wellbeing, filling, and sustenance.
>
> But the snake entered the Garden in Genesis 3 and took this food, by way of the apple, and promised his kingdom to Adam and Eve through dishonest intentions. This same food that was meant to display God's goodness to Adam and Eve was the very same

food that Satan hi-jacked and perverted in meaning so that humanity's parents would fall into sin and judgment. And on that day, the paradise of God that was given in food was given up in food. Up to this moment, nothing had ever been done apart from the life and love of God. Now, suddenly a whole new world opened up. The seed of that forbidden fruit sprouted deep in human hearts, spreading out roots and branches that encompassed the whole of humanity's future, blossoming into pride and envy, murder and deceit. Every crime, personal and corporate, private and public, grew out of this common root, from sex trafficking, to genocide, adultery to petty theft. Life with God was rejected and life without God, embraced. The bite from that fruit was truly the kiss of death. This horror and atrocious fall forever filled food with a mixed message, a message of blessing and message of judgment.

This theme continued in Genesis 18 when God visited Abraham through three men, as He confirmed His promise to give Abraham and Sarah a son to restore the mess that Adam and Eve's sin had set in motion. During the meal He shared that this son would lead to two things. The promised son was to make Abraham a very rich man in blessing and legacy—growing to be as many children as the stars in the sky. Secondly, and ultimately, this promise was to fulfill what God promised through Eve, that a Son (A Christ—Messiah) would come through Abraham's line and crush the head of the serpent; the serpent who had brought sin and death into the world through that forbidden fruit. And so once again over a meal came the promise of a blessing to God's people.

Abraham had Isaac and Ishmael, and soon Isaac had Jacob and Esau. The story tells us that Esau was born first and so by birth order was entitled to the Father's inheritance. The line of blessing promised to Abraham was to come through Esau, but in Genesis 25:29-34 Esau came in hungry one day, and Jacob offered him a bowl of soup in exchange for the family inheritance. Esau snatched the bowl of soup in ravenous hunger, gave his inheritance away in that moment to Jacob, and Esau forfeited the blessings of God all over again over a bowl full of food.

As the Israelite history progressed it brought along men like Joseph who was raised up for a particular time in human history. He was raised up when Egypt was experiencing a historic harvest of food, of which Joseph was put in charge of to steward and store. And not long after this sign of blessing in provision from God came, did God allow famine to come upon the land. The use of food not only supplied blessing but allowed God to display his judgment as well. And due to the famine and Joseph's faithful stewardship of the years of feasting, everyone in all the land came to Egypt to live and survive.

This led to a change in hands in Egyptian leadership, which caused slavery to come upon God's people for 400 years. We all know the story from here. God rose up Moses and called him to go to the Pharaoh speaking the words, 'Let my people go,' and after 400 years of slavery and 9 plagues, Pharaoh still refused to oblige. But on the final plague, God promised to take the first born son of every family in the land as a sign of judgment on the Pharaoh's stubborn disobedience. This plague was to impact everyone unless they obeyed one condition. If the people were to take a Lamb, kill it, and smear its blood over the door posts of their homes, the angel would accept the death of the Lamb in the place of the first born son. That night as the angel passed over the houses smeared with blood He extended grace in light of the lamb, and entered the homes to take the life of the sons of those without this sign. The whole land once again experienced God's dichotomy in *food*. Some family's killed dinner and were spared, and some refused to take God's provision and were judged.

This led to the glorious freeing of the Israelite slaves as they followed God into the desert toward the Promised Land. God had beaten their evil king. God had proven His kingship over His people once again. And as the people traveled toward the promised land God provided for His people. In the desert God provided manna—a bread and meal from heaven for them to eat.

And what Israel had not yet seen was that things would continue to transpire on into Israelite history as it progressed into the times of Jesus. The Israelites (*as future to this moment within Numbers 9)* were carried into slavery once again by Babylon, in which Nebuchadnezzar changed the names of God's people to reflect the worship of his God, and he offered men like Daniel a place at his table. Interestingly enough Daniel didn't mind his name being changed, and he was even offered a position in the King's school of diviners, witches, tarot card readers, and new age psychics, of which he accepted, but the one thing he wouldn't take was the King's offer that Daniel could share in the meals of the King's table. The reason why can be further seen as the Bible's story progresses even on into Esther.

The King's table under Nebuchadnezzar and on into the time of Esther under King Xerxes was a deeply pagan event. The king would throw huge feasts, tainted with sex, drugs and rock 'n roll. Food was linked to the idea of sin, un-cleanliness, revelry and partying among those who gladly took Satan's apples. But once again, the judgment that echoed the Garden was undone by God's redemption. Esther came into the center of all the revelry to plead for God's people who were about to experience genocide from this demonic kingship. She cooked the King and his evil side-kick Haman a meal, all the while pleading for her people. The king relented and the tables of history were turned—literally. A people of Israel were saved from the tyranny around a meal. They celebrated the victory with a feast, a meal called Purim—a tradition still observed in Jewish tradition today.

So when Jesus entered human history in human flesh and was birthed in Bethlehem (*which means "the house of bread"*), and grew up only to be tempted in the desert to sin and give into Satan's false provision like Adam had, by eating food at the start of His ministry (Lk. 4) it was more than just coincidence. In beginning His ministry when He referred to Himself as the Bread of Life (Jhn. 6:35), feeding the 5,000 with bread and fish —linking him to Elijah in 1 Kings 17 when he was fed by ravens—and showing up in Matthew 26:26 on the feast of Passover to offer communion in 'remembrance of Him.' The meaning in the event of the meal was more profound than a simple dinner. In Jesus breaking bread which represented His body, and pouring wine that represented His shed blood, He was alluding to a story much broader and much more redeeming than merely one moment on a cross. The dinner and death of Jesus was attached to all of Holy history; not only to remembering the past but also to remembering His promises for the future.

The future church would begin and grow around a meal (Acts 2:42), and ultimately the whole of human history would end in Jesus' 2nd Coming, when in

Revelation 19:6-9, after all the judgments of the earth had been completed, Jesus hosts the feast and Marriage Supper of the Lamb. This will be the ultimate sign of blessing and of judgment. Those who are invited to the banquet are blessed; those who eat elsewhere are not.

Through one meal, instituted into the calendar cycle of Israel, both the native and the sojourner were to remember one thing and one thing only—The Lordship of God. The meal is like a container that is filled with a gallon of meaning. The meal itself represents what it is to be inside and under God's rule and reign, and it also proclaims that same message to those living outside God's rule and reign under the tyranny of another master. The meal is to exemplify the nourishment and nutritious life and care of Christ, and is to expose the malicious and defeating lies of the enemies' fake façade of provision. It is a reminder which creates an environment that enables everyone to fully ponder the feeling of slavery, and to once again rejoice that sin's chains have been broken and are no more.

The people were hidden beneath the swells of a regal and noble eagle's wings in following God their Father. The Passover meal was to be a *rhythm* in their travels to remind them of such a reality.

In the following passage, Numbers 9:15-23, an additive rhythm to that of the Passover appears as yet another tool for training. The pillar of fire and the billowing cloud of God's leading and protective presence served as another helpful reminder to them of God's gentle hand of Lordship. In a rhythmic fashion, as the Passover served to remind the people in how to think about God and relate to Him and each other throughout the journey, the leading of the cloud and fire trained the people in a rhythm all its own. The method God instituted in how He led His people teaches us how all of reality is to be walked out in the day-to-day journey. Numbers 9:15-23 records:

> On the day that the tabernacle was set up, the cloud covered the tabernacle, the tent of the testimony. And at

evening it was over the tabernacle like the appearance of fire until morning. So it was always: the cloud covered it by day and the appearance of fire by night. And whenever the cloud lifted from over the tent, after that the people of Israel set out, and in the place where the cloud settled down, there the people of Israel camped. At the command of the Lord the people of Israel set out, and at the command of the Lord they camped. As long as the cloud rested over the tabernacle, they remained in camp. Even when the cloud continued over the tabernacle many days, the people of Israel kept the charge of the Lord and did not set out. Sometimes the cloud was a few days over the tabernacle, and according to the command of the Lord they remained in camp; then according to the command of the Lord they set out. And sometimes the cloud remained from evening until morning. And when the cloud lifted in the morning, they set out, or if it continued for a day and a night, when the cloud lifted they set out. Whether it was two days, or a month, or a longer time that the cloud continued over the tabernacle abiding there, the people of Israel remained in camp and did not set out, but when it lifted they set out. At the command of the Lord they camped, and at the command of the Lord they set out. They kept the charge of the Lord, at the command of the Lord by Moses.

The Lord's pattern of movement, long established since the Israelites left the clutches of Egypt, is re-mentioned here in correlation with the Passover because the Israelites were about to become mobile again. The cloud had led them out of Egypt to the base of Mt. Sinai to be taught and organized; to be reconciled in relationship, and to be rehabilitated. Now, the cloud of God was on the move once again toward a different goal. God was not about to lead His people to the base of yet another mountain, but He was about to take His people on a road trip toward the Promised Land.

What Israel could not see, that we as the reader can see, is that the journey toward the Promised Land was going to be one of great trial and struggle. The Israelites needed absolute sensitivity to God's will, God's avenue, and God's timing along the highway if they were going to survive. Anything short of shear surrender and dependence upon God would only result in disastrous outcomes. God's presence in the cloud and in the fire taught them the rhythm of shepherding. God's movement here becomes for Israel like a giant demonstration of God's direction and guidance, and for us today it becomes a giant illustration and parable for how God's people continue to follow God's lead.

The first thing that this section of Scripture teaches us about God's rhythm of leadership is that during the day, His leading is ever so gentle, docile, beautiful, and fragrant; like walking through a clouded mist, or perched on a grassy hill on a beautiful day with wispy clouds dangling in the sky. God is at home in the light, and is light, and His leadership is tender and gentle like that of a cloud. He, like a cloud, may cover the light of the sun for a time, but He keeps no secret that there is always a great hope just behind the fog. At night however, and in all things related to darkness, God is severe and edgy. The fire pierces the darkness with a semblance of light and provides a warning to all. To all intruders it issues a warning that God defends and watches over His people. To His people on the other hand, though it in one manner provides a sense of safety, it in a another capacity causes hearts to think twice before trying to step out from underneath God's leading out into the flames in the dark of night. God is fiercely jealous for all that is His, and the cloud and fire was to shine before God's people and to His enemies to make this known.

These daily reminders and movements of the Lord served to provide a training mechanism of habitual discipline for God's people. When the cloud lifted they moved, and when it settled they stayed put. The verses in Numbers chapter 9 clearly share that the cloud and fire often settled for days, weeks, and even months, but the people were to know that the decision to move or stay was based solely on God's decision. This was a statement to the people underneath God's care that when the way was clouded or blocked by fire, they needed to rest. It is a statement to God's people that when the answers to questions are clouded, they needed to wait. It is a statement to God's people that even though it is seemingly daytime outside, or lit up with fire at night—thus everything looks clear—it does not necessarily mean that God is ready to move. Nor does it mean that all potential danger is far off. The people needed to trust Him.

God fully knew and understood how long the Israelites needed to remain in each place. God's goal in each location, whether His people experienced the rain or extreme heat, is that His glory, His timing, and His purposes be revealed before allowing them to take the next step. In and through this daily repetition of waiting and going, God formed His people's hearts to be dependent and surrendered to His voice. The people quickly learned that as they traveled along the road of the journey that God's hand would not allow anything in or out of His camp unless it was by His authority and design. The people's hearts took courage in this—in knowing that their own initiative and know-how brought about only absolute fruitlessness without God's strength behind it. Their sole source of success came in moving when God moved, and in staying when God stayed.

This is the same message that is conveyed in and through the Passover meal. While in Egypt, the people had undoubtedly clawed and scraped their way around trying to innovate ways of escape, but God settled His mind in keeping them in their imprisonment. He deemed it fit for their good, and He lifted and freed them when He saw that His glory and the good of His people could fully be known, shown, and profoundly experienced in all its love and in all its judgment. God's motivating factor is and always will be the showing forth of His name. This is His priority, not the comfort of His people. In holding the Israelites long enough within His plan, He ensured that His people would not merely experience temporal pleasure, but that they could walk through life seeing the extent of the greatest pleasure that is to be had in Him. The Passover is a giant lifting cloud and release of joy through the waiting. The people during their time in slavery had lost sight of God's ability to ordain and sovereignly maintain control over even the darkest moments of their imprisonment, and here through a cloud and fire, God recalibrates their aching hearts to see the truth of His rule.

The people were about to see more fully that every time God waits it's for the good of His people. Whenever God moves, it's for the good of His people. Anytime the answers seem clouded and unclear, and the path seems blocked, it's for the good of His people. Anytime God burns an enemy or strikes fear and awe into the hearts of His followers, it's for the good of His people. Anytime God's fire consumes those who step outside His charge, it's for the good of His people. God acts upon His perfect nature, and in the honor of His name, only so that He may claim the perfect good for His people. For God to do anything else, and to honor anything imperfect and lower than Himself—above His own praise and admiration—would mean that He becomes an idolater ultimately leading to the destruction of His people—sacrificing their joy in the process.

To communicate the fullness of all that is enclosed within the cloud and fire's meaning, God took His people on a journey of stop and go, ebb and flow, and to and fro. The daily deliverance of the people came in the symbol of God's cloud and fire. Nevertheless, even with such a sign surrounding them, the people's hearts were slow to surrender. Each moment in the journey revealed different crevices of fault and broken thinking. Each pathway, roadway, and highway of maneuver only proved to unearth the pieces of broken cisterns that still lay dormant at the base of the Israelite hearts. Their freedom was secure but their trust in it was still minimal. It took a journey through the dessert to massage the hopeful truths of God's authority into their wounded souls.

SCENE 10

A WEE BIT 'O CELO'BRATION

Before the tents had collapsed and the caravan commenced for the long arduous journey toward the Promised Land, God sent shock once more in cathartic rhythm into the hearts of His people. In Numbers Chapter 10:1-10 God once again speaks to Moses in giving him an altogether peculiar command:

The Lord spoke to Moses, saying, 'Make two silver trumpets. Of hammered work you shall make them, and you shall use them for summoning the congregation and for breaking camp. And when both are blown, all the congregation shall gather themselves to you at the entrance of the tent of meeting. But if they blow only one, then the chiefs, the heads of the tribes of Israel, shall gather themselves to you. When you blow an alarm, the camps that are on the east side shall set out. And when you blow an alarm the second time, the camps that are on the south side shall set out. An alarm is to be blown whenever they are to set out. But when the assembly is to be gathered together, you shall blow a long blast, but you shall not sound an alarm. And the sons of Aaron, the priests, shall blow the trumpets. The trumpets shall be to you for a perpetual statute throughout your generations. And when you go to war in your land against the adversary who oppresses you, then you shall sound an alarm with the trumpets, that you may be remembered before the Lord your God, and you shall be saved from your enemies. On the day of your gladness also, and at your appointed feasts and at the beginnings of your months, you shall blow the trumpets over your burnt offerings and over the sacrifices of your peace offerings. They shall be a reminder of you before your God: I am the Lord your God.'

In the midst of the anticipated and expected move, God throws down a task that seems a bit disconnected from everything else going on. He orders the people to make two silver trumpets in order that they may be sounded as the caravan sets out. Among all the commotion of moving, packing, and loading up, some of the people were forced to stop and take time to fashion, create, and shape these processional instruments. The question that might come to mind at this point is, "Why?"

To understand why God issues this word of instruction we must understand the nature of the trumpet. The trumpet appears at various times throughout Scripture both in the Old Testament and the New Testament, and due to contents contained in passages that also speak about the trumpet, we can derive some insightful meaning into why God includes this here. The trumpet throughout Scripture often symbolizes a turning point (Is. 27:3) and is connected to the idea of a celebration (The Feast of Trumpets, Lev. 23:24, Numbers 29:1).

Pertaining to our story, we can observe that the trumpet is symbolically sounded at the Feast of Trumpets on the day that Joseph was symbolically released from his own prison cell, which inaugurated his day as leader of Egypt. This ultimately led to the release of Israel's captives from starvation and hunger. The trumpet, in a like manner, is not only used here symbolically, but it is also used to portray the release of all of God's people throughout the continuing Old Testament, including the instance here in Numbers (Ez. 37:16-19; Oba. 1:18; Zec. 10:6). As also seen here in Numbers, it is not only a call of release, celebration, and victory, but it is a call to war, a call to assemble, and/or a command to march. This same use of the trumpet quickly appears again at the close of Numbers as Joshua begins Israel's first steps toward and into the Promised Land (at the Battle of Jericho). The trumpet was God's vessel through which He worked to destroy the city of Jericho, when after seven successive days of marching, the people sounded a loud trumpet cry (Jos. 6:4-20) to make the city fall.

Carrying this theme into the New Testament, the trumpet is also linked to various end time prophecies, and its use also precedes the Day of the Lord when the King of kings and Lord of lords comes and inaugurates the Kingdom of God on earth (Joel 2:1; Zech. 9:14-16). When Jesus comes, the resurrection of the dead will be connected to a trumpet blast (1 Cor. 15:52; 1 Thess. 4:16), and the even the seven trumpets sounded in judgment upon the unbelieving people of earth will bring about the demise of the earthly system of Babylon, and will sound forth a processional of Christ's reign—forever and ever.

The most obvious intended meaning for the Trumpet here in Numbers 10 is a sounded alarm, which brings the people together in an assembly to march toward the intended Promised Land. The trumpet's robust symbolism throughout the whole of Scripture must also capture our attention here in order that we may understand the full depth of symbolism and meaning in the passage.

First of all, Israel had spent the better part of their FREE days out from underneath the hand of the dictator, Pharaoh in the wilderness of Sinai. God kept them there to train and teach them, and to establish His cultural ethic of authority in their midst, but now there appears to be a turning point. Israel now begins to be free in how they live and in the pattern of their thinking. In some regard their belief in God has become a living obedience and trust in His leadership. With the blast of the Trumpet, there is sounded an exclamation point. God's work of rehabilitation to some extent had resurrected this dead people into a new type of nation.

This is cause for celebration. God does not desire nor want the ethic of His culture to be one of dreary drudgery that only produces a cerebral and reverent people. He wants a loud and lavishly celebratory people. The Psalms allude to this kind of praise when they command the raising of hands, the shouting of voices, the pounding of drums and the various ensembles of dancing, bowing, kneeling, lying prostrate in joy and surrender, and in fervently overflowing with the joy of the Lord.

Something very real has been done within the wilderness of Sinai. A new people has emerged. They are not perfect, far from it, but their aims have been changed. They are still under construction, as we will soon see in the coming chapters, but this is not a time to focus on their sins, their pains, and the hurts that still remain in their hearts. God intends in this chapter to focus on the battles and small victories that have been won in His people. The Trumpet's connection to feasting, and festival, as seen in the Feast of Trumpets, comes to the surface in all its joyful tone. God's work in His people has been hard and excruciating at times. All they had experienced was like open-heart surgery, but now it is a time for a *rhythm* of celebration. This celebration comes in the wake of a victory and at the beginning of a new chapter. Israel is not to move on from their literal "mountain top" experience only to quickly forget it. They are to savor it and feel it in the sound of the trumpet.

The trumpet's joyful cry quickens and rouses the attention of those who may have forgotten to pay attention to all that had transpired. This trumpet is a transition piece not only to mark the completion of the journey that had already been traveled, but as a remembering tool for the journey about to begin. Quickly we'll see in the following chapters that Israel in their journey will soon forget their joy, which will cause them to turn in complaint toward the Lord — as is so often the case with humanity. The trumpet's sharp and piercing celebration is to arouse any remaining dead hearts to remember. This moment is not only to help the company of God's army to march forth in remembering their own victories, but it is to soon function as a memory they can look back on in their distress and continue to remember the victory of the Lord.

This symbolism is not just paramount in the creation of the trumpet. In many instances throughout Scripture God uses the creative process to create these "pillars" of joy, worship, and remembrance— not only to remember all that had been done, but to rejoice in all that was to come. Here, God's vessel of creation is the trumpet. The people, out of their change, out of their transformation, and out of their joy, are challenged to *create*. This instance here strikes an echo that sounds all the way back into the Garden of Eden when God, who was so overwhelmed with His love, deemed it fit to *create* the world and everything in it out of His overflow. Any enjoyment that God found in Himself caused Him to pour forth in lavish innovation. In the creating of the trumpet, Israel was bearing His image. This act of creating in response to all that God had done also appears through the building of, and the creating of other things in the Old Testament.

The way in which the ancients responded to God was by building *pillars* or *altars*. When Noah came out of the ark on to the renewed earth, he "built an altar unto the Lord; and took of every clean beast, and of every clean fowl, and offered burnt offerings on the altar." It was a signpost of rescue. When Abraham received God's promise and blessing, his communion was in a hostile scene, for "the Canaanites were then in the land." On removing from Sichem, Abraham came "unto a mountain on the east of Bethel, and pitched his tent, having Bethel on the west and Hai on the east: and there he built an altar unto the Lord, and called upon the Name of the Lord (Gen. 12:8)." His altar was a response to God's blessing revealed.

Isaac later came to Beer-sheba with God telling him not to fear.

God promised to remember His promise to Abraham. Then later an angel appeared to Jacob in a dream on the property of the promised land, and when Jacob wrestled with the angel on guard of the Garden and was victorious in his desire for God's continued promise, he built an altar acknowledging God's mercy in keeping His promises integrally (Gen. 31:13-32:22-32). Continuing, when the people were in Exodus due to their rebellion, they built altars and raised pillars when victorious in battle, for God was still faithful (Ex. 17:14). God continued with His people faithfully even in instances when God battled their gods at the altar of Baal through Elijah; forever communicating something new about His power (1 Kngs. 18:30-31).

God clearly states that these altars and pillars were built in places of importance. He says that they are, "places where I record my NAME" (Ex. 20:24). These altars go far deeper in meaning than just building something. They were acts of service, creativity, work, production, and ideas that came as an overflow to what God revealed about Himself. These pillars, wells, and altars stand in places in the journey that will be traveled again. An altar's newness eventually marks the familiar and then fades into tradition.

The Israelite people for example, as we will soon see, come upon Jacob's well as they traveled. This very real place of "newness" for Jacob is now an "old" anchor mark for Israel's memory as it causes them to remember their own love story with God. This goes to show that Israel's journey is not too different than our own. The landmass upon which they traveled seemed large, but in all reality their story is very small and repetitive. As they circled round and round in the land as they traveled—becoming faithless, heartless and whiny along the way—they continually passed by these places that reminded them of the record of God's NAME, and they once again were refreshed by how He had loved them, wooed them, courted them, and pursued them. This is the robust imagery and landscape that God wanted to encourage in the making of the trumpet. This was and is the robust symbolism contained in Numbers 10. This was to be Israel's turning point.

Another clue indicating that a turning point and a new day for

Israel had come is found in the following verses in Numbers 10:11-28. God once again numbered the tribes to march. He had already done this once before as He prepared them in such a way that they were ready for war (which we will look at in a moment). The way in which He numbers them again however, tells us something about what had happened in the hearts of His people.

In Numbers 1, God first numbered His people for the benefit of their protection, their governance, their organization, and their formation around the culture of God's redemption plan. In doing so, the first tribe He accounted for were the tribes that had come from Leah. In Numbers 1, He counted the tribes of Reuben (*see my affliction*), Simeon (*hears my affliction*), and Gad (*troop or invader*) before any other tribe was to be numbered, and then proceeded to count and number the tribes of Judah (*praise*), Issachar (*bears a burden*), and Zebulun (*dwelling*). It was as if in coming out of Egypt God needed to first begin by numbering Israel in association with their *pain*.

When Israel came out of Egypt their pain and shame defined them. It is the first thing God noticed and addressed even in His system of numbering. At the time of their liberation from slavery, Israel was freed by God's hand, but they were neither living nor thinking free. In many ways their view of themselves was one of *pain* and despair. They were a broken people and they defined themselves by their past. Though they were saved and delivered, the freshness of all the wrong they had been a part of was still fresh in their minds. So in like fashion, God too noticed the pain they carried and acknowledged it first, but He did so only in light of the tribes He numbered after Leah's group. In Numbers 1, we see that next, God numbered the tribe of *praise* and *deliverance*, as if to paint a picture for the Israelite tribe that their pain was about to, in some way, be redeemed and used for a greater purpose.

In Numbers 10:11-28, we see that greater purpose as it emerges. God ordered the companies and their leaders to set out according to rank and order. In Numbers 10, as Israel is ordered to embark upon their journey toward the Promised Land, God assembles them in the reverse order to that of Numbers 1–2. Judah, the praise of Israel goes first, as followed by Issachar and Zebulun. Only after this do the tribes of Leah's lineage follow. The reason this shift is important is because it reveals the true intent of this passage. The tribe of Israel had reached a turning point. In coming out of Egypt they had been defined by their *pain*. As God called them out in their pain, He also reminded them in the ensuing tribes of Judah, Issachar, and Zebulun that He indeed intended to reshape them and bring them home to a point of *praise* once again. Though the journey toward praise and healing had not been completely realized within Israel's ranks here in Chapter 10, a large statement is made. God had indeed transferred them from death into life. God was not about to lead a tribe known for death any longer!

Israel was no longer labeled nor defined by their *pain* but rather as a people of *praise*. The people were no longer to walk around with a proverbial "I am a sinner" mantra coming out of their mouths. Their reality had changed. They were loved, they were redeemed, they were protected, they were governed, and they were led by the hand of an almighty and loving God.

This people were to be defined by a new name and a new reality, and God needed to convey this change of scenery to them in how He ordered them for travel. Israel's eyes were to be firmly fixed on God's presence for leadership, and they were encouraged to turn their eyes away from all that was "past."

Even though in large part this nation had experienced deep healing, this did not mean that every heart submitted fully to the Lord in moving toward this new destination. In chapter 10:29-31, we see the tribe of Hobab—one of the sons of Keturah, who became Abraham's wife after Sarah died—displaying hesitation in leaving due to their attachment to the land where they had settled and due to a concern for their family. Moses pleads with Hobab to come with them as he views them as helpers to the entire nation, and He pleads with them to come based on the blessing that God had promised to Abraham and to all his offspring—that He would surely bless them as Abraham's descendants. And in the midst of a celebration of victory, of remembrance, and in a reflection upon the turning point in Israel's history, the tribe of Hobab is roused to think of a vision greater than the vision they had for themselves. Part of the celebration within Israel's ranks results in the fainthearted heart being awakened to faith, reclaiming the blessings that had been promised to them so long ago. This moment in Israel's journey serves to call all peoples to attention to reconsider, repent, and remember the story of God.

Though a few stragglers remained hesitant to Israel's new direction, their detox at the base of Mt. Sinai had worked in them a miracle of redemption, which altered the entire makeup of this nation. And in Numbers 10:34-36 the text again records the rhythm of the cloud as it lifts and sets out upon the road in leading the Israelite people one step closer to the Promised Land. In vs. 35-36 Moses' declaration at their departure and settling is recorded: "And whenever the ark set out, Moses said, 'Arise, O Lord, and let your enemies be scattered, and let those who hate you flee before you.' And when it rested, he said, 'Return, O Lord, to the ten thousand thousands of Israel.'"

Two things were now most real to Israel. First, their lifestyle was going to be a rhythm of a *journey*. They were going to live in waiting and moving, clarity and unclarity, lifting and stopping. This is their rhythm of faith, trust, and dependence in and upon the Lord. And as they moved and traveled along, they were to be reminded through Moses, that armies would flee before them at the sight of the Lord. As a result of God's movement, all things detrimental and threatening to Israel would flee—even if it meant they would experience adversity along the way.

In a second regard, the trumpet now was to define Israel's lifestyle, in that their journey was to be one of eating and celebration— of creating and worshipping. Each time the cloud was to lift, the trumpet was also to sound. Each time the next phase of the journey kicked into action, Israel was to feel the new sound of their next turning point in the soles of their feet. The blaring rouse of the trumpet's voice served as a reminder to celebrate, to remember, and to press forward with great hope. In their waiting, they were to enjoy each other, enjoy the Lord, and eat and celebrate within the cocoon of His fiery cloud. They were to find rest, solace, and peace within His bounds whether they experienced moments of movement or of pause. In their journey they were to sing the trumpet's song of the Lord's freedom as His kingdom advanced before them.

PART II
ACT 2

SCENE 1
COMPLAINTS ARISE

In the next Act of God's drama of deliverance and sanctification, the travel toward the Promise Land commenced. The Lord up until this point had equipped the nation of Israel with great hope and expectation; holding true in delivering on all the promises that He made. He provided for His people, even down into meeting their daily dietary needs through the miraculous manna that rained down each and every morning on the people as literal "bread from heaven." God gave His people great perfection as He delivered to Israel His perfect and infallible laws in which they could place their trust, and upon which they could anchor the delight of their heart. God gave the people His promised presence. He had and would continue to speak to Moses in intimate prayer and conversation, and each and every step along the journey would be a testimony to how He guides His children by the cloud, the fire, and the awe of His presence.

In this, there is great protection and power. Not only had God's arm thrashed and split the Red Sea, but His might pillowed magnificently into the sky before Israel and before Israel's enemies as a warning to all as to what they would encounter if they were to challenge the Lord.

And yet, even after all the Lord had done in chapter 10, we quickly see how Israel's humanity kicks in as they began to respond to all God's goodness in lavish displays of complaint and hostility. It seems that the sound of the trumpet blast had just ended its celebrative and assembling call, and already the people had forgotten its music. In Numbers 11:1-13, the text describes the quick and utter dissolve of Israel's faith and perspective as the journey toward the Promise Land initiates:

And the people complained in the hearing of the Lord about their misfortunes, and when the Lord heard it, his anger was kindled, and the fire of the Lord burned among them and consumed some outlying parts of the camp. Then the people cried out to Moses, and Moses prayed to the Lord, and the fire died down. So the name of that place was called Taberah, because the fire of the Lord burned among them. Now the rabble that was among them had a strong craving. And the people of Israel also wept again and said, 'Oh that we had meat to eat! We remember the fish we ate in Egypt that cost nothing, the cucumbers, the melons, the leeks, the onions, and the garlic. But now our strength is dried up, and there is nothing at all but this manna to look at.' Now the manna was like coriander seed, and its appearance like that of bdellium. The people went about and gathered it and ground it in handmills or beat it in mortars and boiled it in pots and made cakes of it. And the taste of it was like the taste of cakes baked with oil. When the dew fell upon the camp in the night, the manna fell with it.

Moses heard the people weeping throughout their clans, everyone at the door of his tent. And the anger of the Lord blazed hotly, and Moses was displeased. Moses said to the Lord, 'Why have you dealt ill with your servant? And why have I not found favor in your sight, that you lay the burden of all this people on me? Did I conceive all this people? Did I give them birth, that you should say to me, 'Carry them in your bosom, as a nurse carries a nursing child,' to the land that you swore to give their fathers? Where am I to get meat to give to all this people? For they weep before me and say, 'Give us meat, that we may eat.' I am not able to carry all this people alone; the burden is too heavy for me. If you will treat me like this, kill me at once, if I find favor in your sight, that I may not see my wretchedness.'

A people now led out by God's hand through the tribe of Judah—the tribe of praise—now found their mouths to be filled only with complaint. Immediately, in beginning the next phase of the journey, they took their minds and hearts off of all that God had done for them and they looked around and surveyed their circumstances from a skewed and unwarranted perspective. In verse 10 we see the depth of the un-thankfulness in the Israelite hearts.

People were found weeping at their tents. They were found whining, cursing God, waving their fists, and asking the ultimate question that plagues all of humanity, "Why?" This people who are supposedly now defined by *praise,* already began to neglect praise all together and re-embrace their pain. All of this happens in what seems like a matter of minutes. They were dissatisfied with God's approach. Though God clearly and fully had displayed His overwhelming grace to His people, they obviously missed its depths. They wanted more and they were not happy!

One might begin to ask here how the tables turned so quickly. The first section of Numbers seems so hopeful for Israel. It seems as if God's story had been established in their midst. Why such a quick turnaround? Why all the complaining all of a sudden? Though it is true that Israel had been reformed and had been refashioned around true freedom to some degree, God knew that only the journey would truly bring to the surface all the remaining thought patterns of slavery that still remained deep within. The basic and primary principles and rudiments of their new freedom had catechized Israel to a degree in knowledge, but only in performing their learning in real life *rhythm* could everything become a full reality to them.

Much progress had been made in the wilderness of Sinai, but it was now time to apply Sinai's learning to the people's hearts like a scalpel. Like a skilled surgeon, God begins to allow the application of all His truth to begin to work its magic in the hearts of His people as they squirmed and moved against the blade.

In this paramount scene, Israel has the audacity to whine and complain against the Lord for His loving surgery and deliverance. We see them in Numbers 10 lashing out against God in anger and dismay. The text tells us that they began to "complain about their misfortunes in the hearing of the Lord." All they dwelt upon is what they did not have. In seeing only what they wanted to see, they neglected to see what they needed to see. God had provided them with bread from heaven—a miraculous sign of His provision. However, in their view, they could solely and merely see it only as mere *coriander seed*. Its once sweet and sustaining taste had become dry and familiar to them. Their stomachs rejected its simplicity and their conscience despised its uniformity. The rhythm of everything was just too predictable, just too formal, and altogether too regular. It is not that the Lord was not showing His goodness, it's that His children did not like the way it was being displayed.

With fists waving and wails travailing, Israel puts on a pathetic show that resembles the tantrum of a two year old. At their doors they groan. In the streets they make a fuss. They putter about with looks of depression upon their faces; their wails and groans only seeking to draw attention to their poor entitlement mentality. The raucous scene becomes so overwhelming that it not only rouses the anger of the Lord, causing His fire to burn against the people, but it brings Moses and all the leadership to their wit's end. The complaining becomes so severe in fact, that it causes Moses to utter these words in verse 15, "If you will treat me like this, kill me at once, if I find favor in your sight, that I may not see my wretchedness."

The true perversity of the complaining is found in its fruit. It sours the insides of not only the people from which it comes, but it tarnishes everything in its path. It becomes extremely taxing to Moses and to the Lord. The Lord despises the people's ungrateful hearts and sees to the root of such complaints. Their distaste for the manna and for His method of doing things reaches far deeper than merely the pit of their stomachs; it reaches into the stench of their souls. Their slavery mentality comes billowing forth as many of them remember the fatted meals they had enjoyed at the hands of Pharaoh. As they are tempted to remember his meals, they also neglect to remember his torture. They are so senile and childish that they prefer the shallow comfort of a manipulative meal over the generous leadership of their Father. And before God exhibits His love and care once again to His short-sighted people, He awakens and kindles His fiery anger to exhibit His mixed reaction to such a display of discontent. He runs hot at how sinful-mindedness had corrupted His people. His character and Holiness burn hotly against such corruption in order to leave in the ashy path the remnants of anything good that might still remain in His people.

All of this taxes Moses—surrounded by the literal millions of Israel, and everyone is complaining. Their mourning reaches his ears and it becomes too much for him to handle. The effect of the complaints poisons the people, they enrage God, but they are particularly burdensome for Israel's leadership. In one sense, Moses' struggle is the same as that of the people. He cannot bear the road that God chose for them. Moses cannot stand the people that God paired Him with. He is afraid that the discontent of the people might bring to light the discontent that is also in his own soul—his own "wretchedness." The annoyances of the people only seem to expose Moses' greatest weaknesses and proclivities. Moses is human too, and he now struggles not to buckle under the pressure.

In Numbers 11:16-20, a salve to the problem is implemented. More leaders are needed to shoulder the weight of Israel's despondency. Directly to Moses are given words from the Lord's mouth directing the multiplication of leaders (Numbers 11:17). God orders this for a specific purpose. The Lord says in this passage, "and I will come down and talk with you there. And I will take some of the Spirit that is on you and put it on them, and they shall *bear the burden* of the people with you, so that you may not bear it yourself alone." This gathering of over 70 leaders, which foreshadows the sending of the 70 in the New Testament gospels, is a provided solution to help in managing the people's hurts and woes. It is to exemplify the true nature of spiritual leadership and being a follower of God—it's a road of aiding God in serving His people and in helping to "bear their burdens." And this is what their leadership is for. It is not for them to accomplish a vision or to reach their heart's aspirations and dreams. These men are to serve the people in their despair and help Moses, in the same way as the disciples served Jesus—in going to the poor, the weak, and the destitute and giving ear to their concerns. Even though the Lord is angry with Israel's rampant complaints, He responds tactically with the love and the compassionate care of a Shepherd and a Father. His hand outstretches down out of heaven into and out of the hands of His leadership in order to provide the sense of His presence and tender care.

God does not just want just any kind of leadership to oversee this people. He wants people who are displeased when He is displeased and pleased when He is pleased. He needs a leadership that will reflect His character and image to the people. He needs the fleshly hands and feet of men like Moses and the 70 to dispense His spiritual grace. Even as seen here, the people do not deserve to be heard, nor spared by the hand of God. They had pushed God to the very limit of patience in their complaints, so it seems, and yet what continues to show in God's dealing with them is His extraordinary ability to remain tireless in His grace toward this woeful and disheartened people. Though they did not deserve to be spoken to by Moses, let alone addressed by God, God still speaks, and Moses is faithful here to dispense God's love into their hopeless state. The people do not deserve this good news. The people do not deserve this care, but it is there nonetheless.

In verse 25 God comes down and puts some of the Spirit He had placed on Moses onto the 70 leaders who then begin to take on some of the similar gifting of Moses as a result. The text tells us that they all began to prophesy. Most of them became truth tellers for a short time, many became almost fanatical (vv. 26-30), but yet a few of them used their ability to dispense wisdom in and amongst the people in a way that calmed them and built them up in the midst of their shallow perspective.

An even greater predicament arises than merely just medicating and feeding these people's selfish and broken spirits. The people were physically crying out for something other than the manna. They wanted what they had in Egypt (vs. 18). They wanted meat. They wanted meat to feed the multitudes, and yet when Moses and the leaders survey the cattle, they cannot fathom how such a demand can be met. To feed all the people in the way they desire would take more cattle than they currently possessed (vv. 21-23). Moses brings this before the Lord, and yet the Lord responds in saying, "Is the Lord's hand shortened? Now you shall see whether my word will come true for you or not."

In the wake of this statement, the elders are endowed with the Spirit and sent back into and amongst the people. No sooner does this happen then a monsoon wind rises up, which brings quail in from the direction of the sea. The birds begin coming in droves. The text says that the birds flew in such swarms that they covered the ground as far as one could see in any direction—a day's journey in all directions. Each person collected around 60 gallons of birds and the land was swelled to the knees with a depth of birds almost a half foot thick.

The miracle is overwhelming. God met the people's demands and gave them what they wanted. He satisfied their complaining with the exact thing they had asked for. But, was this a blessing to the people? They thought they had received the comfort, the satisfaction, the contentment and the solace that their souls supposedly hoped for, yet in the text, this generous miracle from the hand of God is to be seen as a gift of judgment.

The people wanted more than what God offered to them. They wanted more than what God was to them. The seemingly wonderful and blessed gift of God in quail becomes a reflection only of the people's souls. It is a sign to them to point to the state of their own hearts. The quail lodges between their teeth and it comes out their noses (vs. 33). The birds were far too numerous to consume, and so their rotting carcasses began to stink with the smell of mold and death. The stench and experience became far too overwhelming so the people needed to move from Kibroth-hattaavah (meaning *graves of craving*), to Hazeroth.

The weight of such an experience permeated their thoughts regardless. It remained fresh in their noses, lodged in their teeth, smeared to the bottom of their sandals, and hooked to the very guts of their heart. God wanted to firmly fix in them yet another lesson of His authority. He wanted to demonstrate that any desire of the human soul which seems to want something else more than God Himself can only lead to greater heartache. He wanted to teach the people that He is all they need, but if they wanted to follow at the heels of false hopes and idols He would indulge them in their fantasies and let their own desires lead them to a place of waste.

Though to the earthly taste of the human tongue the manna may have seemed bland, God reminded His people here that His simplest provisions sometimes hold the most profound meaning.

We have discussed in brief already in this book how the simplicity of a meal across Scripture speaks the story of the Gospel. This meaning again appears here. The manna was to be a sign to point to the real reality of God's provision. God's intent was not that the people would supplement the manna in place of him. God intentionally kept the manna simple in order that the people would not become too fattened upon the gifts from God and thus forget the Giver.

The manna challenged in the people their ability to be content in the mundane and in the seemingly trivial matters of the journey. Both the men, who were tired of leading day to day in the mundane and stress of all of this, and to the women who were preparing the manna everyday (vs.7-9) and who were mourning the rich desserts of Egypt (vs. 4-6), God speaks through a megaphone His message of contentment. The message displayed here is echoed in Paul's writings in the New Testament when he exclaims that he's found the secret to being content in all things. Paul's understanding is that the *mundane* things often become the greatest teachers of humility. The *mundane* things often become the greatest warriors against humanity's sense of entitlement. The *mundane* things often tend to expose the deepest places of the embittered and pouting soul, in an effort to lead God's people to a place of real praise in His glory beyond the natural world.

This message, although its primary purpose is to be a sword driven into the depth of the people, also drives to the depths of Israel's leadership, particularly Moses. This served as a reminder to his own human soul that this journey toward the Promised Land was going to be one of great burden, but also one of great contentment. This needed to be the first lesson learned for the people of Israel as they set out across the desert in their once again mobile community. The nature of a journey implies that things were going to be ever-changing, which means that the potentiality for the human soul to become disheartened amid such changing terrain is an intense possibility. Along the highways and bi-ways God allowed Moses to see into their journey ahead to some extent and prepared him for the weight of the task. Though Moses spent many years preparing for this journey before seeing his people freed from Egypt, nothing quite compared to the reality of actually acting it out in real time.

To remain steadfast, the people of Israel and its leadership were going to need to remain conscious of the message of God's redemption story in their encampment, in their priesthood, in their people, in their hearts, and in their central Lord. They were going to need to remember their story. They were going to need to continue to celebrate it. The journey ahead only seems to hold oncoming complication and diversion. These unexpected occurrences sought to either anchor Israel's hope in God and satisfaction in God alone, or the hard terrain would serve to callous the people to these once fresh and inspiring events.

11

SCENE 2

LEADERSHIP ACCUSED

The complaints that came up against the Lord and against Moses from within the ranks of the Israelite nation did not subside in an instant, but rather seemed to grow more intense as the journey itself continued on. One would assume that after a miracle such as the quail and the manna that Israel would quiet down in their objections toward the Lord and toward Moses. Very quickly however, the zoom lens of the story focuses in and pans out to catch a candid conversation that took place between Miriam and Aaron regarding their reaction to the transpiring events. The contents of their conversation are recorded explicitly in Numbers 12:1-2;

> Miriam and Aaron spoke against Moses because of the Cushite woman whom he had married, for he had married a Cushite woman. And they said, 'Has the Lord indeed spoken only through Moses? Has he not spoken through us also?' And the Lord heard it.

As seen here, further contempt and distrust in the hearts of God's people grew, both toward the Lord, and toward His authority as expressed through His human leaders.

At first glance, the accusation directed at Moses from Miriam seems righteous and correct. The content of Miriam and Aaron's talk about Moses disdainfully laments the fact that Moses indeed married a foreigner—a Cushite woman. During their time in Egypt the Israelites learned to hate the Cushites. The Egyptians despised these people and referred to them as "vile Cush." Not only this, but by God's orders, the people of Israel were preserved for holiness and sanctity before God, and many times throughout the Old Testament God's people were forbidden to marry outside of their bounds of faith because doing so would result in the worship of the other gods from other distant families and lands. However, Zipporah, Moses' Midianite wife (Exodus 2.15-22) was a descendant of Abraham through his wife Keturah. Therefore, her heritage is legitimately Semitic leaving no valid objection for her union with Moses. The only thing that can appear to be emerging here in Miriam and Aaron's thinking is their jealousy toward Moses' position as leader.

Though their objection against Moses' leadership seems to masquerade as an objection of noble intent, their faulty problem falls apart in their approach. Not only do they base their objection and complaint against Moses on false assumptions and facts, but the way they went about confronting such a problem is also wrong. They gave way to jealousy and malice, and in verses 1-2 we see them speaking *about* Moses, rather than *to* Moses.

Throughout the Old Testament and into the New Testament (1 Tim. 5:17-19), men in the position of elder and leader are to be spoken to about apparent problems in a reverent and respectful way. Two or three witnesses must be present in a unified case against a leader, and without such unified perspective, an accusation against a leader is not to be entertained. Miriam and Aaron's accusation against Moses was not only ill-founded upon false evidence, but it was handled in the way of gossip and slander, which put Aaron and Miriam in the wrong, not Moses.

Though Aaron and Miriam clearly accused Moses of stepping out from underneath the law and authority of the Lord, they in fact were the ones committing such a crime. Yet another bacterium of slavery mentality surfaces as a people, who spent most of their life blaming the slave masters for their prolific evil, fell into their own hypocrisy in forgetting their own responsibility. Miriam and Aaron participate here in a coward's conversation as they masquerade as heroes who seek to liberate Israel from its tyrannical leadership—under the Lord and under Moses—but in all reality they function like a leprous cancer within the camp. They harm the body, they harm themselves (as they are part of the whole), and their passive tactics of talking behind Moses' back only seems to reveal the inner workings of their heart. They were still resistant to authority.

In the midst of the conversation nevertheless, the text reminds us that God was still overseeing this entire situation. In verse 2, God's Omnipresence, Omniscience and Foreknowledge are clearly seen when He not only allows such a disobedient conversation to take place, but the text makes it clear that He hears every detail. God hears Aaron and Miriam's slanderous speech. He sees them, He knows them, and in the following verses, God calls them out in discipline for the actions. God was in their midst, and though the people thought that their seemingly hidden rebellions went unnoticed, God committed to taking seriously everyone of their little slaps-in-the-face toward His authority. In the minds of Miriam and Aaron, their gossip was warranted and their belittling of the authority seemed even virtuous. But in claiming to be a better authority than Moses, they themselves became the judge of God. God placed Moses in leadership and therefore their gossip was an attack on God's leadership, not Moses.

The only one that truly knows a heart is God. Miriam and Aaron were clearly picking at something they could see in order to discredit Moses. They went after his wife, and yet did not fully understand the situation. It is true that Moses had his frailty and could very well have pled guilty due to the fact that he had not always followed the Lord. He had fled Egypt once before after having killed a man in Egypt. At that time Moses had been raised up in the Egyptian schools, and most likely was influenced in their way of thought. Until God called Him to deliver the people out of Egypt, Moses was not deeply concerned with the ways of God. Therefore, the marriage, though perfectly understandable either way, was perfectly legal.

The motives of the heart are what concerns God. Though Moses' external actions are perceived to be outside the bounds of God's rule book, he was in his heart devoted to the ways of God. It is clearly shown throughout the book of Numbers that when God spoke to Moses, he responded. Here in verse 3 of chapter 12, the text tells us that Moses was "meeker than any man on the face of the earth." This reference to Moses' meekness pays great due to how Moses related to himself and to the Lord. When Moses' honor was touched, and when his name was slandered, there was no man more meek and mild as a lamb in defending his own cause. On the other hand, as in the case when the people were found at the base of Mt. Sinai worshipping the Golden Calf, there was no man more zealous and jealous for God's honor.

The fear of God was the motive of Moses' heart. His great heart-display of humility reflects that of Jesus in 1 Peter 2:23 when it says of the Son of Man, that when insults and accusations were hurled at Him, He did not retaliate. He entrusted Himself to the "One who judges justly." Like Moses, Jesus did not seek revenge, for that would only have come out of bitterness and a desire to punish another for their actions. Rather, like Jesus, Moses released these people into God's handling and righteous judgment. Although this may appear to be an action of weakness, meekness should in no way be misconstrued with what is cowardly. Meekness is an action of great power, for it is an action of great restraint of power. Meekness does not thrive in displaying its power and authority, but it thrives in withholding it out of concern for a greater purpose. The meekness of Christ Himself shines through here in Moses' countenance toward the situation, as Moses does not seek to defend His honor, but entrusts His authority and defense to the Lord.

On the other hand, Miriam and Aaron appear pious and righteous to the people in their leadership, but behind closed doors they allowed their increasingly rebellious hearts to surface in silent disagreement toward God and His choices. Their struggle, though they attempted to hold it together before the nation of Israel, was that they allowed their hearts to question God's authority through Moses. Though they claimed great authority in judging Moses and his office, they lost all weight to their argument through their actions.

The reason for noting the contrast in leadership styles in this passage is to point out the true reality of what it means to reflect God's authority. True authority is understanding the real light that is shining. It is clearly seen in the symbolism of the 7 lampstands, that the nature of the lamps represented the centrality of God as He walks amongst the people. God illumines all of life through His people, and the central figure to all of human history is Jesus Christ.

The only true commitment to true leadership and authority is for humans in any and all circumstances to act in such a way as to point to the light of God. Moses' leadership truly does this. Though he stepped aside as if to appear helpless in defense of himself, his actions demonstrated the greatest authority of all. Moses did not want his own voice and will to resound in this circumstance. He wanted God's ways to triumph. The opposite can be seen to be true in Miriam and Aaron's actions on the other hand. When they were forced to choose between their own perspective and God's sovereign decree, they submitted to their own worldview. This caused them to lose sight of all that God was doing in and through Moses.

In the midst of this whole circumstance, the text clearly states, that as a result of Moses' leadership, God defended him. Numbers 12:5-9 says,

And the Lord came down in a pillar of cloud and stood at the entrance of the tent and called Aaron and Miriam, and they both came forward. And he said, 'Hear my words: If there is a prophet among you, I the Lord make myself known to him in a vision; I speak with him in a dream. Not so with my servant Moses. He is faithful in all my house. With him I speak mouth to mouth, clearly, and not in riddles, and he beholds the form of the Lord. Why then were you not afraid to speak against my servant Moses?' And the anger of the Lord was kindled against them, and he departed.

To authenticate Moses' authority and leadership, God clearly honored Moses before the other people. God said of Moses that he was a man to which God Himself, "speaks mouth to mouth." The image portrayed is one of intimacy. Moses' true weight and heroism as a leader came not from his own ability, nor did it come simply because God chose him, but Moses' true valor and strength came from Moses' life-giving connection to God. The mouth-to-mouth imagery used conjures up in the imagination a picture of a living man keeping a dead man alive through resuscitation. Moses' surrender and dependence on God for survival is one of deepest concern, and is something Moses clung to with all sober mindedness and seriousness. God acknowledged that Moses surrendered to Him in such a way that it would be appropriate to think of them as sharing the same breath.

As the meeting between God and the leadership ended, and God's cloud lifted, Moses was left sustained, but Miriam was left as leprous as snow (vs. 10). Aaron, though unaffected by the leprosy resounded in loud repentance, "Oh, my lord, do not punish us because we have done foolishly and have sinned. Let her not be as one dead, whose flesh is half eaten away when he comes out of his mother's womb."

Quickly the reality of what sin did inside of Aaron and Miriam's heart became exposed through the outward disease of leprosy. The punishment for their belligerence was two-fold. Miriam was given over to her sin and to its physical effects, and Aaron was forced to watch. Miriam's sin affected her physical person, and her punishment comes through bearing the physical toil (much like the curse that was given to Eve as a result of her sin in the Garden). On the other hand, though Aaron's punishment does not appear physically, he was forced to watch the results of his bad leadership as Miriam decayed before him—in a similar fashion to how Adam had to watch Eve suffer physically for his sin.

The ultimate issue comes to light. The man, Moses, who is under God's authority, emerges in righteousness, and Miriam and Aaron, who claim great authority, are exposed in their sin. The real war being waged in this passage is that of light against darkness—sin against righteousness—rebellion and pride against authority and true humility. The weight of sin wrecks the life of Miriam and Aaron, not to mention that it seeks to divide something more deeply important. Miriam is Moses' older sister. Her sin therefore sought to rip apart the very bedrock of God's society—the family! Sin's effects pitted husband against wife, sister against brother, and children against father and mother.

This seemingly insignificant and brief chapter in the book of Numbers records for all of us a chance to see the real threat of slavery. When Miriam and Aaron embraced what they wanted and forgot to consider the ways of God and what everyone else needed, their bound thinking served not only to enslave them, but to divide them. It threatened the very intimacy that families are created to have with one another. It threatened the very intimacy that God desires to have with His people. God already spoke of His relationship to Moses as being as intimate as mouth-to-mouth *breathing*. This interdependence is the depth of relationship that God desires to have as a Father to His own children in Israel. This too was threatened by the manner of Miriam's and Aaron's sin.

Once again, the meekness of Moses emerged as he pled for the heart of God to be revealed toward Miriam and the people. Moses cried to the Lord, "O God, please heal her—please." But the Lord said to Moses, "If her father had but spit in her face, should she not be shamed seven days? Let her be shut outside the camp seven days, and after that she may be brought in again." So Miriam was shut outside the camp seven days, and the people did not set out on the march till Miriam was brought in again. After that the people set out from Hazeroth, and camped in the wilderness of Paran.

Moses could have defended his honor by either defending

himself or by rejoicing in Miriam's punishment; however, his response is one of compassionate intercessory prayer. He exercised his relationship with the Lord in a manner such as to appeal to God's heart. Moses reflects a piece of God's heart in that he did not want Miriam to die in her sin, but rather he wanted her to receive her penalty as a warning so she would be healed and never again be tempted in this area by sin's rebellion.

What took place in the short time of Israel leaving the comfort and safety of the Sinai wilderness is that the people erupted in complaints, and out of bitter jealousy some of the most influential leaders rose up to try and overthrow God's perfect plan.

This tendency of rebellion resides in the hearts of the smallest of child, and its influence reaches all the way up into the heart of the very highest leader of the priesthood. Everyone was and is susceptible to sin's poisonous effects. Everyone is weak before its cancerous spread. Nevertheless, God sets Moses on display as an example to all of how to avoid such leprosy and decay. The only way for any person to continue on in the journey and remain safe is to remain in humility before, meekness within, surrendered unto, and intimate with the Lord.

12

SCENE 3

PRAYER

The only way forward for Israel in the journey is to embrace meekness, dependence, and bold surrender to the Lord and to His ways. The way forward is to preserve communication with God alone. It is to speak with Him and to listen to Him in order to receive His specific commands and instruction for how and where to proceed. It's been noted throughout the book of Numbers that *prayer,* particularly between Moses and God, is a great theme that permeates the book. Prayer's thematic undercurrent rides right below the surface in every circumstance that transpires. The conversation between Moses and God emerges again in Chapter 13 of Numbers, as the specifics of what Israel is to do in their journey is now revealed more fully.

God is about to take His people into the land of Canaan, the land that He promised them. This was His intention from the beginning, and this is the land that has been promised to the forefathers of Israel. It is a land flowing with milk and honey, and a land of rich wealth, rich safety, and great abundance. This land is Israel's home. They had been absent from their home for a very long time, and since their departure, foreign visitors and enemies had inhabited the land of promise. Israel had been exiled and enslaved in Egypt for so long that their absence in the land had allowed for many people to move in that were never intended to be there in the first place.

As a result, in Chapter 13:1, God again speaks to Moses in order to give Him the plans for how they are to reenter and recapture the Promised Land. The Lord speaks to Moses, saying,

> 'Send men to spy out the land of Canaan, which I am giving to the people of Israel. From each tribe of their fathers you shall send a man, everyone a chief among them.' So Moses sent them from the wilderness of Paran, according to the command of the Lord, all of them men who were heads of the people of Israel...

Moses sent them to spy out the land of Canaan and said to them,

> Go up into the Negeb and go up into the hill country, and see what the land is, and whether the people who dwell in it are strong or weak, whether they are few or many, and whether the land that they dwell in is good or bad, and whether the cities that they dwell in are camps or strongholds, and whether the land is rich or poor, and whether there are trees in it or not. Be of good courage and bring some of the fruit of the land (vv. 1-3, 17-20).

What surfaces in these verses is not only a plan of attack, and a plan of the next steps for Israel, but we are also given an intimate glimpse into the specifics of God's conversation with Moses.

God's words to Moses are very specific. God clearly commanded Moses to send out a man from each tribe to spy out the land of Canaan on behalf of the entire nation of Israel. This measure was taken in order to protect the Israelites before entering the land. They needed to have a clear picture of what they were about to encounter in order to prepare for the next phase of their journey. God did not want His people to remain in the dark concerning all that He had planned for them. God also did not want His people to be unprepared for all that He had planned for them. His directions are therefore very clear and specific to Moses in order to demonstrate to His people that He is truthful, and that He is forthright with every intention for them. Before He gave them all that He was about to, He first needed Israel to survey the entire vision. He needed them to consider the land and the circumstance from all points of view before entering.

This is why God's first order for the people is that they send out a group of spies to survey the land. Secondly, and in relationship to the first point stated, God is very clear to His people in speaking to them, as He gives them a clear strategy for proceeding. The people, if they would have rashly rushed off to take hold of the land promised them, would only have met their demise. As a precaution and necessity, God called His people to hold back their anticipations and perhaps doubts, and to wait a little while longer to consider everything. God's strategy is specific and calculated. The reason that He ordered the spies to go first is not because He enjoyed holding Israel in waiting, but His orders forced Israel to be prudent and wise in proceeding into their inheritance. To do this correctly, God chose the people (vv. 4-16) who would go from each tribe. He designed the plans of what they would do and decided the places they would survey.

This clear plan of strategy and attack equipped the nation of Israel with great wisdom—wisdom they needed in order to victoriously move ahead. The first sign of wisdom appears in verse 17-20 when Moses sends the spies out into the land with detailed instructions regarding the information they were to gather. Moses commanded the spies to be very aware of all they would see. He told them to survey the land, and ascertain whether the people who dwelled in it were strong or weak; whether they were few or many, and whether the land that they dwelled in was good or bad. He asked them to consider whether the cities that they dwelled in were camps or strongholds, whether the land was rich or poor, and whether there were trees in it or not. Though God clearly gave Moses the specifics of their strategy, He obviously left some open-ended unanswered questions in Moses' mind. God was very specific in prayer about the strategy that Moses and the people were to take in their next steps toward the Promised Land, but He left gaps in Moses' thinking in order to encourage the people to obey and follow through.

God ultimately is building a rhythm in His people of *faith* and *obedience*. He gave them enough information to keep them safe and moving, but He never unveiled too much for the sake of preserving these two rhythms. His desire was that through prayer they would trust Him and move into their next phase of the journey based on their belief in His character and truthfulness, not simply based on all the gifts they believed they would receive. The medium of prayer also serves to protect the people from seeing things and knowing things that they were not yet ready to handle. If God were to reveal and speak everything to the people, they would either have attempted to march forward in certainty—losing the greatest hope for their souls, satisfaction and dependence upon God, or on the other hand, would have wound up in fear and terror beneath the sheer weight of all they were about to encounter. The people needed to maintain faith. It was a safety to them.

This prayerful interaction led to great wisdom on the part of Moses. He responded to God's instruction prudently, but not hastily, and He chose the men God appointed, cautioning them to be aware of their surroundings in every regard. Moses acted upon God's strategy with great wisdom and diligence. He began to dissect every detail that lay ahead, and issued specific orders to the people as to what they were to look for.

In prayerful conversation, God not only birthed in Moses the correct information along with giving him the next steps to the journey, but he awakened Moses' mind to think through every issue that Israel would encounter. They needed to think through what they were about to experience. They needed to understand the nature of the terrain, the nature of the people, the civility and hostility of the nations and armies in their paths, and the strain of everything in their path. Moses prepared them for the journey ahead, the war ahead, and the promise ahead. Great discernment was needed, and the only way to obtain the correct insight was to consult the Lord.

Moses demonstrated not only his ability to ask good questions in response to God's voice but he demonstrated to the people here what obedience and faith actually looks like. He clearly modeled for the people how the *foreknowledge* of God interacts with human *obedience*. God knew all that the Israelites would encounter, and that's why He gave Moses the instructions that He did. However, even in God knowing what the future held, He knew that His people needed to participate in His journey with Him in order to accomplish the plans He had set before them. This rhythm of faith and obedience, foreknowledge and the unknown, the predetermined plan of God and human will, comes into full view here.

The people's trust did not mean they needed to obey Him blindly without condition or effort on their part. The people were not to follow hastily, but rather proceed with great caution, wisdom, and thoughtfulness. They were to wait on things, sifting them out, and considering the pros and cons of everything the Lord had given them. The Lord asked for faith from them in their allegiance to follow, but He also asked for their faithful loyalty as they continued to walk with Him in faith through obedience. God did not separate the ends of faith from the means of faith. He connected the destination with the journey. Both are equally important to Israel learning to truly follow, love, and trust His leading.

In Numbers 12:21-24 the spies did as they are told and they went out to scout the land. They surveyed the landscape before them, sampled some of the land's fruits (vs. 23-24), and even brought some of its bounty back to the camp as proof of their findings. This scouting mission took 40 days to complete, and once they had done all they had been commanded they returned to the encampment of Israel:

 And they came to Moses and Aaron and to all the congregation of the people of Israel in the wilderness of Paran, at Kadesh. They brought back word to them and to the entire congregation, and showed them the fruit of the land. And they told him, 'We came to the land to which you sent us. It flows with milk and honey, and this is its fruit. However, the people who dwell in the land are strong, and the cities are fortified and very large. And besides, we saw the descendants of Anak there. The Amalekites dwell in the land of the Negeb. The Hittites, the Jebusites, and the Amorites dwell in the hill country. And the Canaanites dwell by the sea, and along the Jordan.'

But Caleb quieted the people before Moses and said, 'Let us go up at once and occupy it, for we are well able to overcome it.' Then the men who had gone up with him said, 'We are not able to go up against the people, for they are stronger than we are.' So they brought to the people of Israel a bad report of the land that they had spied out, saying, 'The land, through which we have gone to spy it out, is a land that devours its inhabitants, and all the people that we saw in it are of great height. And there we saw the Nephilim (the sons of Anak, who come from the Nephilim), and we seemed to ourselves like grasshoppers, and so we seemed to them.'

God sent the people to spy out the land, and His hand of protection oversaw their journey. The spies returned safely from their 40-day journey due to the hand of God upon them.

Upon returning, something interesting is brought to the forefront in the above verses. As the men walked into the encampment, all of them hung their hats on the same peg of courage. They had all obeyed in faith and they had all survived the journey. They were all a testimony to God's grace and faithfulness, and they could all rejoice in the fact that God had used them. However, two different perspectives appear in their view of their journey and of their findings.

The large majority of the men brought back nothing but negative reporting. Fear is sensed in their words as they brought a "bad report" of the land laid out before the people. Though they clearly say that the land was bountiful in produce, like that of milk and honey, their fear of the land's inhabitants overcame them. The Nephilim had struck fear into their hearts. The armies and fortified cities had caused their faith to shrink and had returned them home in a disheveled and disheartened state.

The truth of the matter is that the spies that were sent out had departed on their journey in the mercies of God. They had left under His command and authority and with His stamp of approval. Though they should have returned in confidence in all they had done, the mission had only sought to leave them beaten down and short-sighted. They could no longer see the land as bountiful and free. Their perspective of God's goodness and beauty was blinded by doubt. Their faith had been replaced by worry, and had kept them from seeing God's promises. Not only had their faith become so anemic that it caused them to assuredly give up on the Promised Land altogether, but their discouragement turned their focus inward on themselves rather than outward into seeing God's plans. The end result of such a view led the people to intense insecurity to such a degree that they looked upon the fortified cities and seemingly giant soldiers and said, "we seemed to ourselves like grasshoppers, and so we seemed to them." A prayed-up people going out on God's mission and forgetting His presence along the way caused this shrinkage of faith. The voice of God that seemed so large and correct at one time, had become to them over the 40-day journey an inconsequential mutter.

In Caleb's mind, his confidence in God still remained. He stood before the people to exclaim, "Let us go up at once and occupy it, for we are well able to overcome it." His faith roared stronger than before he had left. Though he'd traveled the same journey under the same direction of the same God as the rest of the people, he emerged with an all-together more complete and victorious perspective. Caleb's faith is proven genuine. The other men were shown in their folly. He anchored his hopes in God's words and never let them leave. He carried them with him in the assignment. He sought God in the beginning not only for direction and future blessing, but he saw God's provision and faithfulness in the means.

What comes to light here is the difference between true faith and obedience, and a belief that is based solely in flimsy platitudes. Caleb's belief is set on God and His Holy decrees—God's authority. The other men's faith is set upon the authority of what they see in front of them. In surveying the land, the larger group of men made the terrain bigger than God. They made the world bigger than God. They made the people, the places, and the fortified cities bigger than God. In doing so, their view of themselves became smaller and smaller. They became self-defeating. They became helpless and bound once again in the chains of despair. The chains this time are not the literal shackles of Egyptian cuffs, but are the shackles upon their paralyzed soul.

Caleb on the other hand stands valiantly and courageously. The journey had only seemed to heighten his belief and trust in God. The fortified cities had only served to awaken his thirst for God. Each challenge Caleb faced became a new chance to see the power of God unfold supreme. Caleb anchored His joy in the glory of God being revealed, whereas the others laid waste to their joy in placing it in only what they could see.

Quickly the difference between a prayerful outlook and faithless perspective emerges in the light of Caleb's response. Prayer is not something that Caleb merely observes in Moses, but he allows the words of God to envelop his soul. The words spoken by God are not merely words uttered in haste, but God's words had become part of him. Caleb allowed the words of God to define his view of reality. He made all other ways of thinking submit to God's plans and decrees.

Prayer is far more forming to the Israelite community conscience than the people could have realized. Moses' candid conversations before the Lord served to shape the communities' life. Prayer is to take a caterpillar and make it a butterfly. Prayer raptures people into the language of heaven and allows them to hear a new vision of reality—much like a caterpillar who never thinks of flying before beginning to look at life through the eyes of a butterfly. This vision shift is true evidence that God's authority has taken hold.

The authority of God is always bearing weight upon the human soul. The words of God are always speaking and ringing loudly in a person's ears. The words themselves always hold the authority to change, transform, and grant faith. The only thing that separates the people away from anchoring their hope and confidence in God's authority is their own embrace of self. When people take no time to awaken themselves to a heavenly vision, the world becomes an intimidating and fearful place because inwardly they listen to themselves. Unfortunately, they can only see what they understand, and though the bounty of God surrounds them in all its beauty and power, they can not see it. Israel could not see it, not because it wasn't there, but because they refused to believe.

13

SCENE 4

THE PEOPLE REBEL

From the Israelite camp was heard a desperate cry (Numbers 14:1). Households were filled with grief and turmoil over what the spies reported. The men stood before the courts of the Lord and pleaded for the safety of their families (Numbers 14:3), The whole congregation of people recanted all that the Lord had done, and are found in Numbers 14 wanting to return back to the slavery of Egypt. Fear had entrapped the people's hearts. All they could see is the threat of the sword and the risk of death before them (14:3-4). And in verse four of Number chapter 14, the people came to the conclusion that they should choose another leader to lead them back into Egypt. Some hesitation on behalf of the people is no doubt understandable in light of all that was reported about the land. The fortified cities standing in their way were a real cause for concern.

Ensuing was the cry that went before the Lord. A cry is the natural posture of a person before a Holy God. A surrendered cry comes from the guts of a person who fully realizes the depth of their inability (Rm. 3:10). On into the New Testament, Titus 3:3-4 reminds us of our condition before the authority of God; "For we ourselves were once foolish, disobedient, led astray, slaves to various passions and pleasures, passing our days in malice and envy, hated by others and hating one another." The very nature of the people's inability and depravity surfaced in their cries, and their hopelessness is not all together unjustified.

Nevertheless, they had never heard the second half of words similar to Titus' exhortation in chapter 3:4-5; "But when the goodness and loving kindness of God our Savior appeared, he saved us, not because of works done by us in righteousness, but according to his own mercy..." The people had forgotten that the saving grace of God is what had delivered them up until this point, and would continue to do it again. Their cry was not based in the right motivation—a cry of dependence. What makes their cries of desperation here in Numbers 14 so vile and repulsive is that their hearts turn toward the Lord in disdain.

Though they cried to Moses and Aaron and grumbled about the reports from the spies to their human leaders, vs. 3 clearly states that there true distrust was directed at God. They exclaimed, "Why is the Lord bringing us into this land." They were passing blame upon God for the land. This blame is warranted in that God was indeed bringing them into the Promised Land, but His intention is by no means to abandon them. His intentions for them were good and pleasing, but once again the people could only see what they wanted to see.

In the forefront of their minds they fretted not their own limitations, but they also doubted God's commitment and goodness toward them and their families. Fear overtook them only as much as they were willing to surrender to it. Fear maintained power over them only due to the fact that they willingly gave it power.

The response of Caleb and from Joshua is one of faith. Caleb clearly saw the power of the men before them, but he also knew that even the Nephilim were no match for the multitudes of Israel who were backed and empowered by the presence of an Almighty God. Unfortunately, the people could not see God's hand. All the years in slavery had burned patterns and habits into their thinking. They learned to believe that God would abandon them and abuse them in their greatest hour of need. But in this case, remaining under God's authority as expressed through Moses and Aaron is to their only benefit. It is for their good.

The verse in Titus mentioned above starts off in vs. 1 saying "remind the people to be submissive to rulers and authorities." These vessels of leadership that God had provided to lead Israel into all His blessings, the very leadership Israel rejected, is the very leadership they needed in order to medicate and soothe their fears—rehabilitating them and enabling them to submit under good intentions.

This is why their cries in Chapter 14 were neither warranted nor righteous. Righteous cries base their desperation upon surrender and blissful hope in the Lord. These cries of anguish stemmed from the hearts of a people who were experiencing depression, anxiety, stress, and worry due to their lack of trust in God's goodness. These people ached not because they were being abused but because of the great care they were under. They were deeply grieved under the helm of *good* leadership. This seemed almost foolish, but their thought patterns were so trained and shaped to function ungratefully at the ends of the whips of slave owners, that the art of good leadership felt abnormal to them—like putting salt on a wound. Though the salt of God's guidance healed their deepest injuries, the sting of it is all they could still feel.

Following in the wake of such response, Moses and Aaron along with Caleb and Joshua, took the demonstration of *good* leadership to the next level in their response to the people's weeping and despair. Numbers 14:5-9 tells us;

> Then Moses and Aaron fell on their faces before all the assembly of the congregation of the people of Israel. And Joshua the son of Nun and Caleb the son of Jephunneh, who were among those who had spied out the land, tore their clothes and said to all the congregation of the people of Israel, 'The land, which

we passed through to spy it out, is an exceedingly good land. If the Lord delights in us, he will bring us into this land and give it to us, a land that flows with milk and honey. Only do not rebel against the Lord. And do not fear the people of the land, for they are bread for us. Their protection is removed from them, and the Lord is with us; do not fear them.'

The leadership of the Israelite nation bared their chests, tore their clothes, and in a dramatized display of compassion felt the people's pain. They understood the weight of fear. They understood all that it could steal, but in the midst of it they pled for the people to believe in their own best. They pled with the people to believe that their greatest safety remained beneath the sheltered wings of God's leadership. Though the temptation to leave God's protection was real, the leaders exhorted the camp in desperation not to pay attention to such evil leadings.

Moses and his team interceded for the people; standing in the gap between them and God in compassion as they cried out for the people's best. This is a far cry from the motive behind the people's cry and screams. The people's cries and screams masqueraded as righteous petitions that they somehow thought were achieving something for their good. Moses and his team clearly exposed the people's evil cries in ushering forth their own pleas. Moses' cry was not based in fear, it was based in His desire that all God's people might walk forward in faith and see the blessing that the Lord will bring. Moses' cry was one of true begging. His motive was to see the people leave their notion that Egypt had what they wanted, and to continue on toward the risky love of God's leading.

The congregation could not hear it, and in verse ten they stood to stone Moses; which, the threat of such an advance, only seemed to ignite the anger of the Lord further, "And the Lord said to Moses, 'How long will this people despise me? And how long will they not believe in me, in spite of all the signs that I have done among them? I will strike them with the pestilence and disinherit them, and I will make of you a nation greater and mightier than they.'" Once again, in the middle of a murderous moment in the hearts of God's people, God's' anger is rightly roused, and in the midst of it all Moses once again emerges in meekness to defend what is truly most important in the situation. The most satisfying result to be had in this situation is not that the glory of the people shines forth, but it is that the Lord has His glory:

> Moses said to the Lord, 'Then the Egyptians will hear of it, for you brought up this people in your might from among them, and they will tell the inhabitants of this land. They have heard that you, O Lord, are in the midst of this people. For you, O Lord, are seen face to face, and your cloud stands over them and you go before them, in a pillar of cloud by day and in a pillar of fire by night. Now if you kill this people as one man, then the nations who have heard your fame will say, 'It is because the Lord was not able to bring this people into the land that he swore to give to them that he has killed them in the wilderness.' And now, please let the power of the Lord be great as you have promised, saying, 'The Lord is slow to anger and abounding in steadfast love, forgiving iniquity and transgression, but he will by no means clear the guilty, visiting the iniquity of the fathers on the children, to the third and the fourth generation.' Please pardon the iniquity of this people, according to the greatness of your steadfast love, just as you have forgiven this people, from Egypt until now.'

Moses appealed to God's justice. In prayerful conversation, Moses spoke to God regarding God's commitment to His own name. God's name is still the most important thing in this situation. This is a courageous act of love and responsibility on the part of Moses. The audacity to approach a Holy God and appeal to God's goodness in all that was happening demonstrates a tremendous boldness, and also a merciful love for God's people. Moses was willing to trust that the Lord would listen to His prayers, and He also was willing to receive the Lord's rebuke. He was truly "taking one for team." He was willing and bold enough to challenge the Holiness of God on the basis of God's own commitment to His own glory and name.

This is the only ground that Moses stood on. Any other approach to question God's Holiness is an act of treason and disobedience. If Moses were to have done this in the same manner as the people, He would have become just like Israel—questioning God's authority with hate and doubt. Moses' own desires were not what drove his cry, but rather Moses' approach to God in questioning is in hopes to persuade God to act on behalf of His own name. This is how Moses spoke with God. This demonstrates the correct understanding that Moses had in how he related to God's authority. Moses knew that God's authority willingly interacts with us, and often God even listens to us and submits to us as the servant King that He is. God will not and cannot flex to preserve any other cry over His own.

This prayerful conversation here between God and Moses is one of the most terrifyingly beautiful passages in all of Scripture. In one moment we see the humble intercession of a leader unto God on behalf of God's people, and in almost the same breath, Moses speaks directly and openly with God about what he would hope to have happen in the situation.

The most shocking thing is that the only God of the universe, the only One of great power and glory, would actually listen to Moses' petition. In vs. 20 the Lord says, "I have pardoned according to your word." God clearly responded to Moses' petition that God's name be shown forth and be made known. God answered to Moses' authority and request in showing forth His mercy upon the people as Moses asked.

The story does not end here, however. Though Moses' cry is reverent and done with the authority of God, His request is still human. Moses only understands in part how God's name and authority can be shown in all its fullness, and in the following verses

God continues on from His initial answer to Moses in a long detailed description of the totality of how He will exalt His own Name:

> And the Lord spoke to Moses and to Aaron, saying, 'How long shall this wicked congregation grumble against me? I have heard the grumblings of the people of Israel, which they grumble against me. Say to them, As I live, declares the Lord, what you have said in my hearing I will do to you: your dead bodies shall fall in this wilderness, and of all your number, listed in the census from twenty years old and upward, who have grumbled against me, not one shall come into the land where I swore that I would make you dwell, except Caleb the son of Jephunneh and Joshua the son of Nun. But your little ones, who you said would become a prey, I will bring in, and they shall know the land that you have rejected. But as for you, your dead bodies shall fall in this wilderness. And your children shall be shepherds in the wilderness forty years and shall suffer for your faithlessness, until the last of your dead bodies lies in the wilderness. According to the number of the days in which you spied out the land, forty days, a year for each day, you shall bear your iniquity forty years, and you shall know my displeasure. I, the Lord, have spoken. Surely this will I do to all this wicked congregation who are gathered together against me: in this wilderness they shall come to a full end, and there they shall die.'

The men whom Moses sent to spy out the land had returned only to make the entire congregation grumble against him by bringing up a bad report about the land. These men who brought up a bad report of the land were sentenced to die by plague before the Lord. Of those men who went to spy out the land, only Joshua the son of Nun and Caleb the son of Jephunneh remained alive.

On one hand, Moses pled for forgiveness, love, and mercy to be shown to the people so that the people would see God (v. 18). In partiality, God did in fact respond to Moses' request with an act of deliverance, patience, and compassion. Moses prayed for mercy upon a merciless people and did the opposite of what most leaders would do. Because of Moses' reaction to such a coup, God declared that Caleb and Joshua—the faithful spies—be allowed to see the land God promised. This is a great victory and answer to prayer. On the other hand however, Moses did not take the people's offense seriously enough. For God's name to be fully shown, it was not only to be known in mercy and love, but also in judgment, wrath, and anger.

The people had ignored God's signs (vs. 22), they had tested God in not trusting in, listening to, and following after His voice (vs. 22). They despised God in their grumbling (vs. 26), and they had brought their groans into an entire nation and lineage of people (vs. 33). Such an offense, to go without consequence, would prove to be devaluing to God's Holiness. God's Name is offended. Though He remained patient with the people in order to exalt His patience, it was now time to show forth the other side of His Majesty. The judgment needed to fit the crime (vs. 34). God's promise was to be as equally fervent in extending mercy to the people through word and promise as He would be in His commitment to also discipline and rebuke. He commits to pardon as much as He commits to fully discipline (vs. 36-38). God is true to every word and to every facet of His character, and this circumstance provides no exception.

The paramount lesson of this scene is found in God's approach to the people's groaning. God allowed for the people to voice their doubts and sinful perspective. He did not silence their rebellion immediately, but He listened patiently even though He knew what was in their hearts. His patience also allowed the righteous prayer of Moses to intercede on behalf of the people's defense. The people were heard, Moses was heard, and still God's name remained central. God's response to both, one in judgment, the other in grace, demonstrates the supremacy of His authority and sovereignty over all situations. Even in His allowance of things that may not fully align with the full weight of His glory, He still works with His people.

This answer from the Lord seems to ignite a quick response from the people. Following God's words, the people mourned again greatly. This time, their mourning appears to be on behalf of their own sin in the situation, not merely toward losing what they most wanted. They wailed through the night and they rose early in the morning in order to commit their steps to the Lord. "We will go up to the place that the Lord has promised, for we have sinned," they proclaimed. The people apparently responded in repentance, or did they?

Moses saw through their fancy façade and drilled right into their false presentation. Moses says, "Why now are you transgressing the command of the Lord, when that will not succeed? Do not go up, for the Lord is not among you, lest you be struck down before your enemies. For there the Amalekites and the Canaanites are facing you, and you shall fall by the sword. Because you have turned back from following the Lord, the Lord will not be with you." The people of Israel in the aftermath of God's judgment put on a *fake display* of repentance. They were not concerned with following God before, and now only after He pronounces judgment did they want to get off the hook for their sin. Their motive for *not* going into the land in the first place was for the same reason that they wanted *to* go in now. Disobedience!

When God said go, they said, "NO!" When God says, "O.k. you are under judgment now for your disobedience," the people said, "Well that can't be true either—we don't believe that's the case." Their fake repentance is purely shrouded defiance.

The clear lesson rises to the surface here in that we see that to truly be under the authority of the Lord is to accept His answers when they come. One must also be willing to accept God's judgments when they come even though we may also raise objections. The key factor is that all cries must be made with the intention to see God's name made great; fake repentance on one hand, and fake obedience on the other cannot bring about such a result.

Though God is still in the people's midst in Numbers (vs. 44), He clearly did not intend to bless their work and false displays. When the Israelites acted upon their *fake response* to the Lord in going up against the Amalekites and Canaanites in *fake obedience*, they were soundly thwarted (vs. 25). The word of the Lord had spoken and the people had clearly not listened. Their rebellion to God's command only brought defeat.

14

SCENE 5

A PLEASING AROMA TO THE LORD

The most disconcerting thing about the nature of Israel's rebellion is that they already had begun to desire and seek after the promises of God more than the promise of God Himself. It is very apparent in their groaning against their leaders and in their sheer defiance in waging war against the Amalekites and Canaanites, that their desire for the Promised Land far outweighed their desire to obey God in obtaining it. In their hearts, God's promise became the paramount of their worship. They did not want the God of the land, they only wanted their own little version of heaven.

In order to accomplish such a task, they began to devise ways in which the kingdom would best suit them. This led the people to begin to fight for a path and a paradise that best suited their preferences. The kingdom and paradise of God no longer represented to the people a place of rest within the shelter and reign of God, as it had in the Garden of Eden. To the people, their paradise was a place that existed under their own authority—where they could do whatever they wanted—a paradise gained by their own devices, and secured by their own innovation.

The nature of such desires are sinful at best, for a kingdom without the goodness and safe protection of God's overarching banner of love is like a party without the wine; a feast without the chef, and a book without pages and story. What quickly transpired in their brief journey since leaving the wilderness at Sinai is that the people had already forgotten the redemption story that is far bigger than a mere plot of land. They forgot what had transpired in Egypt, and they had forgotten that the work of God is the sole means that had safely brought them to this place. In forgetting this work of God, the people began resorting once again to their self-sufficient slave mentality. They began clawing to the top and fighting for their best interests at the expense of another. They began treating the beautiful work of God in redemption like a whore that is only to be used for a time and then to be discarded when a better lover appears. This is how Israel treated God.

The next scene in Numbers 15:1-31 is penned as a result of the above reality. The camera lens zooms out after focusing upon Israel's groaning, and zooms in again upon the work of the temple. As the nostrils of the people flared in hostile dissatisfaction, the billowing fire stacks from the altar's sacrifices and offerings still rose brilliantly into the sky. The priests still walked around in garb that proclaimed God's story, the Nazarite and leper still modeled the lessons to be learned from sin and self-righteousness, and the encampment and tent of meeting itself still proclaimed the live drama of God's saving authority.

This perspective was to quickly balance the short-term memory of Israel as they moaned and groaned and carried on. Once again, God needed to plop down a little reminder of His purpose into their journey. He did this by zooming in on the wide variety of the offerings being made on behalf of the people and by the people. The different offerings made amongst the people were:

The Burnt Offering: Lev. 1; 6:8-13; 8:18-21; 16:24.
Elements Given: Bull, ram, bird, pigeon, dove wholly consumed
Practice: It was a volunteer act, given for the poor (a pigeon) and

for the rich (a ram). The animals were put on the altar to be wholly consumed, and their sprinkled blood put on a door, along with their skin being sold.

The Grain offering/First fruits: Lev. 2; 6:14-23.
Elements Given: Grain, fine flour, oil, incense, backed bread
Practice: It was a volunteer act, given without sin, in recognition of God's provision. The items were to be a first fruit, a pouring of oil; given with an added amount of salt, and a measured gleaning.

The Peace Offering: Lev. 3; 7:11-34.
Elements Given: An animal without defect—a variety of breads
Practice: It was a volunteer and communal act, including free will offerings of thanksgiving that were provided without fat.

The Sin Offering: Lev. 4; 5:1-13; 6:24-30; 8:14-17; 16:3-22.
Elements Given: A young bull (for whole congregation), a male goat (for the leader), a female goat (common person), and a dove (poor).
Practice: This was a mandatory communal act, including free will offerings for intentional and unintentional sins (vs. 22-31).

The Trespass Offering/Guilt Offering: Lev. 5:14-19; 6:1-7; 7:1-6.
Elements Given: Ram
Practice: Restitution for unintentional sins and defilement and to alleviate guilt.

. . .

The Freewill Offering/Wave Offering: Exo. 36:3-7; Lev. 7:16; Duet. 16:10.
Elements Given: Variety
Practice: Given willingly, at special moments, spontaneously as hearts were stirred.

The focus placed upon offerings serves to provide the story with a lift and an encouragement. As the stench of Israel's misguided disobedience rose into the nostrils of the Lord, it aroused His anger and His fury, but the smell of the offerings came to Him as a sweet aroma.

Their disobedience is profane to His taste, their fake repentance is disgusting to His heart, and though so much had been done for them, the people still reveled in their darkened commitment to their past slavery. The waft and smell of rebellion was illuminated and covered only by the smell of sacrifice. The promise and hope of God was set right before them in all its goodness and beauty, and the people still refused to see anything hopeful because somehow they could only see their past. Their fear arose, their faith was filled with doubt, and their pain once again clouded their praise. The ever-present scent of Israel's strife and self-righteous pursuit of God's promises permeated the camp in the smell of disobedient works.

Nevertheless, the sacrifices and offerings themselves were a pleasing aroma to the Lord. This phrase is repeated throughout the chapter of Numbers 15 to create another way of looking at the story of Israel's grumbling and hostility. The offering and sacrifices were provisions for the very sins in which Israel now indulged. While their disobedience only incited God's wrath, the offerings before the tent of meeting allowed the scent of payment into the presence of God the scent of payment. Each offering serves as a symbol of redemption for every guilty complaint that Israel made. Every work put forth out of the Israelite's own strength in order to obtain the Promised Land on their own terms is counteracted and covered by the perfect work of God's commands in the tent of meeting.

For the purpose of moments like these, due to the reality of sin dwelling in the people of Israel, God ordained these offerings. They ultimately foreshadow the necessity and abundance of the coming Messiah. The Messiah is the ultimate burnt offering—to pay for the people's failings. He would come voluntarily to rescue the rich and the poor in being mutilated upon the fire of the cross. He would be the ultimate grain offering given without sin as God's first fruit; the anointed One that would repel death, clean impurity, destroy the power of temptation, and preserve His people. This Messiah would be a Lamb without defect, given communally, freely of His own volition, for the purpose of purchasing our peace and repentance before God. This King would be the mandatory sin offering for the whole of the world, and the restitutionary "One," enabling freedom from guilt, and the purifying of defilement. He would be the new song, the free will offering, and the spontaneous art of heaven sent down into all of life's moments in order to make them special. This Messiah is Jesus.

Jesus is the one toward which the offerings point. His light is the centerpiece to the entire Israelite community and way of life, and the focus upon the offerings here in Numbers 15 reminds the people and the reader of His place within the journey of Israel. Israel's hope is tied only to the hope of God's work on their behalf. They are anchored and secured to the very same gospel hope that is ultimately delivered in Christ. This is what they needed to remember. They forgot this reality and they were standing on the precipice of walking right back into their own methods of operation once again. They were already becoming a threat to themselves in forgetting the work and offerings being done on their behalf. Because of their forgetfulness, they made the bone-head decision to once again go ahead of God's orders in trying to take matters into their own hands.

It is as if God is picking them up and dusting them off and pointing His finger back up into the sky to draw their attention back to the scent and the billowing smoke of the fire coming off the sacrificial altars. In pointing to consistent payment being made continually to reconcile their sins before God, the people needed to see that though in their own thinking they were waging war against God's perfect ways, His ways were still in fact the only thing keeping them alive. This was the pleasing aroma to the Lord.

Almost as quickly as God points His finger to the towering covering and beacon of forgiveness in the sky, Numbers 15 captures the finger of God pointing to yet another occurrence that was to remind the people of their place before Him:

> While the people of Israel were in the wilderness, they found a man gathering sticks on the Sabbath day. And those who found him gathering sticks brought him to Moses and Aaron and to the entire congregation. They put him in custody, because it had not been made clear what should be done to him. And the Lord said to Moses, 'The man shall be put to death; all the congregation shall stone him with stones outside the camp.' And the entire congregation brought him outside the camp and stoned him to death with stones, as the Lord commanded Moses.

This snippet almost appears to be disconnected from the whole of the context unless we actually take time to analyze what is going on the heart of God's people. God's people were caught up in striving. They were clinging to their belief that they could outperform God's decrees. They were succumbing to the lie that being under His leadership was constricting their freedom, and that to gain the Promised Land, they only needed to do it on their own terms. Yet, though their confidence appeared to them to be so strong, in the context here in Numbers we can see that the tribe is plagued by fear, intimidation, and insecurity. Though they claimed to be confident in their own ability to lead and wage war, it only masked and covered the true fear that rested in each of their hearts. They believed they could do it on their own, but not really. In some fashion their search for peace and rest had stolen all their peace and rest. In holding tightly to their ability to work themselves out of the situation, they had become a frantic, stressed out, and burdened people.

This appears to be the reason that a quaint little quip about the Sabbath enters here in Numbers. Apparently, a man caught working on a day that God had ordained for rest was, in this instance, punished by a severe stoning. It is not for the fact that this man was working on the Sabbath that created a cause for concern, but it was his motive in his working. Jesus even says in the New Testament that the Sabbath is made for man not the other way around (Mk. 2:27).

The Sabbath was made for man to rest and enjoy. It is a day to cease from striving and a day to work hard at enjoying God's creation and the relationships within God's family. This man however, was not working hard at building God's family, he was hard at work picking up sticks and trying to shore up his own security. His strife on the Sabbath Day is what awakens a cause for concern. This man's strife on the Sabbath Day also provides a warning to the Israelite people in light of their own violation of God's rest. God warned the people to cease from their own devices and their own matter of obtaining God's rest. God warned them not to violate His peace and authority by introducing into the mix their own methods for advancement. The seriousness of such an offense, as portrayed to the Israelites through this example of the man working on the Sabbath, is an offense that deserved stoning and sudden death.

God values His rest with great intensity, and the jealously He has for His rest is for the good of the people. In the previous chapter in Numbers, the people had forsaken God's rest and leadership and gone out to fight on their own accord and had only met defeat. In leaving the safe arms and directions of the Lord, the people only found what was crippling to them. It was a sad and defeating thing. This "parable" about the Sabbath here proves to be an important filler piece in the drama unfolding in Numbers 15. The people needed reminding regarding the God who protected them and allowed them to experience blessing even in light of their sins. The people also needed to be reminded of the consequences of forsaking and leaving such rest.

In one last pictorial image God tries to remind His people of all He had tried to do up until this point. He finishes His warning in ordering the people to make *tassels* for their clothes. These tassels were to hang from the corners of their garments. These tassels were to be "for *them* to look at and remember all the commandments of the Lord, to do them, not to follow after *one's* own heart and eyes, which they are inclined to whore after. So *they* should remember and do all God's commandments, and be holy to *their* God." (Italics added) God proclaimed to them through the tassels; "I am the Lord your God, who brought you out of the land of Egypt to be your God: I am the Lord your God." Like the offerings and the Sabbath punishment, these tassels provided a way for the people to remember God and to visualize all that He had done and would do. These tassels were to remind them of their propensity toward strife and of their depravity and *whoreship*. They were to remember their propensity to leave God's presence and to pursue other lesser ways of life. They were to remember their inclination to sleep with the world rather than remaining in relationship with God. These tassels reminded them of their holiness, of God's Lordship, and of God's character and commitment to them.

God speaks to His people through these displays of art and visual message. He taught of His forgiveness by wafting billows of smoke in the sun-scorched sky. He taught, through these pillars of fire, of His ability to make or break His people based on His own terms. He taught through the harsh punishment of a man breaking the Sabbath law that the mode of a person's heart should be to operate in a state of grace and peace, not in a state of worry and strife. And the tassels that dangled from their daily dress were to point to their call to be Holy, and to warn and remind them of their human tendency for having a taste for whoring pleasures.

15

SCENE 6

KORAH'S REBELLION

Though the gracious warnings from God's hand continually came to Israel in the form of God's artful and colorful presentations, the hardness of Israel's heart continued to sharpen. They were given much grace and reminded of much grace, and yet their fake repentance continued to linger. The leadership rebelled at the sound of the Lord's commands, and all the people only seemed to listen to the Lord when their own security was threatened.

The people are lukewarm in their obedience and though it looks pious to some degree in our reading of Numbers, it is fake. Though their repentance looks sincere, it masks only their true motivation for their own self-preservation. As a result, the tribes witnessed the birth of yet another rebellion. This time it came through a man named Korah. Numbers 16:1-3 records the scene for us;

> Now Korah the son of Izhar, son of Kohath, son of Levi, and Dathan and Abiram the sons of Eliab, and On the son of Peleth, sons of Reuben, took men. And they rose up before Moses, with a number of the people of Israel, 250 chiefs of the congregation, chosen from the

> assembly, well-known men. They assembled themselves together against Moses and against Aaron and said to them, 'You have gone too far! For all in the congregation are holy, every one of them, and the Lord is among them. Why then do you exalt yourselves above the assembly of the Lord?'

Korah is a distant cousin of both Moses and Aaron. Though the previous chapter records the corporate rebellion of Israel as a whole, here in Chapter 16 of Numbers, Korah serves as a typological example of the depth of rebellion that resided in the individual hearts of the people. The depravity that had continued to brood in Korah's heart toward the Lord and the Lord's authority finally welled up within him to lead to his utter rejection of all that the Lord was doing. Similarly to the rebellion of the Garden, the text tells us that the first group of people that were affected due to Korah's impatience were his very own family. His rebellion began right under the hands of those within his household. He rejected the environment of the home and he put to shame the attempts of others—bringing discord into their homes.

Like the people, Korah was not getting his way in this whole deal. His discontent and bitterness fueled his passion for change. In the eyes of those throughout the rest of Israel he could see his own bitterness, and the time to act upon rebellion was now.

The people were about to enter the Promised Land. They were now undergoing the very real journey it would take to get there. Rather than submitting and welcoming the Lord's process in returning them to their place of rest, the people saw the opportunity as primed for upheaval. Everything was already moving and changing, and Korah put his finger right on the pressure point of unrest and began to surmount his coup against the Lord.

Korah, who was well known in the community (vs. 2), gathered with him others who also possessed his influence and talent of leadership to rise against Moses. The team of malcontents raised their voice against Moses' leadership and his seemingly foolish ways.

Their bitterness made them loud, impossible to console, and full of anger.

The book of Hebrews tells us that bitterness is like a root that sprouts up and becomes a tree that defiles many, and that is exactly what happened to those in the Israelite army (Heb. 12:14-16). The people began busy-bodying around with each other. The malice, slander, and discontent spread like a wild fire as their choice morsels of gossip and hatred sank to the very depths of the people's souls. Out of the poisonous wells that sprung up from within the people came a faction of rebel leadership, and they deemed Korah as their new leader. Korah's message of rebellion appealed to the Israelite people, and to any of those who were not persuaded, their fear of Korah and of the people outweighed their fear of the Lord. Many who were not rebellious at heart were now being quickly persuaded to malice because of their cowardice. The people were no longer guarded and guided by the peace and encouragement of the Lord's leading, but their bitterness drove them into the waiting arms of a destructive leader. Korah's every intention was to lead the people astray, and yet the people could not see it because their eyes were too blinded by their fear and hidden secret passions for what they wanted.

In an about face, the community of redemption that God had fashioned and freed in delivering them from Egypt was now returning to slavery in the formation of a new community ethic. The people began to band together in their cliques and isolated huddles. They began to surround themselves with the council, not of those who would challenge their perspective, but of those who would affirm that "they were o.k." in their validation of their cause. The communities of bitterness that formed began to affirm each other with the mantra, "you deserve more." The environment was pregnant with sin, and was a hotbed for every kind of impurity.

Developing in the community of Israel was a mind-set of bondage that was about to land them back into the hands of yet another false master. Their entitlement thinking began to spread like a cancer, and brought the people before Moses and Aaron uttering this toxic statement; "You have gone too far! The whole community *is holy*, every one of them, and the Lord is with them. Why then do you set yourselves above the Lord's assembly?"

Out came the real reason for the people's rebellion. The people in their deepest soul defined themselves as "holy and good people." They believed their goodness did not depend on the Lord but that it resided apart from God within their own hearts. They believed in this passage that they did not need God's leadership or the oversight of Moses. They ignored God, ignored His voice, and refused to heed to the commands that were prayerfully coming from God through Moses to the people. All their anger and pent up aggression was based only in their own belief that they were entitled. They believed they were entitled to all the milk and honey of the Promised Land—the good life—and they believed it so deeply that they embraced the thought that they should and could have all God's blessings in doing it without Him in the picture.

The same attitude emerging here in Korah is the same attitude that caused the people in Numbers 14:44-45 to go to war against their foes and do it without the leading of the Lord. The people were so arrogant, and had grown that way ever so much in such a seemingly short amount of time, that they believed the Lord was with them in their battle even though they were clearly living on their own terms. The people, and Korah, had already forgotten the results of their previous fake repentance. Perhaps they even still blamed their defeat on God at the hands of the Amalekites and Canaanites. They blamed it on God not because God had done it, but that He had allowed it. Their sense of entitlement could not permit them to trust a God that could allow their demise. They were a good people! A Holy people! They were exempt from the rules—so they thought.

The truth of the matter is that amidst all the complaining and false attempts at humility, Korah and his crew were living in pride. The fact of the matter is that they wanted more of their own authority. The text even tells us that they went so far as to appoint council members (vs. 2). They wanted Moses' position, the priesthood position. Ultimately, even the Levites were dissatisfied and wanted God's position (vs. 8). Yet in the process, what was completely hidden to them is that in their attempts to leave the shade of God's protection they were forsaking the *all* that they had under God's leadership. God's people were succumbing to the mere table scraps that fell from the table of their own thinking.

When Moses heard this uproar, his response was to fall before the people on his face in a plea of true humility. He did not defend his own leadership, but rather appealed to the Lord's validation on his behalf. He said to the people, "In the morning the Lord will show who belongs to him and who is holy, and he will have that person come near him. The man he chooses he will cause to come near him. You, Korah, and all your followers are to do this: Take censers and tomorrow put burning coals and incense in them before the Lord. The man the Lord chooses will be the one who is holy. You Levites have gone too far!" Moses' appeal was that the decision of leadership be left to the Lord. Korah wanted to validate his own leadership, but Moses left his affirmation to the Lord's approval. Korah advanced his own cause in bitterness, but masked it under the guise of false humility and righteousness. Moses, let all of his brokenness hang out before the people in a display of his own inability to defend himself. This authentication was going to be left up to God. The reason being, is that it was against the Lord that the people "banded together" (vs. 11).

Korah's response to Moses' challenge came with the same cowardice that drove the rebellion in the first place. In vs. 13 a subset of Korah's crew was challenged to come up before the Lord for His authentication and they answered, "We will not come!" (vs. 12). The people threw yet another holy temper tantrum and acted as if they were strong, even though deep down they knew of their weakness. They knew of the Lord's holy displays of real power—they had witnessed it. They knew that they were merely like a rickety shack trying to bear the weight of a hurricane. Like a shack, the people were deceptively considering themselves to be standing firm in cool weather, but deeper still, they knew when the power of God's judgment was to appear, they would be soundly thrashed by His winds.

Moses' decision to allow the Lord to speak on his behalf thus proved wise. Instead of dealing with the people of Israel, and even instead of trying to right the wrongs that were in his own *family*, he simply released and surrendered his right to try and explain himself. In fact, the only anger that appeared in him was his absolute frustration at the rebellion of the priesthood. In verse 15 he tells the Lord, "Do not accept their offering. I have not taken so much as a donkey from them, nor have I wronged any of them." His anger only seemed to amplify his meekness, for again he was not angry at his own name being slandered, but rather he was concerned over the fact that the Levites were bringing an offering before the Lord that was not worthy of His Holy Name.

Thus, Moses left the people to their own work and drew attention to the fact that their own work utterly exposed them. He let the work of their hands be the source of their own crippling, and in verse 23-48 of Numbers chapter 16, their work did just that.

> The Lord said, say to the assembly, 'Move away from the tents of Korah, Dathan and Abiram.' Moses got up and went to Dathan and Abiram, and the elders of Israel followed him. He warned the assembly, 'Move back from the tents of these wicked men! Do not touch anything belonging to them, or you will be swept away because of all their sins.' So they moved away from the tents of Korah, Dathan and Abiram. Dathan and Abiram had come out and were standing with their wives, children and little ones at the entrances to their tents.
>
> Then Moses said, 'This is how you will know that the Lord has sent me to do all these things and that it was not my idea: If these men die a natural death and suffer the fate of all mankind, then the Lord has not sent me. But if the Lord brings about something totally new, and the earth opens its mouth and swallows them, with everything that belongs to them, and they go down alive into the realm of the dead, then you will

know that these men have treated the Lord with contempt.'

As soon as he finished saying all this, the ground under them split apart and the earth opened its mouth and swallowed them and their households, and all those associated with Korah, together with their possessions. They went down alive into the realm of the dead, with everything they owned. The earth closed over them, and they perished and were gone from the community. At their cries, all the Israelites around them fled, shouting, 'The earth is going to swallow us too!' And fire came out from the Lord and consumed the 250 men who were offering the incense.

The Lord said to Moses, 'Tell Eleazar son of Aaron, the priest, to remove the censers from the charred remains and scatter the coals some distance away, for the censers are holy— the censers of the men who sinned at the cost of their lives. Hammer the censers into sheets to overlay the altar, for they were presented before the Lord and have become holy. Let them be a sign to the Israelites.'

So Eleazar the priest collected the bronze censers brought by those who had been burned to death, and he had them hammered out to overlay the altar, as the Lord directed him through Moses. This was to remind the Israelites that no one except a descendant of Aaron should come to burn incense before the Lord, or he would become like Korah and his followers. The next day the whole Israelite community grumbled against Moses and Aaron. 'You have killed the Lord's people,' they said. But when the assembly gathered in opposition to Moses and Aaron and turned toward the tent of meeting, suddenly the cloud covered it and the glory of the Lord appeared. Then Moses and Aaron went to the front of the tent of meeting, and the Lord said to Moses, 'Get away from this assembly so I can put an end to them at once.' And they fell facedown.

Then Moses said to Aaron, 'Take your censer and put incense in it, along with burning coals from the altar, and hurry to the assembly to make atonement for them. Wrath has come out from the Lord; the plague has started.' Aaron did as Moses said, and ran into the midst of the assembly. The plague had already started among the people, but Aaron offered the incense and made atonement for them. He stood between the living and the dead, and the plague stopped; but not before 14,700 people died from the plague. This number was in addition to those who had died because of Korah. Then Aaron returned to Moses at the entrance to the tent of meeting, for the plague had stopped.

When the Israelites had displayed fake repentance in battle, the Lord gave a condition. He was patient with the people and he allowed them another day. Even here in this passage He allows a condition when he beckoned the spouses to "step back." Sadly, in the case of Korah, their judgment was final. He had been patient with them and had allowed them to survive to some extent while still remaining hateful of His ways. But not here! He allowed the extent of their rebellion to literally swallow them up that they might not live anymore. Korah's team and family were swallowed up in response to their leader's disobedience. Even the innocent lives of their children and wives were taken because of their display of grumbling and anarchy.

This is the result of sin. It takes the lives of the innocent. It steals the lives of those who could have lived to see a better tomorrow.

God left *conditions* with Israel in His patience, as long as His Holiness would allow. However, for Him to hold back His judgment forever against such a test of His leadership would only serve to affirm rebellion. Not only this, but if He continued to remain silent, His love to those who were being perverted and hurt by the rebellion would have suffered as the cancer spread. In this passage God acts on His own love for His people, and His own commitment to His righteousness—and He did it all at the same time. The day of conditions had passed. The day had ended where Israel could remain stagnant in their complaining, their hatred of authority, and in their prideful stance. Korah became an example of how the patience of the Lord can only suffer so long with wickedness until His wrath ends all *conditions* and renders a *final* judgment.

In this particular case Korah was swallowed up by the earth, along with his followers (vs. 31). His payment was paid and it was final. Moses was then told to create censors from the ashes of the flames as reminders to the people of all that had taken place, and however shocking it may seem, the very next day, before the dust had even settled, after these censors were placed as a daily reminder of God's judgment, the people rebelled again. Korah's fire had not even cooled, nor had the pleasing scent of the 250 incense bearers been swept away, when the next day the people of Israel return to the courts of the Lord to once again sound their complaints of fear and concern. God's fury awakened once again as He shouted, "Get away from this assembly so I can put an end to them at once."

Again, Moses, in a sign of intercession between God and the people, fell facedown before the Lord in desperation and ordered Aaron to take the censor's contents and quickly offer unto the Lord a pleasing scent of atonement on behalf of the people. Verse 47 tells us that God initiated a plague that was already spreading amongst the people, killing 14,700 people in all (vs. 49).

In addition, a curious phrase appears here in relation to Moses' and Aaron's action, for it says, "He stood between the living and the dead, and the plague stopped." Moses cried out in intercession unto God for the people in repentance on behalf of the people, but the plague did not cease until Aaron, the high priest, ran into the midst of the people to carry the healing agent that would calm God's wrath. Moses stood before God on behalf of the people in prayer and Aaron stood between God and the people in a mediatory role. In doing so, the plague of God's wrath was quenched and satisfied and no longer had to rend its work among the people. Aaron's work on behalf of the people satisfied the wrath of God and foreshadowed the role of the coming Messiah in Jesus.

A great drama unfolds in Numbers 16 in Korah's rebellion. The undercurrent of such an event is driven by much more than hostility against leadership. There was an ultimate battle of good and evil going on. The righteous decrees of God were being challenged and profusely protested to such an extent that it awakened God's justice. The jealousy of God did not so much burn over the doubts and complaints that welled up from amongst people, but His frustration was enflamed when His people's heart's desired to act on their rebellion; trying to make their own way out from underneath His authority and leadership. The people's perspective still had not yet afforded them the luxury of seeing beyond themselves and into the journey ahead. They had yet to see what God sees. They had yet to see their need for Him in the battles they would wage, and the territory they would enter. God's jealousy for them was due to His own desire that His people would have His protection and haven of leadership going forward.

SCENE 7
THE BUDDED STAFF

The Lord grew tired of the Israelites and their constant grumbling. It seems that the further they traveled away from the clutches of Egypt's hand the more quickly they forgot all that God provided. It seems that even though God's care had quickly come to the aid of the Israelite people in the wilderness of Mt. Sinai, and in God establishing the people in truth and with tangible symbolism of redemptive artistic imagery, the people had lost sight of the beauty of the story. They had already forgotten their leader and forgotten where they came from. They had already forsaken their authority in their heart. Though they dwelled within this culture, this encampment, this city, this body of delivered souls, it became increasingly apparent that the hardest thing about learning God's LORDSHIP was the very act of having to submit to His leading in every step of the journey. Learning about the principles of God's authority proved to be the easy task, but submitting to them required real belief and love for God's intentions. Though this broken Israelite people were all led by the glorious and majestic leadership of God's hand, and experienced some of the common grace and benefits of His hand, true atonement and peace could come only to those following and believing His word.

Again the Lord's word appears in chapter 17 when the Lord speaks to Moses and gives him instructions on what to do next:

> The Lord spoke to Moses, saying, 'Speak to the people of Israel, and get from them staffs, one for each fathers' house, from all their chiefs according to their fathers' houses, twelve staffs. Write each man's name on his staff, and write Aaron's name on the staff of Levi. For there shall be one staff for the head of each fathers' house. Then you shall deposit them in the tent of meeting before the testimony, where I meet with you. And the staff of the man whom I choose shall sprout. Thus I will make to cease from me the grumblings of the people of Israel, which they grumble against you.'

Though the people still scoffed at Moses' authority and questioned his motives for taking such a position, God all the while affirmed Moses' leadership in conversation. God did not speak His word directly to the people, He spoke it to Moses. He established a friendship and a relationship of trust with Moses. Moses was privy to the interworkings of heaven, and God allowed Moses to see into His most intimate of plans. This was a privilege that was not granted to the people of Israel in the same manner. Though they claimed the rod of authority for themselves and grumbled under the weight of their entitlement, it was Moses and Aaron who still possessed the real sign of power. Authority did not come from titles and or self-proclaimed leadership in loud displays of complaint, upheaval, and grumbling. Authority did not come through exerting oneself as leader. Authority did not come even in taking captive the minds of a nation and persuading them toward action and boycott. True authority only came from the Word of God as spoken to and through His servants—in this case His servant being Moses. For as God gave the orders, Moses obeyed:

> Moses spoke to the people of Israel. And all their chiefs

gave him staffs, one for each chief, according to their fathers' houses, twelve staffs. And the staff of Aaron was among their staffs. And Moses deposited the staffs before the Lord in the tent of the testimony (vs. 6-7).

Moses not only heard the commands of the Lord but he listened to God's instructions, as evidenced in his immediate action in response. God laid down the gauntlet with the people. Though they simply deserved His sharp hand of discipline once again, God was willing in His lavish grace to indulge the people's moldy unbelief. God commanded each leader to place the name of his tribe on a staff and submit it to Moses for authentication. God's authentication process was that all the staffs were to be placed in the temple, and the one that God placed his seal upon would confirmed who He affirmed as leader.

The chiefs of each tribe did as Moses asked and gave up their staff to be tested. In this test, more was tested than simply the genuine authority of Moses amongst the people. The hearts of the people were challenged. They gave up their staffs arrogantly *"knowing"* and deceptively thinking that they were the chosen ones for leadership. They were wise in their own eyes. Whereas Moses surrendered himself to God's commands in order that God's strength might be seen through him, the people surrendered themselves to God's commands only that he might reveal their own strength.

A similar act of obedience took place both in Moses and the people. Both responded to God's word in action, but God only approved of obedience done correctly. To be a true *doer* of the word, one must go to the Lord for wisdom James 1:5 tells us. One must remain steadfast under trial and adversity (James 1:12), one must lose sight of their own desires and sacrifice on behalf of others without grumbling (James 1:27), and one should be controlled in their tongue and passions (James 3:2, 4). True faith and "doing" produces works of righteousness and displays of God's strength, and it produces unconditional rather than partial love (James 2). This love leads only to the ability to trust God with all our tomorrows (James 4:13-17). However, it is increasingly clear here in this passage that Israel did not trust God. They could not control their desires and passions. Their concern was not for the good of the nation, but only for themselves, and they most certainly were buckling under the weight of the pressures that lay before them. This caused them to turn to their own devices and know-how for wisdom.

Moses on the other hand remained steady holding his tongue and trusting the Lord's guidance, and once again did not defend himself in order to validate himself before the good of the people. The men delivered their staves into the tent and returned to their homes to sleep through the night, all the while awaiting the morning light when God's authentication was to be revealed. In Chapter 17:8-11 the following passage describes the result of God's endorsement:

> On the next day Moses went into the tent of the testimony, and behold, the staff of Aaron for the house of Levi had sprouted and put forth buds and produced blossoms, and it bore ripe almonds. Then Moses brought out all the staffs from before the Lord to all the people of Israel. And they looked, and each man took his staff. And the Lord said to Moses, 'Put back the staff of Aaron before the testimony, to be kept as a sign for the rebels, that you may make an end of their grumblings against me, lest they die.' Thus did Moses; as the Lord commanded him, so he did.
>
> When the people gathered around the tent of meeting at dawn's early light, the spectacle before their eyes was that of a miracle. The 12 staffs, representing the leadership of Israel, lay dead upon the ground, whereas the staff of Aaron had budded, sprouted, blossomed and even produced mature almonds.

The budded staff became another artful representation of a very real spiritual reality. The reality was that God's rule was leading this group, and only God could confirm it through the likes of a miracle.

Moses nor Aaron could have fabricated this act, but God's verification of His word had been affirmed.

This is the fruit that follows the correct and righteous obedience of Moses. Moses allowed the Lord to become his defense and in return Moses experienced God's validation and affirmation. The result of Moses' act of righteous trust is that it produced a plentiful crop. Like a seed tossed into good soil, Moses' obedience planted richly into God's decrees and as a result the nourishment of God made the rod bud. The fruit of Moses' obedience produced a plant that budded quickly and "early"—thus God's plan and ways were confirmed in a timely manner.

Moses quickly experienced God's sense of peace in the situation. Though the long night had preceded the morning, and the results did not quickly appear in the moment that Moses obeyed, God quickly confirmed His call and decree to and through Moses. This rod not only budded, but it blossomed and matured. It produced not just any fruit, but it produced a crop of almonds. Almonds, in the mind of an Israelite, symbolized old age (Ecc. 12:5). Though they were associated with age, they were also known to bloom early in the season. It was a sign to the people that God's decree of leadership came from ages past, but was also alive in the present moment. His plans sprang up from old, and they did so immediately.

Moses' confidence was intensely stirred by such a display of God's miraculous approval. Even though Moses knew that God's call on his life was secure, the human tendency to doubt and question such a call was still present. He experienced great grief over the complaints of the people, for the text even tells us that a number of times Moses fell on his face before the people in absolute abandon. In the same way the budded rod became an artistic expression that enabled the people to visualize God's blessing upon Moses' righteous obedience, the budded rod also became a visual symbol of judgment to those that had obeyed only out of wicked motives. The fruit of Moses' obedience was given, and now the fruit of false obedience and submission appeared. The people in Numbers 17:12 shouted, "Behold, we perish, we are undone, we are all undone. Everyone who comes near, who comes near to the tabernacle of the Lord, shall die. Are we all to perish?" The people, in the wake of their disobedience, were revealed for what they really were. Dead! Their hearts lay bare and exposed, and their outward righteousness revealed for the inner filth that it was.

The fruit of their disobedience was not greater faith but despair. They did not need God to tell them of their heart motive, for they knew it within. This miracle of the budded rod only proved to expose the structure of rebellion that held their souls ever in slavery. The budded almond became for them a sign of judgment upon their inner rebellion. It revealed the real weight and reality of their faith and work. Like fire burns up a hay field, the fire of God's exposure shines light on their souls and scorches all their inner fields to the point that nothing remained. This rod, when lifted up, became a symbol of power and protection, and to the Israelites it etched in their hearts and minds a warning of punishment to which they were to submit.

The word of God powerfully went out. As discussed before, the weight of this scene is initiated and completed by the very word of God as it is spoken to Moses. God gave a decree to Moses and it was followed with real power (1 Cor. 4:20). The real power of the miracle that God performed in the budded rod was not in the miracle itself, but rather in what the miracle revealed in God's people. God's word brought to the surface either belief or disbelief. It exposed submission or rebellion.

The authority behind all that happened is most certainly God's. The message of the rod tells us an even greater message. Whereas the rod was dead, and was brought back to life; whereas the lifting of the rod looses the powers of both life and death (Acts 2:23-24); whereas the lifting of the rod justifies and verifies Moses' faith (Rom. 4:25); whereas the rod symbolizes the qualification of God to lead and to judge (Rom. 14:9); and whereas the rod preserves access between the people and God through the priestly office (Eph. 2:18) and enables them to continue toward their inheritance in the Promised Land (1 Pt.

1:3-4), the awaited Messiah is the one who becomes the ultimate fulfillment to such a display and symbol.

The glorification of such a Messiah is the content and the power of God's voice. Not only does the budded rod speak of the power of God, but the power of the rod is really in the person that it points to—the Messiah. This Messiah was to be planted, He was to bloom and mature quickly in order that He would produce a wealth of harvest that extended into ages past, as well as springing early, producing a crop long into the future.

The authority of God's word came to Moses through the mode of prayer, and this was indeed a contributing factor to Moses' authority. Not only did the word of God speak, but the power of the message is what drove the response. God did not merely speak *any* words to Moses, but He spoke and alluded to one *Word* (Jhn. 1:1) that would come into the world and reveal the true power behind the voice that spoke to Moses. This Word was and is the true authority.

17

SCENE 8
THE LEVITES

The word coming from the mouth of God set the stage for a widespread panic. The last verses of Numbers 17 portray a people coming face to face with their own disobedience. They failed to obey the word of the Lord despite all His good advances and all His patient allowances. The people, who had spent so much time defending their rebellion, realized the weight of punishment that their constant disbelief deserved, and their cries rang out, "Behold, we perish, we are undone, we are all undone. Everyone who comes near, who comes near to the tabernacle of the Lord, shall die. Are we all to perish?"

They were brought to the point of dismay and despairing again. Their awful works brought about their consequence, and the Israelite nation knew only one pattern of response—to grovel and expect death. In Egypt, were they to do anything wrong or malicious toward authority and been found out, they would surely have been punished. Even Moses, after killing a man, left Egypt at once for fear of his own life (Ex. 2:15). Egyptian ethic deemed it right that disobedience be dealt with blood for blood. The Israelites had grown expectant of this type of punishment, and therefore their only gut response to the situation now before them was to believe that the Lord would deal with them all the same. The people's hearts had not learned to trust His hand. Even in their supposed fear of Him they failed to embrace His deepest intentions. They failed to learn the depth of His heart. The Israelites clung to their habitual and patterned response of terror toward leadership—a rhythm they had learned in Egypt—and they all but forgot the new rhythm that God had brought about in His new and redemptive national culture.

It became increasingly apparent to the Lord that His people needed a shock to the heart in order to remind them of the realities that they had forgotten. The zoom lens of Numbers 18 focuses sharply in on the Levitical priesthood once again for the purpose of reminding the people of the provisions God made for Israel's blunders. Even the Levitical priesthood themselves had been sucked into the charisma and idle leadership of Korah, and they too needed to be reminded of their role unto the Lord and before the people. The Levitical lineage and legacy reached deeply right back into the heart and foundation of Egyptian rule, as we have discussed briefly in earlier portions of this book.

When God had judged Egypt for their rejection of His command, God plundered them with 10 plagues, the last of which being the one that took the first-born son of everyone in the land. Nevertheless, those who trusted the Lordenough to accept His provision of a sacrificial lamb in place of their son went free. Out of this miraculous deliverance, God delivered the first-born children of the family's of Israel, and these children became the set-apart tribe of Levi. Their very history and lineage reminded them of God's ability and desire to preserve them, not punish them. The Levites were a symbol to the people of God's real heart and desire. Not only did they embody His message of second chances but their role within the temple proclaimed God's rescuing plan in forgiveness.

In Chapter 18:1-2 of Numbers God spoke to Aaron and proclaimed once again their call and purpose and reminded them that their role and ministry before the people and among the people was to "bear their iniquity." They were to guard the temple from impurity and outsiders who did not respect the tent of meeting and the presence of

God that dwelt there (vs. 4). The role that they played, in making sacrifices to the Lord on the people's behalf, was designed by God to testify to God's desire that the people be free from their bondage of un-forgiveness. The animals that were offered were meant to remind the people of God's posture of forgiveness toward them, even in their gravest rebellions. The Lamb being slain in Egypt to spare the Levites from God's wrath was representative of all the animals that the people now brought to be slain for the same purpose. Numbers 18:5 records God saying, "You shall keep guard over the sanctuary and over the altar, that there may *never again be wrath on the people of Israel.*"

These words are the words that provide the salve of healing to the Israelite's hearts. In the wake of their recent rebellion they stood terrified at God's wrath and justice. They stood fully aware of God's ability to bring down on them the full weight of their guilt and shame. In this instance, the message they needed to hear was that of God's continued offering of forgiveness. God needed to remind them that the ethic of Egypt—blood for blood—was still in place, but the glorious good news, hidden in the fabric of God's culture, is that the animal now pays on behalf of the people's sins. They were correct in believing that wrath and death are due them, but they were near-sighted, forgetting the bigger picture that God had outletted their punishment on the bird and beast.

The Levites needed also to be reminded of this mystery of payment and appeasement. They were to remember the message of God's grace in their ministry. As they stood there offering sacrifices to the Lord before the altar on a literal kill floor—bloodied and bludgeoned like battered war veterans—they were to remember that their office was awarded to them as a gift and is also a gift to the people (vs. 7). The swing of their knife was to sober them to the reality of God's wrath toward them apart from payment, and the flow of the blood from the animal was to remind them of the blessing they received in spite of their constant disobedience.

This was the message that is supposed to keep the people from returning to their place of shame, and returning to the recoiled and cowardice of their slavery-like thinking. Everything about their mistakes seemed to force them to return to their past and re-embrace its calloused misery and bondage, and yet the icon of the Levite—the icon of the slain lamb—was the thing they were to constantly look toward and experience as a reminder of their own forgiveness. It is a gift to them (Heb. 10:11; 1 Pt. 3:18).

The gift that God provided was not only a gift that the people could receive, but it was a gift that demanded their response in giving. They could bring their fruit, a wave offering, a grain etc. In light of all they had done in transgressing the Lord's leadership under the leadership of Korah, their contributions brought a reminder of all that was in place to ensure payment for their mistakes. Their hearts were freely saved despite all their treacherous actions. God's wealth extended to them despite all their greed, and though they acted shamefully and became nothing, God allowed them the preservation of their dignity. This tribe was forgiven much, and to those who received this forgiveness, they were expected to forgive much. Their acceptance of such forgiveness was to well up within them into a grateful display of generosity.

Though many of God's commands required that an Israelite give up to 15% of their income in response, many brought 25% of all that they had. The clear take away from observing such a percentage, is that the foundation of Israelite giving was done out of a gracious response to the grace received. The zoom lens of God highlighted the ministry of the Levites and the nature of the offerings in order to salvage the despairing perspective that the people quickly embraced. God refocused them and reminded them that His culture of authority is much different than what they had previously experienced. In His kingdom there was no room for despair, only celebration.

Following God's reminders and loving prodding, He then instructed the Levites in how they were to handle the contributions and the offerings that came in as a result. Though the Levites possessed no land or inheritance from which to give from (vs. 20), God reminded them that the grace that was extended to the people also came to them through the very contributions from the people.

God said, "All the holy contributions that the people of Israel present to the Lord I give to you, and to your sons and daughters with you, as a *perpetual due*. It is a covenant of salt forever before the Lord for you and for your offspring with you." In verse 21 God said, "To the Levites I have given every tithe in Israel for an inheritance, in return for their service that they do, their service in the tent of meeting." Out of these contributions made by the people, the Levites responded to the Lord's grace in the same manner—giving a tithe of the tithe (vs. 26). The people's work brought about a plentiful harvest that allowed them to give freely of all they receive, and the Levites were also not to be muzzled as they treaded out the grain. They too were given their perpetual due, not as a sign of their worth or earned payment for hours rendered, but their *perpetual due* was given to them so that they will not miss out on the joy of giving in response to God's mercies.

Clearly what is being communicated is that though a division seemingly remained between the inner and outer courts of the tent of meeting, and there was a clear separation between the common man and the calling of the Levite, each person was to depend equally upon the mercies of God through the provision of His forgiveness. The entire nation of Israel was indebted to God's grace. The entire world was still in existence due to this lavish and wondrous grace. Though all of Israel had experienced the one-time call of salvation out of the hands of Egypt, God reaffirmed the salvation that was still available to them even in light of their slip-ups throughout the journey. His salvation had saved them, and His clear-cut mercy would preserve them in order to enable them to grow into a belief that would deposit them into a better tomorrow.

18

SCENE 9

A HATRED FOR THE UNCLEAN AND ANYTHING DEAD

God's statement to affirm life and forgiveness permeated through the encampment. The scene that followed must have been a spectacle. Families emerged from their homes with a little spring in their step. The community took on a certain pleasing odor. Though there remained a greater stench of blood in the air due to the sacrifices, subdued morale and thankful offerings, and the odor of forgiveness filled the heart. Though the Israelites soon traversed back into their dismay, their hearts were now full and grateful for the opportunity to simply live and see another day.

This is the simplicity of life that God wants for His people under His authority. He wants forgiveness to envelop them. He wants the stench of His sacrifice to bleed into their hearts, and that out from them will waft a beautiful aroma of contentment. He did not want Israel worrying about the next step. He did not desire for them to fret over or figure out what the next phase of the journey would hold. He simply wanted them to live in the quiet embrace of each day; knowing that their days are numbered and that they were blessed by the opportunity of experiencing a new sunrise each morning. This outlook of contentment is an outlook ensuring that Israel would keep their eyes on all the riches that were to be had in His kingdom. This outlook ensured their joy and happiness, and would keep them from falling prey again to thinking that there was something more pleasurable outside the bounds of God.

Though a tender shift can be certainly felt in the atmosphere around Israel's encampment, their forgiven and encouraged hearts also needed to pay fair warning to all that God had allowed to happen should they ever feel like giving into such rebellion again. In Numbers Chapter 19-20, as they came to a close in their wandering, and were about to begin their trek in entering the Promised Land, God focused in on the theme of all that is unclean and all that relates to death. He did so in order to sober His people to the only hope that rebellion can promise should Israel continue to pick from its tempting fruit.

Israel time and again demonstrated their proclivity toward rebellion, and the land they were about to sojourn into was a land under rebellion—not yet released unto the freedom of God and His rule through His people. They needed fair warning not only as a correction to their past, but as an admonishment toward their future. God hates rebellion. God hates rebellion because He hates impurity and death, and rebellion always leads to both. Since the beginning of time in the Garden of Eden, death and impurity have contaminated God's perfect creation. It had tarnished his human vessels and image bearers, and it had reduced the world down to utter meaninglessness. Though God is not surprised by death (Job 14:5), He is more emphatic and intentional about the course of the living (Acts 17:38).

The idea of living does not simply include someone who is breathing and walking around healthy and virile. Death begins with impurity. Any impurity that entices God's people toward rebellion is infuriating to Him. In Numbers 19:1-10 God's displeasure with all that is impure and unclean is voiced to the Israelites. Not only did He remind them about the nature of His forgiveness and grace, but He explained to them why He was so passionate about them submitting to His authority. It was not only that they experienced abundant life, but that they also avoided impending death and defilement.

The people were to avoid death like they were to avoid the outside of the encampment. Outside the camp is where the priests would travel to slaughter the unblemished red heifer on behalf of the people's sins. The sacrifice was made to ensure the purity and forgiveness of the Israelite people. In doing so, the priest was exposed to the "unclean" and therefore was to remain there, and only after washing was he to re-enter the camp. Upon re-entering the camp, the ashes were to be brought on behalf of the people to sprinkle in the water. This was to symbolize their own need for purification; "And a man who is clean shall gather up the ashes of the heifer and deposit them outside the camp in a clean place. And they shall be kept for the water for impurity for the congregation of the people of Israel; it is a sin offering."

The act of impurity is linked to the idea of death. Impurity and uncleanliness brings about death. God warned the people in regard to their impurity. Though they were alive, and had been spared from judgment and execution under the leadership of Korah, they were still to recognize the reality of what might happen should they embrace anything again that would attempt to cloud the perfect holiness of God.

Death is not just an end of life, but it can contaminate the means of life through uncleanness if one is not careful. Death is a final end, but impurity is a slow fade. Death can come into a camp if a people again start participating in "dead things." Dead things are anything that seeks to tarnish a person's awareness of the dignity, the value, and the worth that God extends to His people. This is what they had forgotten in lieu of Korah's honeyed words of false teaching. God encouraged His people not only to be scared of death as an end, but to be repulsed by anything that could rob them of His sweet authority and protection in the present.

To avoid the risk of being short-sighted in His advice, God brought forth a command in Numbers 19:11-20 regarding all things actually dead. Anyone who contacted anything dead was to be purified for seven days and washed on the 3rd and 7th day in order to be clean. The slime of death was so repulsive that every open vessel in the vicinity of someone who died, whether in a tent or out in the fields, was to be discarded like bio-hazardous material. The reason for such harsh measures to be taken is that God needed His people to understand the seriousness of impure promises. He could not have His people once again believing the toxic lies of another enemy, only to find out that their enemies' sugared promises were like a chocolate covered ball of toxic poison offered to them—the outside tasting smooth and silky, but the inside and end result only containing elements for asphyxiation.

With these words of warning neatly tucked away in the people's minds, the Israelites in Chapter 20 traversed ahead into the next phase of the journey as they settled in the wilderness of Zin at a place called Kadesh—a dominant question still looming in the reader's mind as Israel pulled into their new pit stop: "Though the Lord's warning is clear, did the people fully listen?"

It was here in the wilderness that God again put His words to the test in the hearts of His people. His curriculum of education taught the Israelites to believe Him fully. He first taught them His ways and truths, and then He provided environments of testing for them that would actually expose their hearts whether they embraced the warnings or not. He again allowed their hearts to be exposed to the very realities that God's words had described, in order that they would fully embrace them and actually participate in complete surrender to them.

It seems that in Chapter 20, as the people of Israel settled in Zin, that they indeed encountered the testing of God. The course of the chapter is laid out in short little micro-scenes that play out the drama of all that took place in the aftermath of God's warning. In the first little micro-scene, within Scene 8 of Act 2, their beloved matriarch Miriam died. Miriam's death shattered the hearts of those camping amongst Israel. She was the family member of Aaron and Moses, and also part of the trifecta of leadership that led Israel out of slavery in Egypt. Micah 6:4 later affirms her influence in naming her as a leader; "For I brought you up from the land of Egypt, and redeemed you from the house of slavery; and I sent before you Moses, Aaron, and Miriam." Her death brought about great mourning in the tribe of

Israel, and as follows in Numbers 20:2-9 we do see the people quickly begin to grumble again, not only at the fact of her death, but regarding the lack of water in the land. It must be considered that the apparent and instant despair of Israel in the aftermath of God's warning must have been intensified by Miriam's death. Not only had one of their leaders died, but they were once again suffering in the land. This was not what they expected to happen.

Death's effects quickly resurfaced. The reality of Miriam's death awakened mourning and grief within the camp. The result of death only brought tears and sadness. Likewise, the lack of water in the land revealed death and impurity once again in the hearts of the Israelites as they cried out in painful cries of woe and grief. The distrust that they held in their heart toward God was as blackly sorrowful as the death of Miriam. Their continuous and doubtful demeanor toward the Lord again reemerged, and they once again began their track toward igniting God's jealousy and fury.

Moses, who grieved over the death of his sister Miriam—her being a great leader and matriarch of the nation—was again given a command by the Lord to silence the people's whining by bringing water from a rock that could quench their thirst. Moses responded to God's command by taking the staff in his hand and *telling* the rock to produce water (vs. 20:8-9). Moses gathered the assembly together before the rock, and he said to them, "Hear now, you rebels: shall we bring water for you out of this rock?" And Moses lifted up his hand and struck the rock with his staff twice, and water came out abundantly, and the congregation and their livestock drank.

Though a miracle had again come from the Lord, Moses out of his own grief had given into the impurity of his heart. Instead of speaking to the rock like God had commanded, Moses struck it in anger and pent-up sorrow. Just like that, just as one of Israel's leaders (Miriam) had passed on, Moses' integrity in following the Lord also received a deadly blow. In response, God said to Moses and Aaron, "Because you did not believe in me, to uphold me as holy in the eyes of the people of Israel, therefore you shall not bring this assembly into the land that I have given them." These were the waters of

Meribah, where the people of Israel quarreled with the Lord, and through them He showed Himself Holy.

Death took Miriam and was responsible for all the pain and sorrow that had come into people's hearts. Death rose up in the hearts of the people to bring them to a place of hollow unrest. Now, death tarnished the leadership of Moses. In his anger, he failed to uphold the Lord as Holy. Impurity's goal is as it had always been: to attempt to shadow the holiness and perfection of God. Moses was a representative for God, and death caused him to fail at accomplishing his assignment.

It seems that Israel had now become a live illustration and drama for all that death and impurity could do to a people. Death was and is the source of all human sorrow, all human grumbling, and all human disobedience. It took Miriam, it touched the people, and it even touched Moses.

As Israel passed through the land of Edom, the effects of death and disobedience on the world surfaced even further in the response of the king of Edom. As Israel kept moving they came to Edom and were met by the king.

They humbly exclaimed to the king,

> You know all the hardship that we have met: how our fathers went down to Egypt, and we lived in Egypt a long time. And the Egyptians dealt harshly with us and our fathers. And when we cried to the Lord, he heard our voice and sent an angel and brought us out of Egypt. And here we are in Kadesh, a city on the edge of your territory. Please let us pass through your land. We will not pass through field or vineyard, or drink water from a well. We will go along the King's Highway. We will not turn aside to the right hand or to the left until we have passed through your territory. But Edom says to him, 'You shall not pass through, lest I come out with the sword against you.' And the people of Israel say to him, 'We will go up by the highway, and if we drink of

your water, I and my livestock, then I will pay for it. Let me only pass through on foot, nothing more.' But he says, 'You shall not pass through.'

Edom came out against them with a large army and with a strong force. Edom refused to give Israel passage through his territory, so Israel turned away from him.

God led them into Edom only so they could pass through the land into the Promised Land, but the impurity and death that remained in the heart of the king of Edom silenced any compassion he could feel for God's people. He could not permit anything good for them or for their God because he did not honor nor respect the ways of Yahweh. Because of this, the people of Israel were driven back by the threat of war and the large army of Edom (war being another result of the presence of impurity and death in the world). And if the people were not torn up enough after everything that had happened, Numbers 20:22-29 records the death of Aaron. He was stripped of his priestly garments as the leadership passed to Eleazar, and the people again suffered at the hands of yet another loss. Their losses at this point became so great that they wept over Aaron's death for 30 days (vs. 29).

One by one Israel's pillars fell. Miriam died, Moses sinned and disobeyed, Aaron died, and amidst all of this their pain, and their wounds, was amplified by thirst and war. All of these things are the result of the uncleanliness and impurity remaining in the world and in the hearts of humans. In a live fireworks show of death and sorrow, God allowed the very pinnacle of His words to transpire. He spoke to the people and warned the people of all that death and impurity cause. He warned the people of all that would lie in the shadows of sugar-coated promises. To test the maturity of His people, and to weigh how deeply they'd considered His words, He allowed the realities of death and impurity to corrupt the camp. He allowed the people to come within the greenhouse of His protection and parental hand in order to experience the lengths of even the worst of the world's promises. He allowed the people to become intimately acquainted with the full-orbed facets of it all. They tasted death, grief, shame, despair, disobedience, leader failure, war and hardship, and greater still, they were faced with the still ever-present reality of their own tired and critical souls. God made all allowance so the people were able to taste from the buffet of what is *incomplete.*

Only in visualizing the death of their hopes, could they fully embrace the fact that their only residing hope rested in God's nature of *completeness.* Upon entering the Promised Land, the people's hope was to be ever grounded in God's perfection. Any lesser anchor would only prove fatal for Israel.

PART III
ACT 3

PART III

ACT 3

SCENE 1

BABY STEPS

The Second Act of Numbers commences with the tragic disobedience of Moses and with the death of Miriam and Aaron. As the chapter of wandering comes to an end for Israel, the next phase in Israel's journey toward the Promised Land is filled with possibilities. Though much had been lost to Israel in pain, tragedy, sin, and disobedience, much had also been gained. Israel had grown into a great nation and currently had realized the promise and covenant blessing made to Abraham that God would make His seed a blessing, and would number His offspring more than the number of the stars in the sky. Each apparent setback that Israel encountered, much of it resulting from the evil they brought upon themselves, seemed only to continually multiply their influence. What once was a poor, disheveled, and authority-less people now had become something altogether different. This nation, though still like a newborn baby in many ways as we will continually see, slowly had become a toddler; standing to their feet and beginning to walk. In Numbers 21 a number of occurrences take place that really captures the whole of Israel's growth both as people and as a nation.

In coming out of Egypt, one of the first things that God did for His people was to number them for war. This was done in order to set their expectation rightly upon what kind of life that was in front of them. God wanted them to know that He is their Deliverer and their Defender, but also that the enemy that lay before them was very real indeed.

Though they banded together, their hands were not held in trust and love for one another. In Numbers 21, with Israel yet again facing the very real threat of war in the King of Arad, a different kind of process and outcome emerged. Maybe the difference was a result of default, or maybe even a fluke, but it is my conclusion that Israel's response to king Arad gives us hope that they indeed were making progress—be it ever so small.

Numbers 21:1-3 reads this way,

> When the Canaanite, the king of Arad, who lived in the Negeb, heard that Israel was coming by the way of Atharim, he fought against Israel, and took some of them captive. And Israel vowed a vow to the Lord and said, 'If you will indeed give this people into my hand, then I will devote their cities to destruction.' And the Lord heeded the voice of Israel and gave over the Canaanites, and they devoted them and their cities to destruction. So the name of the place was called Hormah.

What seemed to be another lost battle and disappointment to Israel, as they were bruised by Arad, appears to be an experience soliciting a different response. This time, unlike before, in the wake of all their tragedy, Israel's response to God in their loss resembled something of a formed unity and trust. Israel's word to the Lord is this; "If you will indeed give this people into *my* hand, then *I* will devote their cities to destruction." Notice the emphasis Israel's response places upon the word *my*. Their once disunified front and wounded hearts had indeed been trained in some matter of speaking. They had walked out of their isolation and were now thinking as a team—a unified unit. They realized that they were interconnected to one another and that they were also dependent on God for their unity. They pled with God to deliver them and recognized that even in their defeat that He was the only one with the true ability to free them once again.

At least for the moment, Israel did not complain about the initial results of their war. They apparently trusted God with their outcome and believed that even in their capture there was a plan for a greater victory. Could it be that Israel had ever so slightly started to lean upon the sovereignty and plan of God in directing their baby steps of faith? Could it be that Israel recognized that God intended to go before them and would allow only things, both good and bad, that would ultimately lead them to a greater promise and hope? Whatever the conclusion in the long-term, it is clear here that Israel trusted God in this circumstance. Even in their prayerful request, they together went before the Lord and not only asked in confidence for His deliverance, but they resolved to devote their enemy to destruction.

What the people sought to allow God to do in their prayers is to decide how they were to be best defended and delivered in the situation. Their hearts had been trained on their arduous journey to know how to fight. Not only was their trust in this instance placed in God to deliver them if He so desired, but now Israel was ready to respond to His actions in holy obedience. Along the journey they so quickly had partnered with the sins, idolatries, and the evils of the tribes dwelling in the land, but here they were resolved to do as God would do. They resolved not to allow evil to move freely, but to take it captive fully and put it to death so that everything good could live again.

This decision on Israel's part is good, to say the least, but even more profoundly, it points to the initial purpose and creation for humanity—*the imago dei*. Israel expressed the *image of God* in how God intended it to be revealed. They chose to live in holiness and expose evil, not partner with it. They were unified as one person in accomplishing such a task—not divided—and their bond together was brought only through their trust and love of God. This was the original intention of the Garden.

Future to Israel, this was to be true again, only in the perfect sense of God's son Jesus, as He was soon to come as the true Israel to lay perfectly "all things under his feet," (a commonly used phrase in the New Testament). Israel's prayer to God to deliver things into their hands, is a foreshadowing of God declaring through Jesus that He would place everything in "*His*" hands" and would allow the "*I*," Jesus, to devote all the world's evils to destruction. Both in the future, and in the present, the Lord answered the intercessions of Israel and responded to their faith, and the battle against Arad was won.

Israel learned to take their first baby step—*they learned the next phase in trusting in God in their war.* As they emerged victorious from the clutches of the king of Arad, and moved from Mount Hor to go by way of the Red Sea around the land of Edom in order to reach the Promised Land, Israel quickly found out that the terrors of war needed to be experienced and defeated in the human soul as well as the human world. Immediately after leaving their victory, the Israelites faced yet another baby step which revealed how far their maturity had come.

Once again, directly following a profound victory both in war and in growth, Israel spoke against Moses once again for they became impatient in their travels toward the Promised Land. The people spoke against God and against Moses, "Why have you brought us up out of Egypt to die in the wilderness? For there is no food and no water, and we loathe this worthless food" (Num. 21:3-5). Though God had been good in victory, the temptation was much too great, and the people again complained about their displeasure in the food that God had provided for them. This time, God responded to them differently and less favorably than He had in Arad when the Lord sent "fiery serpents among the people, and they bit the people, so that many people of Israel died" (21:6).

This is a curious response to the people's complaining. In sending the serpent into their midst, God allowed them to experience all over again the horror that took place in the Garden of Eden. There, Adam and Eve became discontent with God's ways and provisions and decided to go their own way. In taking of the forbidden fruit, they allowed their *discontent to give way to evil.* That's exactly what God allowed among Israel in this scene. He allowed their discontent to bring about all its fruits, and the serpent's bite provides a visual image into what they had allowed into their hearts.

> The people came to Moses and said, 'We have sinned, for we have spoken against the Lord and against you. Pray to the Lord, that he take away the serpents from us.' So Moses prayed for the people. And the Lord said to Moses, 'Make a fiery serpent and set it on a pole, and everyone who is bitten, when he sees it, shall live.' So Moses made a bronze serpent and set it on a pole. And if a serpent bit anyone, he would look at the bronze serpent and live (21:7-9).

Why such a unique response to the Israelites complaints? Not only does God allow the snakes to come upon the people in judgment like He had in the Garden, but why then does He instruct Moses to form a snake and erect it on a pole so that the people could look at it and be healed? Why does the image of judgment—the snake—become the image of healing?

Perhaps God wanted the people to remember the horrors of Egypt and wanted to call attention to Moses' staff that had performed the miracles of God to free them. When the diviners of Pharaoh's house had produced snakes to threaten Moses' request to allow God's people to go, God had turned Moses' staff into a large snake which devoured their petty attempts at trickery (Ex. 7:12). Perhaps the people just needed a reminder of Egypt's "bite" in order to remember the sweet taste of all God did to free them from bondage.

Maybe God's intention was to again draw attention to the nature of what complaining does in and amongst them. Their sin bites like a snake. In erecting a bronze snake perhaps it called them to see the seriousness of their outward sin in the innermost parts of their soul. Perhaps as they looked up at the snake while being bitten by other snakes they would remember where their place of sin and suffering in Egypt had become their place of redemption.

God was directing them to look upon their struggle, both in Egypt and here amidst the biting serpents in order that they might find redemption. God wanted their greatest pain to serve as a reminder, perhaps even in the bite marks running up their legs. That pain was not to be remembered for its goodness, for in and of itself it was not good, but rather the healing of God was what should be rejoiced in. This is the way in which intense places of *pain* can be glorious places of *praise*.

Perhaps even further, we can take an interpretive cue to how to make sense of this occurrence from listening to the later perspective of Jesus in John 3:14-15 when He proclaimed this raised staff to be a testimony to his own grace; "Just as Moses lifted up the snake in the wilderness, so the Son of Man must be lifted up, that everyone who believes may have eternal life in him." Therefore, the snake upon the staff was raised up, not being good or bad in and of itself, but the snake on the pole *pointed to a greater reality of God's deliverance and grace*. Therefore, the image of the snake is not bad, for it points to the greater reality of God. This way of looking at it keeps in line with God's use of imagery throughout the entirety of Numbers.

It would take the death of King Jesus to fully deal with the penalty of sin and to do away with it—crystallizing it in a bronze covering which would demonstrate its final hardening, punishment, and ineffectiveness. This Jesus, like the serpent, would have to become a representative of the people's sins and evil, and Jesus, like the bronze snake, would stand in the place of all that sin and bear the weight of its evil in order that all who looked upon such a sacrifice would experience victory.

This seemingly weird instance in Israel's history became a profound baby step toward them maturing in faith and trust in their God. They had learned to trust Him in *war*, and now they were learning to believe in Him through *temptation*.

They experienced the bite of their sin, but they were allowed to see that the place of their greatest struggle is where the victory of

God rings its chorus of loudest song. Their place of failure is His place of victory. Not only did this become an incredible artful expression of God's help toward them, but it served to become a landmark that they might never forget. Time must serve to remind them to never again return to bondage. The serpent was to remind them not only of what they experienced in a loss of dignity in their slavery, but to help them rejoice in the healing and freedom of what they had been given.

After this,

> ...the people of Israel set out and camped in Oboth. And they set out from Oboth and camped at Iye-abarim, in the wilderness that is opposite Moab, toward the sunrise. From there they set out and camped in the Valley of Zered. From there they set out and camped on the other side of the Arnon, which is in the wilderness that extends from the border of the Amorites, for the Arnon is the border of Moab, between Moab and the Amorites. And from there they continued to Beer...'

Israel after experiencing a full victory in trusting the Lord in *war*, and after receiving a reminder of their victory through *temptation*, God again began to move Israel in their journey toward the land of promise in quick spurts of encampment. In movement, God trained the Israelite's hearts to stay alert.

With every move, the Israelites packed up their entire camp. They had already become proficient at erecting and disassembling tents and living structures. They corralled and led their cattle and herds with proficiency and with great loving kindness. They became familiar with children screaming "are we there yet" as their constant moving evoked many challenges ranging from parental hardships to marriage spats, on into work-related stress, worry, uncertainty, a sense of homelessness, and many other issues of like manner. Their movement was another way in which God trained His people in baby steps. Each time they moved they were forced to re-order their things, throw away unnecessary baggage, work with diligence, develop routines and discipline, and all in all develop a rhythm of life that helped them in following God.

Israel became quite accustomed to such a rhythm. Through *war, temptation,* and *movement* God kept His people enough on their toes to expect great things from Him, but enough on their heels to where they did not know what to expect next. God built into them a rhythm of trust through their travels, and Israel slowly learned a lot more about faith in the simple activities.

God's education plan for Israel was to return them to the mundane and the ordinary. Their constant moving forced them to see their routine chores and household duties in light of something greater. Every day as they washed dishes, worked in the marketplace, ate, washed, and experienced the small moments of life together, they were constantly able to see their little movements in light of the whole picture of the Promised Land. Everything they did in the *small* things was moving them along to a *large* home. Everything they did had significance. Though the little things seemed to be very insignificant indeed, each effort brought them one step closer to their anticipated new reality.

The sheer load of it all took its toll upon their soul. Upon arriving at an ancient site in Beer, the people were encouraged to rest for a short moment in the journey, and in resting they sang with great joy as God provided little moments not only to train their soul, but to give them rest. Numbers 21:16-18 says,

 ... they continued to Beer; that is the well of which the Lord said to Moses, 'Gather the people together, so that I may give them water.' Then Israel sang this song: 'Spring up, O well!—Sing to it!—the well that the princes made, that the nobles of the people dug, with the scepter and with their staffs...'

This brief scene of solitude was refreshing for Israel. The faithfulness of God not only had kept them, defended them, and led them

through hills and valleys, but also His loving kindness had given them places of restoration in between their work. This well was a place already established for them. It was a place that God had already forged by the work of his own hand, and the people, who had been keeping up with God's leadership as they worked and traveled, were now given a moment by God's foresight to recoup.

This rest, a rest well needed, propelled Israel into the next moments of war with the King of Sihon and Og (Num. 21:21-35), who again fought against the people of Israel as they sought to possess the land that God had promised them. But indeed, their ranks had been strengthened both physically and spiritually in the baby steps that God had allowed them to take. They were able to surmount hostile tribes, terrible temptation, and laborious journeys, and God's rest was a reminder to them that from His springs alone come the source of all victory. Any pleasurable outcome that Israel experienced was not because of them, but it was all in spite of them. The hand and protection of God was the sole reason Israel experienced these victories. God's authority, as "they went in and possessed the land" (vs. 35) was the only thing that won for them the territory, as well as what kept them from quickly watching it fade. They needed to remember this and embrace this in order to stand firm through what would come next.

SCENE 2
THE ENEMY

U p until this point, the narrative of Numbers, as it traces Israel's journey to the Promised Land, has kept its focus primarily upon God's working in and through Israel. In the ensuing chapters (22-24) the focus shifts and begins to detail what transpired within the other nations as Israel traversed through the land. In Numbers 22:1-19 the camera zooms out and pans left to capture what was going on in the nation of Moab. The reason for such a perspective shift relates to the overall theme of Numbers in teaching authority, but to explain the reason for such a change, the next section of the story must unfold.

The nation of Moab and its leaders had seen what Israel had done to annihilate the Amorites, and fear surged through their veins in seeing Israel's approach to their land. The text tells us of their fear and details what they did in response;

Moab was in great dread of the people, because they were many. Moab was overcome with fear of the people of Israel. And Moab said to the elders of Midian, 'This horde will now lick up all that is around us, as the ox licks up the grass of the field.' So Balak the son of

Zippor, who was king of Moab at that time, sent messengers to Balaam the son of Beor at Pethor, which is near the River in the land of the people of Amaw, to call him, saying, 'Behold, a people has come out of Egypt. They cover the face of the earth, and they are dwelling opposite me. Come now, curse this people for me, since they are too mighty for me. Perhaps I shall be able to defeat them and drive them from the land, for I know that he whom you bless is blessed, and he whom you curse is cursed.'

So the elders of Moab and the elders of Midian departed with the fees for divination in their hand. And they came to Balaam and gave him Balak's message. And he said to them, 'Lodge here tonight, and I will bring back word to you, as the Lord speaks to me.' So the princes of Moab stayed with Balaam. And God came to Balaam and said, 'Who are these men with you?' And Balaam said to God, 'Balak the son of Zippor, king of Moab, has sent to me, saying, Behold, a people has come out of Egypt, and it covers the face of the earth. Now come, curse them for me. Perhaps I shall be able to fight against them and drive them out.' God said to Balaam, 'You shall not go with them. You shall not curse the people, for they are blessed.' So Balaam rose in the morning and said to the princes of Balak, 'Go to your own land, for the Lord has refused to let me go with you.' So the princes of Moab rose and went to Balak and said, 'Balaam refuses to come with us.'

Once again Balak sent princes, more in number and more honorable than these. And they came to Balaam and said to him, 'Thus says Balak the son of Zippor: Let nothing hinder you from coming to me, for I will surely do you great honor, and whatever you say to me I will do. Come, curse this people for me.' But Balaam answered and said to the servants of Balak, 'Though

Balak were to give me his house full of silver and gold, I could not go beyond the command of the Lord my God to do less or more. So you, too, please stay here tonight, that I may know what more the Lord will say to me.'

The text paints a vivid picture of what went on in the hearts of Israel's enemies as they approached their land. God had indeed been faithful to Israel in keeping His covenant promise to multiply them; so much so, that the on looking nations trembled in fear. Israel's sheer numbers could very well have overwhelmed their land and agricultural resources. The multitude of Israel posed a seemingly dire threat to Moab and their nation. Moab, as a new character in this subplot is brought into the narrative of Numbers to add color to the unfolding drama.

Appearing in the short record of the aforementioned nineteen verses, there are four major characters introduced to God's story: Balak, the Messengers, Balaam, and the Moabite Princes. To begin, Balak was King of Moab. In standing out on the peak of an overlooking cliff he saw the vast number of people coming into his land. Reports of Israel's strength and expertise in war had reached the ears of Balak by this point, and not only was he consumed with dread over their size, but he knew what the people of Israel were capable of beneath the direction of their Lord the King.

Balak was the overseer of his people. He led them in similar fashion to how Moses led Isreal. He was entrusted to lead and protect his people. And in his eyes, this land was also his to protect. In his mind, these were his resources and this was his kingdom. Though the people of Israel were mightier than he, something needed to be done to Israel in order to communicate to them regarding his seal of approval over this kingdom.

As a response he took matters into his own hands to communicate such a message to Israel and sought out the guidance of a diviner to direct him in his next steps. Balak reached out to the only hands of power available to him in the form of the local spiritists. As Moses sought his direction from the Lord, Balak sought out the guidance of anything else. Thus the very nature of Balak's intentions toward God and Israel are revealed in this narrative, for he was an evil king. Balak was also an opposing power to the people of Israel and to God, and as the antagonist character within the story, he is pitted in comparison against the leadership style of Moses.

Though Moses was a very meek and humble leader who led in righteousness and drew from a holy and powerful source in Yaweh, Balak was a man of pride and wicked intent. The well that he drew his power from was filled with evil ambition and conceit.

Balak's thinking in regard to himself was filled up with idle notions of his own power and ownership of the land. He fell prey to the belief that everything was his. In verse 6 his view of himself grew so detached from reality that he claimed for himself and his nation the Abrahamic promises that God made to Abraham and Israel. He believed that God was on his side to bless all those he blessed and to curse all those he cursed. He acted on this false belief and assumption not only in thought but also in action. In order to ensure that his nation received the promises of blessing that he deemed fit for his rule, he appealed to his messengers.

These messengers were Balak's task force and they were commissioned to do his bidding. They were sent carrying the fees that pay the diviner for his services, and these messengers were to act in accordance with Balak's desires. Out of Balak's evil intent these missionaries of falsehood were sent. This legion and task force that were sent out from Balak's midst to journey toward the place of the diviner's residence were endowed with great kingly authority, great kingly riches, and with them they brought the intentions of their evil king.

Their journey and task led them to the doorstep of Balaam, (the 3rd character introduced in our story), a diviner and a spiritist. He resided in an area of the land that at the time was known for divination, and he was chosen because he was the best of the best. When the messengers of Balak arrived, Balaam invited them in and entertained their predicament and determined what he might do for them. The messengers carried with them a lot of money and goods for payment from King Balak. Balaam provided them with something for their trouble so that they would leave him with these riches. Balaam turned to the men and beckoned them to stay the night under the guise that he would seek the "lord" and come back to them the next morning with his answer to how they should deal with Israel.

The reality is, that Balaam was not a God-fearer, and most likely did not seek the true God of Scripture for his answer, but his possible pantheistic view of plural gods enabled him to go and make an attempt to speak to the Lord.

The shocking reality of the story is that the true God of the Bible in fact showed up to speak with Balaam. God's omnipresence, also present in leading Israel in the cloud, went before Israel simultaneously and spoke with their enemies on their behalf. This story gives us our first real glimpse into God's actions as He goes before the people of Israel. All that Israel had seen to this point was the cloud of mist guiding them by day as well as the pillar of fire by night. On ahead of God's billowing presence however, all along, He had been preparing the way for Israel in the presence of their enemies. God had led His nation as they followed behind Him, but had also defended them and warded off their enemies out in front of them.

In a peculiar scene, the God of the Bible revealed His ability not only to direct the goodness of His own people, but also to influence even the most evil of forces.

As God spoke with Balaam about what Balaam was to do with Balak's orders, Balaam held a real conversation with the real Yahweh. Though Balaam's conversation was based on false beliefs and pretenses, God was greatly eager to interact with him. God asked Balaam about the messengers and their purpose, and Balaam in verse 10-11 explained the plot of Balak to curse and destroy these people. The Lord's response was that Balaam should refuse such an order from the king. God directed Balaam to send the men on their way.

When the next morning came, Balaam piously delivered the Lord's decrees to the messengers and sent them back to Balak to deliver his decision. In delivering the message, Balaam appears to carry with him a self-made righteousness. He carried the message of the Lord, but behind his actions he carried a false motive for his obedience. He had kept these men through the night not because he wanted them to know God's will, but that he wanted the payment that they brought from the king.

Upon hearing the news of Balaam's refusal, Balak, in his pride, did not accept such an answer, and he proceeded to mount a bigger missionary tribe in amassing an even larger group of travelers—this time sending out his Princes to do his bidding (vs. 15). These men, far more honorable and influential than that of the messengers, were sent to sway the hand of Balaam. Balak's army of evil not only carried with it the power of messengers sent to do his bidding, but it also included very real Princes that were equipped with polluted wealth. The imagery pointed to the presence of evil as it directed Balak's steps in and through his people. As God dwelled in and amongst His people in Israel, the very real presence of something altogether different dwelt amongst the people of Balak. This force motivated Balak's armies all the same.

In approaching Balaam the second time, Balaam held firm to the orders given to him by the Lord. He once again told the Princes that the Lord would not lend his hand to blessing their evil plot. Though Balaam spoke the right words, he again made the mistake of keeping the princes over night, for the wealth that they brought with them was far too great a temptation to him. Rather than immediately sending the princes on their way, fully knowing that the Lord had refused them, Balaam entertained evil intentions in hopes that the Lord might change His mind. Even in his obedience to the first decree of the Lord, Balaam was double-minded as his lust for the payment of the king caused him to urge the men to stay one more night. This decision on Balaam's part did in fact prompt an answer from the Lord, but it did come as a result of Balaam's belief. In making this decision to accept their payment, Balaam revealed his true wickedness, unbelief, and greed before the Lord (2 Pt. 2:15; Jude 1:11).

That night, in response to Balaam's greedy and hasty compromise, the Lord visited Balaam telling him, "If the men have come to call you, rise, go with them; but only do what I tell you." Though the situation clearly turned into a web of deception and false intent, God commited to work even within this little game in order to bring about a greater result. In God telling Balaam to go, the Lord was by no means validating Balaam's dereliction of duty, but rather in vs. 22, the text tells us that as Balaam set out to go with the men, as the Lord had commanded him to, the Lord's anger was kindled against him because he went.

What is happening here in the story? Does God give a command to Balaam and then suddenly change His mind? In giving the command for Balaam to go, is God hoping that Balaam would disobey? The answer to these confusing questions can be found by looking deep into the recesses of Balaam's own soul. Balaam's heart was not intent on obeying God out of righteousness, but he went out only at the whim of his repulsive and greedy heart. Balaam clearly revealed his commitment to his own pleasure over and above his desire to see the Lord's will come about. The Lord here simply demonstrates how He deals with such evil intent. In one sense the Lord demonstrates His *active* will in telling Balaam what he should do. The Lord all the while saw Balaam's motives and simply gave Balaam over to his greed by enabling him to give into his own desires. However, the Lord, clearly displeased with Balaam's evil heart motives, moveed to *actively* speak to Balaam. In His *permissive will*, He enabled Balaam to go and pursue his own human evil intent.

When Balaam set out to "obey" the Lord, an angel of the Lord came and stood in the men's way as they traveled. The angel was not an angel of blessing, but an *adversary*. As Balaam and his servant's journeyed toward Balak's land, their plot to do so caused an angel to stand in their way as an opposing force. Ironically the story rather than spiraling instantly downward allowed a humorous chain of events to take place in order to fully highlight the stupidity of Balaam's course. In Numbers Chapter 22:22-30 the Lord communicated His disapproval toward Balaam through the donkey that Balaam was traveling upon:

 ...the donkey saw the angel of the Lord standing in the

road, with a drawn sword in his hand. And the donkey turned aside out of the road and went into the field. And Balaam struck the donkey, to turn her into the road. Then the angel of the Lord stood in a narrow path between the vineyards, with a wall on either side. And when the donkey saw the angel of the Lord, she pushed against the wall and pressed Balaam's foot against the wall. So he struck her again. Then the angel of the Lord went ahead and stood in a narrow place, where there was no way to turn either to the right or to the left. When the donkey saw the angel of the Lord, she lay down under Balaam. And Balaam's anger was kindled, and he struck the donkey with his staff. Then the Lord opened the mouth of the donkey, and she said to Balaam, 'What have I done to you, that you have struck me these three times?' And Balaam said to the donkey, 'Because you have made a fool of me. I wish I had a sword in my hand, for then I would kill you.' And the donkey said to Balaam, 'Am I not your donkey, on which you have ridden all your life long to this day? Is it my habit to treat you this way?' And he said, 'No.'

What a humorous sight this must have been as the servants of Balaam were spectators to this odd occurrence. None of the men could see the angel standing in their way, and perhaps they were too hard hearted by their own desires to see the angel. As the donkey slowly responded to the angel by first leading Balaam off the road and into a field, and then by leading him between two walls where he was pinned in without a means of escape, the weirdness of the whole event must have caused Balaam's servants to chuckle at the fact that Balaam did not even know how to control his own donkey.

In his frustration and humiliation Balaam cusses and carries on as he beats his steed ever increasingly—still the animal would not listen. By this time the servants were rolling in the road laughing at what was taking place. In a final act of utter stupidity, as if Balaam did not look foolish enough, the ass spoke to Balaam. God opened up the stupid mouth of an ass to show Balaam what an &#$ he was being.

The irony of this scene is so thick it can be cut with a knife. God clearly needed to demonstrate to Balaam's own heart the depth of his own foolishness. Balaam stooped so low in his evil pursuits as to do things that even a donkey would not do (vs. 30). The donkey himself pointed out Balaam's folly, and in paramount fashion Balaam came face to face with his own stupidity. His sin had led him off the path and had taken him completely in the wrong direction. It scraped his foot, hurt his pride, and it had pinned him to the extent that there was no escape.

In that moment, his eyes became clear and he finally saw the angel of the Lord standing before him. The Lord opened his eyes and upon seeing the brilliant angel standing before him with sword drawn in his hand, Balaam's every motive of evil was exposed as he bowed before the angel in terror. The angel of the Lord spoke and said, "Why have you struck your donkey these three times? Behold, I have come out to oppose you because your way is perverse before me. The donkey saw me and turned aside before me these three times. If she had not turned aside from me, surely just now I would have killed you and let her live." To such an accusation, Balaam did not respond, but he did see the foolishness of his ways. Seeing his idiocy led him to grovel in his sin (vs. 34).

Three times he had been challenged toward righteousness, and three times he had missed the advances of the Lord. Like the future Simon Peter in the New Testament, Balaam's three-fold denial of God's advances led him to a bitter place of recognition of his sin. The whole experience brought him to a place where he was ready to finally go to the princes of Balak and share only what the Lord intended for him to say. This man that denied the Lord three times was now prepared to surrender to the voice of the Lord. Balaam aimed to become God's powerful mouthpiece in announcing God's plan to the evil kingdoms of Balaam.

This experience and change of perspective came to Balaam just at the right time, for Balak heard that he was close, and Balak came out to meet him. Balaam appeared disheveled in the aftermath of such an experience. His feet were torn up, his eyes were swelled as if he'd been crying, and he appeared before the king in dismantled fashion as he delivered God's words to the king; "Behold, I have come to you! Have I now any power of my own to speak anything? The word that God puts in my mouth, that must I speak."

Balak, apparently excited that Balaam had come, quivered at Balaam's honeyed words, expecting to hear only good reports from Balaam's mouth. In preparation to hear the curse that the Lord would pronounce on Israel, Balak proceeded to usher Balaam up to a spiritual high place at Bamoth-baal, so that Balaam could see the faction of the people (vs. 41). The battle between Balak and the multitude of God's people, in what once appeared to be a merely human struggle, now fully attached itself to spiritual realities. Balak was merely an instrument in the hands of evil powers, and his struggle to stop Israel was exposed in its deepest intent. Evil always intends to stand in opposition to the Lord.

To amplify such a battle between the holy power of God and the perverse powers of the kingdom of darkness, Balaam ordered Balak to bring seven bulls and rams up on the altar of worship in order that a worship service might take place unto the gods. Balaam exhorted Balak that as the offerings were burned the Lord would come and meet with them and speak to them His decree. Balak proudly obeyed such an order and once the arrangement and religious display were set, Balaam's mouth was opened to speak his first oracle from the Lord:

> From Aram Balak has brought me,
>   the king of Moab from the eastern mountains:
>   'Come, curse Jacob for me,
>   and come, denounce Israel!'
>   How can I curse whom God has not cursed?
>   How can I denounce whom the Lord has not denounced?
>   For from the top of the crags I see him,

> from the hills I behold him;
> behold, a people dwelling alone,
> and not counting itself among the nations!
> Who can count the dust of Jacob
> or number the fourth part of Israel?
> Let me die the death of the upright,
> and let my end be like his!

The truth was spoken. The Lord was not going to curse His own people. The Lord's intent was only to bless and redeem His people. This reality was apparent as they gazed down on the multitude of what God had developed in His nation. Balaam, dumbfounded at the numbers, was perhaps persuaded himself by what he saw before him.

Balaam saw the sheer grandeur of the people of Israel and uttered, "Let me die the death of the upright, and let my end be like his!" Balaam, who perhaps still waged a war of faith within himself, was still not fully a believer in God's kingdom and ways. He spoke as God's mouthpiece, and it is clear that his heart was longing to join into the people of God. In staring at such a multitude his desire was not to overtake them, but to join them.

At this Balak was furious; "What have you done to me? I took you to curse my enemies, and behold, you have done nothing but bless them." He did not accept such a verdict, and another attempt to sway such a decision had to be made. Balak in Chapter 23:13-30 quickly moved the religious display to another high place in hopes that the decision of the Lord might this time change in his favor. Once again the offerings were made, and Balak, gasping, turned to Balaam in an effort once again to summon the words of the Lord. Out of the mouth of Balaam came the second oracle from God:

> Rise, Balak, and hear;
> give ear to me, O son of Zippor:
> God is not man, that he should lie,
> or a son of man, that he should change his mind.
> Has he said, and will he not do it?

Or has he spoken, and will he not fulfill it?
Behold, I received a command to bless:
he has blessed, and I cannot revoke it.
He has not beheld misfortune in Jacob,
nor has he seen trouble in Israel.
The Lord their God is with them,
and the shout of a king is among them.
God brings them out of Egypt
and is for them like the horns of the wild ox.
For there is no enchantment against Jacob,
no divination against Israel;
now it shall be said of Jacob and Israel,
'What has God wrought!'
Behold, a people! As a lioness it rises up
and as a lion it lifts itself;
it does not lie down until it has devoured the prey
and drunk the blood of the slain.

In speaking again, it becomes clear that the Lord was not intent on attacking Israel, but on boldly proclaiming to Balak the motives and intent of his own heart. Despite Balak's religious displays of false-failed devotion, it only seemed to amplify his commitment to his false belief that God could somehow be manipulated. Balak still believed he was the supreme king and owner to his land and that God could be persuaded to obey his agenda. At the heart of Balak's attempts were his desire to change God's mind—to fit God into his mold and shape the eternal plans of history to fit his desires. His spirituality did not work. His devotedness to his own beliefs were shown to no avail. Not only in the first and second oracle was he denounced, but following came two more oracles that exposed his folly. In Balak's third attempt to sway the Lord, Balaam this time experienced the spirit "coming upon him" to speak:

 The oracle of Balaam the son of Beor,
    the oracle of the man whose eye is opened,

> the oracle of him who hears the words of God,
> who sees the vision of the Almighty,
> falling down with his eyes uncovered:
> How lovely are your tents, O Jacob,
> your encampments, O Israel!
> Like palm groves that stretch afar,
> like gardens beside a river,
> like aloes that the Lord has planted,
> like cedar trees beside the waters.
> Water shall flow from his buckets,
> and his seed shall be in many waters;
> his king shall be higher than Agag,
> and his kingdom shall be exalted.
> God brings him out of Egypt
> and is for him like the horns of the wild ox;
> he shall eat up the nations, his adversaries,
> and shall break their bones in pieces
> and pierce them through with his arrows.
> He crouched, he lay down like a lion
> and like a lioness; who will rouse him up?
> Blessed are those who bless you,
> and cursed are those who curse you.

Balaam, still teetering on the cliff of faith himself, now was able to hear the Lord. He bowed to Him, obeyed Him, acknowledged Him, and even conversed with Him, but never embraced Him. It can be argued that Balaam was in fact falling into the hands of the Lord as a believer even as he stood before the nation of Israel and prophesied to them their own blessing with words of beauty. Not only did he re-tell and voice the story of God's work in and through the people of Israel, but he came to agreement within himself that the Abrahamic covenant was for them and on their behalf.

Balak still claimed the covenant of blessing and cursing as his own. He was led astray thinking that he could have the promises of God without believing in the God who makes the promises. Balak wanted what was not his, and so also had Balaam. They both sat in the chair of perverse authority, thinking that the riches and wealth of the land were theirs for the taking. Their false belief was the result of their fake assumption that the Lord would bless and keep them even if they opposed and lived outside of His ways.

But in fact, this was not the case. It was not the case for Balak and his kingdom, or for any other nation. Balaam's fourth oracle in Numbers 24:15-25 focuses in on all the other nations and addresses their claims and commitment to their own rights. They all were to hear the word of the Lord and they all were to submit to His plan, lest they experience the same heartache and defeat that was now coming to Balak's false kingdom:

And he took up his discourse and said,
'The oracle of Balaam the son of Beor,
the oracle of the man whose eye is opened,
the oracle of him who hears the words of God,
and knows the knowledge of the Most High,
who sees the vision of the Almighty,
falling down with his eyes uncovered:
I see him, but not now;
I behold him, but not near:
a star shall come out of Jacob,
and a scepter shall rise out of Israel;
it shall crush the forehead of Moab
and break down all the sons of Sheth.
Edom shall be dispossessed;
Seir also, his enemies, shall be dispossessed.
Israel is doing valiantly.
And one from Jacob shall exercise dominion
and destroy the survivors of cities!'
Then he looked on Amalek and took up his discourse and said,
'Amalek was the first among the nations,
but its end is utter destruction.'

And he looked on the Kenite, and took up his discourse and said,

'Enduring is your dwelling place,
and your nest is set in the rock.
Nevertheless, Kain shall be burned
when Asshur takes you away captive.'
And he took up his discourse and said,
'Alas, who shall live when God does this?
But ships shall come from Kittim
and shall afflict Asshur and Eber;
and he too shall come to utter destruction.'

Then Balaam rose and went back to his place. And Balak also went his way.

Any and all kingdoms that opposed the Lord were to come to the same realization as Balak. Anyone who resists the Lord's authority in and through His people would come to utter destruction and will either decide to partake in the Lord's kingdom or will only be left the option to "go on his way." The way of every nation set against the Lord is to be "utter destruction." There is no nation, no man, and certainly no king that can stand against the all-consuming powerful God of heaven and earth. Israel as a nation was like a lion roaring in pursuit of its kill. Its fierce roar came with God's power and was to ward off all enemies and devour everything in its path. This Lion, this lion of Judah, was to be the coming *one* that would break and bind up anything that is evil.

Unknown to the people of Israel was that all this had taken place in the land of the Moabites. As the Israelites wallowed in their complaints and their constant dissatisfaction underneath the calm and cooling direction of God's hand, God led and defended them. He remained present in Israel's midst, but was equally as present in and amongst the enemy camps that lay in Israel's path. God's voice was speaking and acting out His will and decree over and above the perverse desires of evil characters such as Balaam and Balak. Israel was unaware of all the powers of evil that sought to destroy them.

They were a naïve and misled tribe, as they thought they could stand on their own two feet. Nevertheless, God was committed to giving all His resources to His people despite their ever-shallow perspective.

As the zoom lens of God's narrative pans briefly away from Israel's story in order to capture the stories going on around them, it reveals the nature of an entire kingdom and world outside the safe haven of God's protective authority. It is a world of very real kings, princes, messengers, and false diviners of evil intent. It is a magical kingdom in that it appears to be authoritative, real, and often times even threatening. The true reality appears however when the dust of God's power settles around the interworking of this false and pretentious kingdom. Its powers are revealed for the cowards and powerless bootlickers that they truly are. Its threats are exposed in the idle and empty promises that they purport. Their false beliefs of holding claim to God's promises and blessings are revealed in regard to the reality of their false footing. God's omnipresence is presently among them. He devours them and lays waste to them as they seek to devour all that He creates good. His righteousness works to deceive them and throttle them as they seek to deceive the nations.

To remain outside of God's authority of peace is not to avoid the authority of the Lord, for His authority is equally present amongst His enemies—yet in a different way. His authority, is expressed over and above evil, and works as an *adversary* to His enemies. He stands in the path of their intentions and limits them by His active will, and allows them to work themselves into a trapped bondage at His permissive will. All in all, everything comes under God's direction and His sovereignty, and the story teaches us regarding what will come our way depending on which hand of God's authority we choose.

21

SCENE 3

SEX

The hand dealt to Israel in Act 3 of the drama painted for us reveals God to be gracious in extending a hand of possibility to the people of Israel. The people were given the upper hand even against their enemies—unbeknownst to them—and even though the seemingly invisible hand of God continued to operate off stage and behind the curtain of Israel's forthright journey, the people refused to see the direction. Most assuredly their sinful humanity was unable to comprehend such a God of love. As the pursuit of God's love, discipline, justice, and constant lasting leadership remained overlooked by the people, the people begin to waste themselves in their own pursuits. Numbers 25:1 records the nature of the people's pursuit, by cataloguing their sexual exploits with the Moabite people. The word God chooses to attach to their sins is that of *whoring*.

In taking their eyes off the love and care of God, the people's affections went looking for a perverted imitation of intimacy. What their hands reached to find was the dejected and deplorable forms and wiles of the Moabite women; women which the Proverbs might describe as "loud and wayward, with feet that do not stay at home; now in the street, now in the market and at every corner they lie in wait ... with much seductive speech she persuades him; with her smooth talk she compels him. All at once he follows her, as an ox goes to the slaughter, or as a stag is caught fast till an arrow pierces its liver; as a bird rushes into a snare; he does not know that it will cost him his life."

With their honeyed words of deception, their false promises of respect and looks of desire, and with flattering tongues that lap in the crags of murky water, these women pulled the hearts of Israel's leaders and protectors into their grasp. Numbers tells us that these women invited the people to the sacrifice of their gods, and the people bowed to their gods. The people here not only partook in sexual encounters, but also yoked themselves in syncretism to the worship and affections of the object of the people's allegiance. The bed of Baal of Peor was not just a mere bed of ecstasy, orgasm, and ejaculation, but it was a bed of worship; an altar of sacrifice and adoration unto the created form of the human body rather than an altar of pure worship unto the Creator.

Clearly from God's vantage point, this act, committed on behalf of the people, was much more than a perversion, but it was treason against the most High God. The people attempted to replace their affections for God with the graven and created images of human sexuality. God ruled Israel as their leader and King, and this act of adultery broke and undermined His law of love for the people. The people's infidelity was not an affair to remember, but an act of thievery and murder, intended to steal from God what is His in order to use it for their own purposes. This was an attempt to break people in every way using sex as a sword, not as a marital blessing. Their whoring was not merely a sexual act a crime committed against God. Numbers paints this grotesque picture of what truly happens by utilizing the imagery of a *yoke* and a *whore.*

God's people were and are always to be like oxen—tied to God as their stronger ox in order that they might work together to pull a load. However, the people shook their ties to God, and came up underneath the wooden shoulder piece of the Moabite way of life. In yoking themselves to the Moabite people and their gods, their defiance and degradation allowed them to tie to the practices of the Moabite people. Once the yoke was fastened to them, the people move in step similar to two oxen move once tied together. The Israelites united sexually to Moab, but sex becomes the very thing that turned their course toward an entirely different path altogether.

Their sexual union was made on a bed of *conformation* on which they turned into, became like, and morphed to fit the mold of those with whom they were having sex. They united mentally, physically, emotionally, spiritually, and socially with the Moabite way of life and value system, and thus became conformed to their image. The people no longer rested in the yoke of unconditional love and covenant with their God, but instead chose new thinking patterns to reframe their lives. Instead of embracing the character of God and living out a vision of service and covenant, apart from conditions and strings attached, the people took on a vision of selfish contract—a mentality that assured them that they would get what they needed and when they needed while falsely avoiding responsibility and consequence.

The unity and bond created with them and the Moab nation went far deeper than mere mental and physical adhesion. The bond of sexual unity brought spirits together to form altars of worship and honor unto pagan gods. The act of sex united their emotional makeups so that they might further validate their use of each other for selfish gain. It formed value systems of disrespect and a low view of human worth, and it perpetuated social relativistic norms; whereby the people rationalized their behavior as being normal and o.k.

In verse 7 of Numbers 25, Phinehas rose up in anger at it all, not only at the whoring and sexual perversion, but at the fact that despite the Lord's displeasure, some of the people still persisted to bring these Midianite women into their family.

His anger is righteous! He models the real image and response of the Lord in all of this in rising up to stop it. The Lord would not partake in such an event, but would punish it. In verse 4-5 God's anger rose in disapproval, and he ordered the men to be hanged. Phinehas echoed such a motion by going into the tent of the Israelite and his prostitute and pierced both of them through to enact justice on their disobedience to God's law.

Phinehas saw and understood what the perversion of sin brings. He saw the result of its cancerous spread, as it took hold of a vital organ and then soon prevented the whole of the community from life. Sin entered homes and it defiled marriage beds and the innocence of children's eyes. The sin of Israel's men was not a privatized sin even though it seemingly took place behind closed doors in isolation without anyone knowing the difference. Sin's game was to play isolation only as one card in the deck, but the whole of the deck was polluted by one rogue part. These acts leaked a legacy of death and destruction into the community, in that infidelity touched the whole of Israel (vs. 6). 24,000 of them died from plague, not to mention the countless scars of distress that continued to pervade the psyche of the generations of children who watched such an event.

In verse 10, when the Lord finally brought the tension to a resolve, he spoke this of Phinehas; "Phinehas the son of Eleazar, son of Aaron the priest, has turned back my wrath from the people of Israel, in that he was jealous with my jealousy among them, so that I did not consume the people of Israel in my jealousy. Therefore say, 'Behold, I give to him my covenant of peace, and it shall be to him and to this descendants after him the covenant of a perpetual priesthood, because he was jealous for his God and made atonement for the people of Israel.'" This pronouncement over Phinehas' lineage stands in direct contrast to what followed as God announced an altogether different decree over the life of the man whom had brought the woman into the encampment. God said, "The name of the slain man of Israel, who was killed with the Midianite woman, was Zimri the son of Salu, chief of a father's house belonging to the Simeonites. And the name of the Midianite woman who was killed was Cozbi the daughter of Zur, who was the tribal head of a father's house in Midian." God declared a eulogy of death, and a declaration of remembrance, as he marked this event by recording it in His story. Phinehas was to be forever marked with honor, and Zimri and Cozbi, along with their families were to be associated, labeled, and identified only with their shame.

Phinehas' legacy was not that of compromise and faint half-hearted pleasures. Phinehas took pleasure in the jealousy of God for righteous reasons, rather than taking pleasure in the wickedness of man for all the wrong ones. The chiefs and prominent leaders succumbed to the pressure of the mob and watched the perversions take place without raising their voices to fight against the injustice. Phinehas' response was like an electro-shock paddle to the heart of the dying Israel perspective. He roused them to see real heroism once again, and He roused them to remember their God. His actions were not dictated by his own comfort, or even out of concern for his own advancement, but his resolve was to defend and honor the Lord.

The bottom line for Israel, despite all the seeming challenges, still remained the same. The question being asked of them was "where does one's allegiances lie." Israel's journey continued to challenge them in their affections. The Israelites' hearts were continually probed regarding the source and spring from which they drew from in order to find water and quench their thirst—a thirst for belonging, for rest, for justice, restoration, and deliverance, and their thirst for legacy and eternity. Despite all God's advances to make them His people—like a spring in a desert to satisfy them—they insisted on dipping their hands in a well full of sun-scorched sand to draw out a handful of chalky dehydrating death.

While trying to avoid pain, the Israelites kept putting their hands back in the cookie jar—a jar only filled with a giant bear trap. While trying to find rest the Israelite people fell onto the empty breasts of women whose hearts were pillows of iron. While trying to find legacy and a future, the people of Israel continued to waste themselves in lost perspective, rabbit trails, and black holes of promise that only served to seduce them like prey for the purpose of sucking them down to the bottom of an endless pit.

So why such an excursus and detour in the story? Why did the first part of the Numbers saga begin with the rehabilitation of these Israeli slaves, only to lead them through a journey of complaining in the wilderness, and now turn to highlight the enemy encampments and allure of deceptive culture? The answer lies again in the journey of authority. The only cure for a slave-like phobia is that of a slow journey toward a bigger goal. God's authority gave Israel a protection and the promise of a new beginning—a land and a home. The journey toward such a goal had its way of allowing for detours and fowl ups. In every pot hole one stepped foot in due to sin and depravity, one found another nugget of truth that could be mined out regarding the treachery of the human soul. The human soul veers naturally in its affections toward lesser loves, and it whores itself out to things that will brutalize it rather than restore it. This is the life of a slave.

God's test was not to give the people a list of dos and don'ts and leave it at that. God's goal was to give his people an image of something better. His goal was to give them gold to replace their cavity; His aim was to give them purity as a better hope than perversion, and His aim was to anchor their sights on a vision of a better land and kingdom in order to dissuade His people from falling prey to the false of hopes of other kingdoms. This test amongst the Moabites was allowed by God as one more stepping stone on the journey toward home. It was a test to prepare God's people for what was ahead in the Promised Land. He allowed their true affections to be exposed, and He blanched them with a hot iron in their place of misdirection. He exposed their need for Him like a healing ointment. God slowly prodded their hearts to allow them to see their sinfulness and His sufficiency, so that at the feet of their false and brutal lovers they might come to their senses and be taken over by the savory flavor and smell of grace.

22

SCENE 4
PROGRESS

In the wake of such a tumultuous up and down journey everything finally came to a hault. God's leadership walked His people through creation's elements as they moved and departed at His command. The hand of God kept them through a food crisis, water shortages, plagues, leprosy and venomous vermin, idolatry and countless attempts of the human imagination to envision something better than God. The journey put the Israelite people into the path of enemies such as Balak and Balaam, and the seductive tribe of the Moabites.

God's plague against the Israelites subsided in the wake of all that took place in the Moabite camp, and now it was time for God to renumber His people once again. The reason for this, first being, a plague had just wiped out a big part of the population and they needed to recount for military reasons—to number their soldiers for war (for they are still journeying in hostile land where war was inevitable). Secondly, the Lord had something to reveal to the people in the numbers. He wanted them to take courage in their numbers and in the truths they once again revealed.

In Numbers 26:1-50 as God numbered His people once again, the counting revealed that the tribes of Reuben (meaning *affliction*),

Simeon (meaning *heard my affliction*), and Gad (meaning *troops or invaders*), had shrunk in population since their previous numbering in Egypt. Though the Israelite spirit was still deeply affected by the recent immorality invasion and plague, the hope of God hid still amongst His people. Though heartache, affliction, and opposition still remained, as it had when they first came out of slavery, God, by His grace, steadily remained faithful to shrink their struggle subtly but surely. In verse 8-11 an interesting mention also appears once again of the tribe of Korah (the man who rebelled against God and His leadership).

As is made clear in Numbers 16:1-40, Korah was clearly punished for his rebellion when God sent fire from heaven to consume him and 249 of his fellow deviant partners in crime. Dathan and Abiram also died when God caused the ground to split beneath their feet and swallowed them up into oblivion, along with everything they owned. This incident led to the Israelites' to rejecting the Lord's response to the matter and they rebelled against Moses. They found themselves staring down the business end of God's paddle as He inflicted about 14,000+ of them with plague and punishment for objecting to Korah's destruction.

We may ask why this diversion of thought is in the middle of God reminiscing about Korah during a time of reordering and reorganizing. The idea here is that Korah's descendants had left a legacy, a legacy that God had prospered regardless of Korah's shame. Many associated with Korah went on to write some of the Psalms included in the Bible, leaving a legacy of song and worship for future generations. God showed Himself most just in allowing Korah's faction to die, and He remained most merciful in sparing a line that grew up to praise and exalt God's name. Just as God had done in Rueban, Simeon and Gad, He had done in Korah. He brought forth juicy fruit from bitter roots.

God's power of redemption is evident here. Even though His people were fresh off of a disappointing defeat at the hands of lust, adultery, deception, idolatry, greed, rebellion, and even murder, God took the time to point out His continued faithfulness to His people.

God reminded His disheveled people that His promises made to Abraham were still in force. In fact, Isachaar (*burden carried*), Judah (*praise*), Zebulun (*dwelling*), Ephraim (*fruitful, an increase*), Manassah (*forget*), Benjamin (*son of the right hand*), Dan (*judge*), and Asher (*happy*) all had grown in number since the exile out of Egypt.

Amidst their judgment and human frailty, God stayed faithful to His promise to multiply them, bless them and make them a great nation. God did away with much of their affliction and the journey slowly gave the people more victory and reasons to praise Him than they had before. Their burden in large extent had been carried: they had been placed in homes, they had increased, God had forgotten their iniquities, and God had taken them on a journey toward becoming a people that would be wielded as a sword in battle—a powerful and sharp sword.

God's people are human and with humanness comes sinfulness. With sinfulness comes nearsightedness, and God's people lost sight of what God had been doing all along because they diverted their own attention toward lesser loves. But, like the meaning of Nephtali (*my wrestling*), the people of Israel had been cattle roped and wrestled to the ground. In many ways they had been conquered and many had gladly allowed their hearts to come under the different culture that was created underneath the hand of God's Lordship!

In numbering the people, God brings our attention here to His glory. He magnifies His power in highlighting how His purposes and plans thwart and far outreach any plans that man can devise or come up with. The sins of the people slowly chiseled away at their numbers, and in the midst God had birthed others, a new people in their stead, to slowly grow the community into a stronger whole. This was a process and a journey!

God is faithful and also generous and good. Numbers 26:15 says, "The Lord speaks to Moses, saying, 'Among these the land shall be divided for inheritance according to the number of names. To a large tribe you shall give a large inheritance, and to a small tribe you shall give a small inheritance; every tribe shall be given its inheritance in proportion to its list. But the land shall be divided by lot. According to the names of the tribes of their fathers they shall inherit. Their inheritance shall be divided according to lot between the larger and the smaller." Though the people rebelled continually, God kept for them an inheritance not on the basis of their merit or will to preserve their own future, but based on His commitment to His own word, His upholding of His own power, and His loyalty to His own truthfulness. Even Levi, with marks on their record in Nadab and Abihu (vs. 61), who appear to have been given no inheritance in vs. 62, became the line into and through which Jesus Christ is born. Jesus ultimately finalized the covenants made to men like Abraham in His becoming Israel, a perfect and whole person, in whom we now live *through* as His beloved people.

Though in vs. 63 to the end of chapter 26 God makes it clear that only Caleb and Joshua were to enter the Promised Land from the original group, not one person escaped the wilderness before God allowed. God's goodness allowed the Israelite children, and their children's children, to survive and take hold of what they lost. This procurement was not one of effort or goodness on behalf of Israel, but a shear means of grace—an undeserved gift from God.

As this scene closes with the reordering once again of God's people, the camera angle shifts. Rather than shifting over to the past, God pans to the future. The journey had prepared His people, and though they were still frail, they had made progress. It was now time to make the final push to the Promised Land, the land and place of God's full authority and ownership—this land being a symbol of great freedom and the hope for a consummated kingdom.

SCENE 5
SUBMISSION

The tide has shifted completely in this story. Israel is a people that still owns nothing, and they were about to move to a place where they possessed everything. The mentality of the sojourner and nomad is much different than that of a homeowner. Israel was about to settle, and their arduous journey of mobility was hopeful in coming to an end.

In Numbers 27 their mentality starts to change. They sense that the tone and pace of God's movement is beginning to change. God had tightly held things closely to His chest. He had provided food for them, shelter for them, and had decided when they were to move and stay. The reason for this is that if they were immediately given some measure of responsibility in such things their slave mentality would have taken over and it would have turned into an anarchical free-for-all.

God, still intending to rule His people sovereignly and solely in a more visual fashion, now began to move them into a land. This land would produce food by the hands and efforts of the people. Their plan to ditch their mobile structures and the hopes of building mighty bulwarks, homes, and settlements was beginning to become less a dream and more a reality. The motion of their journey was about to slow to a daily walking pace of living and move underneath the cloud and fire of God rather than tracing His heels. God's authority was to rest in the land despite all these changes but He was about to give His people of land of their *possession*. They were about to move from renters to homeowners.

It makes sense in this mentality shift that women would be the first to come forward and recognize all that this would entail, for they are powerful and mighty in the hospitality, mission, and advancement of the home and family. In Numbers 27:1-11, a few of the widowed and orphaned daughters of Israel came quickly forward to address Moses and the Israelite leadership with the following dilemma:

> Then drew near the daughters of Zelophehad the son of Hepher, son of Gilead, son of Machir, son of Manasseh, from the clans of Manasseh the son of Joseph. The names of his daughters were: Mahlah, Noah, Hoglah, Milcah, and Tirzah. And they stood before Moses and before Eleazar the priest and before the chiefs and all the congregation, at the entrance of the tent of meeting, saying, 'Our father died in the wilderness. He was not among the company of those who gathered themselves together against the Lord in the company of Korah, but died for his own sin. And he had no sons. Why should the name of our father be taken away from his clan because he had no son? Give to us a possession among our father's brothers.'

Moses brought their case before the Lord. And the Lord said to Moses,

> The daughters of Zelophehad are right. You shall give them possession of an inheritance among their father's brothers and transfer the inheritance of their father to them. And you shall speak to the people of

Israel, saying, 'If a man dies and has no son, then you shall transfer his inheritance to his daughter. And if he has no daughter, then you shall give his inheritance to his brothers. And if he has no brothers, then you shall give his inheritance to his father's brothers. And if his father has no brothers, then you shall give his inheritance to the nearest kinsman of his clan, and he shall possess it. And it shall be for the people of Israel a statute and rule, as the Lord commanded Moses.'

An inheritance about to be divvied out amongst the people of God caused the daughters of Zelophehad to recognize what this meant for them. In a culture that already had a propensity to undervalue the voice of women, these women were about to be sorely overlooked and homeless under the current system.

Israel was a patriarchal and a male-led society, and that meant that inheritances were passed to sons and fathers of sons, not to daughters. So the daughters of Zelophehad raised their voices in protest of their situation. Their father had died in the tragic surmise of Korah and had wrongfully been associated with such rebellion. Though the daughters note the justice in their father dying because he was in himself a frail man riddled with sin like any other man, it was in fact an injustice that his name be cut off forever because he was wrongly associated with Korah's exploits.

The women sought justice, and the way they sought justice in this situation in particular is telling their human authorities. A few things must be noted. Firstly, the daughters of Zelophehad possessed a humble disposition in presenting their requests. The daughters were urgent, bold, and even a bit forceful with their submission, but their disposition was of great gentility and honor. They could have resorted to bitter gossip, slander, and ridicule of their circumstance, but in this situation went right to Moses and Eleazar with their request. Their response is humble and at the same time bold because they took the proper action and utilized the proper channels. Their hearts maintained a bent toward authority that sought to truly honor those to whom they were submitting their request.

Secondly, the women were not concerned so much with their inheritance as they were with the inheritance of their father and family. Their focus was on rightful justice and an upholding of human dignity and memory. Many attempts to solicit authority were often done in a manner that sought to promote selfish ambition and gain. However, the women's disposition toward Moses and Eleazar was clearly one of respect. They were not seeking to voice disgruntlement in a complaint and selfish outburst of a few women who were not getting their way. They sought to preserve a legacy. The grounds on which they approached leadership with their submissions was favorable for they sought the Lord's heart, not their own desires.

Thirdly, they went to Moses and Eleazar with their requests recognizing the position in which God had placed them. They did not seek to bypass their leaders and sneakily work around people to get what they wanted, but the Lord noticed their method in approach as much as He noticed the dilemma itself. Once again, in Moses speaking to the Lord, Moses prayerfully submits the request himself in a bold and humble way for answer.

The response of the Lord is very complimentary, for God notes the righteousness and rightness of the daughter's plea. A God who is able to dispense both justice and mercy is here able to dispense His mercy, and in doing so, He acts most justly. God not only heard their request, but establishes a law in the daughter's favor; that all women caught in their situation from this day forward shall receive a favorable inheritance in response to their predicament.

What is going on in this circumstance goes much deeper than a few women desiring claim of an inheritance promised them. The above eleven verses link to the following twelve verses that go into detailing the situation and conversation held between God and Moses. The circumstances that cause the conversation between God and Moses are different in many ways from that of the daughters' dilemma, but in other ways the approach is remarkably similar. Numbers 27:12-23 says,

The Lord said to Moses, 'Go up into this mountain of Abarim and see the land that I have given to the people of Israel. When you have seen it, you also shall be gathered to your people, as your brother Aaron was, because you rebelled against my word in the wilderness of Zin when the congregation quarreled, failing to uphold me as holy at the waters before their eyes.' (These are the waters of Meribah of Kadesh in the wilderness of Zin.)

Moses spoke to the Lord, saying, 'Let the Lord, the God of the spirits of all flesh, appoint a man over the congregation who shall go out before them and come in before them, who shall lead them out and bring them in, that the congregation of the Lord may not be as sheep that have no shepherd.'

So the Lord said to Moses, 'Take Joshua the son of Nun, a man in whom is the Spirit, and lay your hand on him. Make him stand before Eleazar the priest and all the congregation, and you shall commission him in their sight. You shall invest him with some of your authority, that all the congregation of the people of Israel may obey. And he shall stand before Eleazar the priest, who shall inquire for him by the judgment of the Urim before the Lord. At his word they shall go out, and at his word they shall come in, both he and all the people of Israel with him, the whole congregation.' And Moses did as the Lord commanded him. He took Joshua and made him stand before Eleazar the priest and the whole congregation, and he laid his hands on him and commissioned him as the Lord directed through Moses.

Recorded above is possibly one of the most candid conversations in all of Scripture. The conversation between the Lord and Moses in Numbers 27 is also one of the most disappointing conversations in all of literature. Within the conversation there are some telling links between the interaction Zelophehad's daughters had with Moses, and the byplay Moses is now having with the Lord. Many of the same variables and dynamics of authority and submission are present in the conversation above, as are with the Zelophehad predicament. Before we note them specifically, let's understand the situation.

There is a drab horror in thinking what it must be like for Moses to look at the Promised Land after all he's gone through in leading God's people, and still realize that he was about to die without entering. The conversation is nonetheless endearing—maintaining a hint of tragic comedy and a scent of deadly romance. Moses, the meekest man in the entire world, had lost his temper in the desert and shown his imperfection. Moses' temper had always been a problem, even when it had gotten him into trouble when he had killed the Egyptian slave master that was beating a Jewish slave. Yet even after running into the desert to hide from his shame and his God, God found him in a burning bush and made from Moses' a shame brilliant piece of artwork that displayed His redemption. He called Moses in His frailty and humanity. He knew Moses walked with a limp (insecurity), and even then God used Moses to be one of the most powerful leaders of all time.

But the Promised Land is here withheld from Moses because of a simple temper tantrum; a tantrum seemingly so small when measured against that of murder. Moses, after being changed into a man seeking after God, seemed to have it all—a perfect life—the model citizen—a good person. By God's standards however, good and bad aren't the measurements, perfect and imperfect are. Moses had failed the test of being a Savior figure and a Deliverer to God's people. He could not enter the Promised Land with the criminal record he had because Israel might then be tempted to sell themselves short and give credit of their inheritance to the glory of Moses, rather than await the glory of Christ—perfection—the man who is the land.

Once again Moses displayed his meekness, for he did not argue with the Lord. He accepted the Lord's direction and guidance as best. In theory this seems to be an easy decision when on the outside looking in, but the camera angle must zoom in on the scene in

Numbers 27. Moses, peeking his head up over the mountain, saw the land he'd dreamed of all those years. He saw the lush grass and trees and was drawn to worship when he thought of the years of complaints and troubles he had suffered to get God's people to this place. He was leading a bunch of slaves, and at every turn they had tried to enslave him—trying to make him turn back. All those years of Moses fighting for the "good life" and now he stared out over the promise knowing he could not have it. It was like drinking a sip of salty water. The water that was meant to bring refreshment only brought sorrow and disappointment. Moses could not go in!

All throughout the story we have observed the humility of Moses' surrender to the Lordship of Yahweh as juxtaposed against the backdrop of Israel's frailty and complaining, and it is no different here. Israel plays the fool most of the time and fell into destruction again and again. All the while, their leader had in many respects stood firm and valiant. Even in his prominence and integrity, Moses still fell short. He was o.k. with falling short, nonetheless. Though his heart burned with human longing to go in, he let the vision die in him in hopes that he was about to embrace something greater. God had killed his dream, but God had erected a better vision in its place ... Moses was to meet God. Moses was about to meet his friend.

That's all Moses wanted. In the frank conversation here in this chapter Moses did not argue nor complain, but he modeled what true authority and freedom is. He modeled in his pain what the people were to be in their prosperity. He modeled to them that true freedom is not about arriving at a place of independence from the Lord—out from underneath His decree and authority. Rather, true freedom is reaching a place of knowing who one is when compared to who God is. Moses' freedom came in knowing who he was in standing before God—He was nothing. He thus was able to surrender freely to God's decree with release and freedom, for to obey the Lord's decrees and commands, and to have the Lord call the shots is the truest place for freedom.

In this moment one can only imagine what was going through Moses' head. I know what would be going through my head. I'd be bitter, begrudged, angry, disillusioned, etc. Perhaps, maybe Moses was too, but the words out of his mouth are not ones of doubt, but they sound a little something like this, "Lord, give a leader to these people."

Such audacity, such boldness, such leadership! This conversation helps one to see into the very gut of Moses' relationship with the Lord. They are friends. Moses trusts his Father, and to follow Him is a joy! He did not begrudge it, but even in his final moments he received the Lord's authority and decision. The last thing he requested ... the last thing ... his dying wish ... his final breath: "Lord, give them a leader to lead them so they will not be like sheep without a shepherd!"

Moses' last cry was that his people would have protection and compassionate headship over them. His last desire was that God's people would not lose all the ground that they had gained. His last fear, if he had any, was that they would make the trek into the Promised Land, and would not re-embrace their slave mentality; turning again against the Lord and electing some tall, dark, and handsome leader not out of a motivation to follow the Lord, but simply to grasp at their version of freedom. Moses' plea goes deeper than a mere leadership change. He was pleading that God would lead them, so that they might receive His blessing, and not be placed once again under a tyrant.

In a sweet and benevolent way, the Lord answers him. "Take Joshua the son of Nun, a man in whom is the Spirit, and lay your hand on him. Make him stand before Eleazar the priest and all the congregation, and you shall commission him in their sight. You shall invest him *with some of your authority,* that all the congregation of the people of Israel may obey." Not only was Moses looking for authority to be placed over the people of God, it was a reflection of God's deepest desires as well. It was God's intention that His people be free under the shade of His protective umbrella, not left out in the rain by their lonesome.

God worked through Moses in his final moments to lay hands on Joshua (Yeshua—meaning *salvation*—the foreshadowed Jesus) to lead the people into the Promised Land. This was for a purpose. Even though Moses did not receive what was promised, God provided something better (Heb. 11:39). Joshua was to be the continuation of the journey. Moses played his role. Moses took his bow, and Moses made his exit off stage so that the other actors in God's redemptive drama could take the stage. Moses delivered God's people from slavery out into a wandering and suffering desert. Joshua delivered God's people to a land flowing with milk and honey, a perfect picture of the one to come.

This is the trajectory of God's leadership. This is the promise in His covenants and loyalty. His journey does not meander meaninglessly, it is filled with glorious tension and resolve that pushes toward a glorious climax and paramount ending. God's people are His characters in His play and are not to be confused with the playwright Himself. His play is to speak of Himself, and Moses and Joshua understood the bottom line of their heavenly Director and Producer. They allowed Him to call the shots, pick parts, and set apart leadership on His own whim. To Moses and Joshua this was a privilege to be involved in such a thing and to submit to it willingly was to make sure that the correct story was told.

In drawing to a close, this particular scene in the Israelite journey brings to the surface a strong theme of submission. First, it shows the protective mantle of protection of male headship in dispensing justice to the daughters of Zelophehad, who may have lost everything had they not been able to appeal to Godly and compassionate leaders. Secondly, it shows the interchange that those in submission must have with human leadership. The women did not remain silent, but they presented and submitted their requests to their overseers for a protected and wise decision, and their thoughts were considered thusly. Their position was not considered to be one of weakness, but of great strength. God heard their requests and wrote laws based on their voiced struggles. The same timbre is represented in the conversation between Moses and God Himself. God provides Moses with accountability and responsibility and did so all under His Sovereign rule and decree. God made sure that Moses had a mantle of authority to submit to so that he could best care for and love God's sons and daughters.

God gave Moses a listening ear and demonstrated all throughout the book of Numbers that our voices do come before Him, and are heard with due consideration. Secondly, Moses did not seem to harbor any fear in submitting and making his requests known to God. Throughout the book of Numbers we see that God was equally balanced in His answers to the people and Moses. Many times their pleas were answered in a way pleasing to them, and many times their pleas were answered in a way they wouldn't have chosen nor expected. Fact of the matter being, their submissions were always heard and considered.

God wanted His people to learn the nature of His interaction between human and heavenly authority so that all those in submission—which is everyone—can humbly and boldly come! The big idea and big picture in God's narrative here in Numbers 27 is to set the tone for how Israel was to live all of life in the Promised Land. He wanted a safe life for them lived in the freedom of knowing they could have candid conversations with their leaders and with their God. It was a place to be governed by mercy and justice, and God being perfect was the only one to determine what was most merciful and what is most just.

Additively, they were about to become homeowners, and God wanted them to have their inheritance, but He wanted them to maintain a demeanor of gratitude for all He was giving them despite their un-deservedness. In this way, this scene reflects God's action plan in bringing Israel out of Egypt. Once they were a people broken and arrogant and distrustful toward all things in authority. Here they have, through all their brokenness and complaining, developed a slowly emerging trust in the Lord. In coming *out of* Egypt God needed to detox their pride, and rehabilitate their trust. Coming *into* the Promised Land, God needed now to highlight their dawning humility and affirm their growing trust in Him. This fragmented people were still broken, but they were far more beautiful than they had once been.

24

SCENE 6

RHYTHMS

A new phase in any journey requires new practices, new schedules, new habits, and new rhythms. In Israel's case, practices needed to be revisited and resurrected. Israel's schedule had grown chaotic and unpredictable (God had made it this way so they would be dependent upon the cloud and fire for leadership), and as everything in life shapes a person, their journey had shaped them. It had shaped them to be on their heels, it had shaped them to be on the defensive, and it had shaped them to always expect the unexpected. All of the stop-and-go rhythms were God's attempt to form the people to find one anchor amidst the storm!

Israel was now entering a new land and a new phase in the journey. No longer were they wandering in circles, but new opportunities and joys were on the horizon. Anticipation was present though it was reluctant. Hope filled the people's hearts though it was tentative. Nevertheless, God needed to frame their new hopes into the right shape, to give them a proverbial glass to pour themselves into so that when he began to pour in the blessings that were coming, the people were be able to hold it and drink it in.

It is not a surprise that God's people had developed a tendency to forget Him when times got good, all the while running to him when times got bad. God began their new schedule by setting for them a rhythm of worship and remembrance; a rhythmic liturgy that would ensure in Israel's conscience a recognition of their God. In Numbers 28:1-8 God began by requiring Israel to give to Him daily offerings of sacrifice and worship. The motivation for doing so was not solely that the people might sacrifice their possessions, but it was so they would remember where all their blessings had come from. God made it very clear when He said in vs. 2, "it's my offering, my food, my pleasing aroma ..." The people were to offer a lamb sacrifice at daybreak and at twilight hours of the night. These sacrifices served as bookends to the daily routine of Israel's communal life. In the middle of such offerings there was to be 3 liters of flour, a ½ liter of oil, a ½ liter of drink offered in correlation to the animal sacrifices throughout the day. Imagine the amount of cattle that would have their blood spilled over a month's time. Multiply the amount of flour, oil, and water that was given to the Lord over a month's time. The sacrifice that God daily required as "pleasing" is significant and it is for a purpose.

This spectacle was a daily and habitual rhythm that was to shape and form the lives of God's people. Imagine the scene each day in the camp. Every morning and night there was the smell of death in the camp—burnt flesh and a pillowing smoke tower rocketing into the sky for all to see, taste, and feel. As the people worked the soil they were moment by moment treading out grain for offerings, grinding down wheat into flour in the their homes for offerings, and remembering even in their celebrations and drinking to the Lord who is Lord and the Giver of all things. God shaped His people to hold loosely to their prosperity in the land, for the land was only to be a symbol. They were to save their best for God as a community—helping each other to do so—and giving all they had in time and energy. These daily remembrances ensured that the people remembered God's new mercies *every morning* (Lam. 3:22-23), that in the morning they heard His voice (Ps. 5:3), and that in the cool of the evening they would be conscious of the Lord walking around in their midst (Gen. 3:8). Everything in their daily rhythm was designed to shape the people into being tainted by a perspective of sacrifice and honor unto God. God completely wanted to craft their perspective to work unto Him and not unto man. Their schedule and liturgy provided to them was intentional, calculated, and intended for their safety.

Out of this, in Numbers 28-29, came God's initiative to remind the people of their weekly rhythms through Sabbath observance. This rhythm extended all the way back to the rhythm of the first land God had prepared for man in the Garden of Eden. In the beginning, for six days, God spoke and Creation worked in response. The lights took their place, the fish swam around, and the land pole-vaulted into the sky to create the mountain's timberline. Mt. Everest exploded, Canis Majoris ignited, and the Great White Shark whisked around playfully in his new home. It can be reasoned and debated that when the seventh day arrived, it wasn't God Himself who was tuckered out and tired, but the Creation itself. It had been hog-tied, stripped, ordered, re-shaped, and changed in dramatic fashion. The Bible therefore does not purport a God who on the seventh day *needed* sleep as if He was tired from the work, but it would seem fitting that He knew a rhythm of work and rest must fill all of Creation for the betterment of its own maintenance. So after God poked and prodded and unleashed His power on an un-expectant world, God gave it rest.

When he fashioned Adam out of dust and breathed into him the Triune image and life, Adam's first experience on earth as a living being was to hear God *speak*. God sounded His voice into Adam's restful and waiting ears and God filled Adam with the same ethic for work. In Genesis 1 He tells us Adam is to have dominion over the animals, to be fruitful and multiply, to fill and subdue the earth, and to cultivate for provision and life. Before Adam even kicked back a yawn and ate his cream of wheat, God woke him with his alarm-clock voice. Adam had been officially placed in creation as a gatekeeper. Theologians call Adam here the Federal Head. He was the source from which all other humans would come. The mission and work given to him would be the work of his children. Adam, this man, was to take the provisions of God and provide for the animals. This man, who had been given a safe haven of protection, was called to subdue the uninhabitable unprotected wilderness around him and make it rich like the Garden—a haven of safety.

As the sixth day passed, and Adam's commissioning was over, he awoke on the seventh day to start his new job. What we must realize is that Adam awoke on the seventh day when God rested. God's last day of creating, was Adam's first day of serving. The seventh day ended God's work. When man came along, rest BEGAN his work. Man didn't have to work *for* anything, but rather worked *from* everything. Man had been given everything and this rest was a symbol to Adam that he did not have to do anything, and the mentality served to shape his attitude in how he would do everything. There was no striving in the Garden, no competition, no vain conceit or passion. Adam and his wife Eve had everything, and the mentality of working "for the weekend" evaded them; they worked from the *week beginning*.

God, from the beginning of creation, and from the beginning of His people's entrance into the new Promised Land wanted to embrace this new idea of His effort being the driver for their management. The Sabbath Day was to set in place a weekly rhythm, not to work towards, but a mentality to work from! Work was not to be demeaning or degrading, it was not be to meaningless, it was not to be a sole source of identity and pleasure, and it was not to be a calling either, work is to be solely an extension of a meaning, a worth, an identity, a pleasure, and a calling already found in God. God crafted this into the people. Daily they were to remember that all is HIS, and weekly they were to remember in essence the same thing. In all this, God wisely recognized the Israelite and human track record of forgetting the source from which they came.

In Numbers 27:11-15 God then moved into shaping the monthly rhythms of the Israelite nation, and then in vs. 16-31 He moved into shaping their annual celebrations and special occasions. The first two highlighted events are that of the Passover and that of the Feast of Weeks.

The Passover was to help the people remember their Deliverance at the hand of God out from underneath the tyranny of Egyptian rule. The people were to commemorate the *work* of God in doing their salvation for them. The Feast of Weeks was to be a following celebration of the *rest* they now enjoyed. They were to celebrate, feast, and rest in peace.

Following, in verse 29, the Feast of Trumpets was not far behind, coming in the fall months (most likely around September). In the Feast of the Trumpets, the faithful devout Jews went up to worship. The unbelieving Jews continued at work gathering their crops along with the Gentiles around them. The unbelieving Jews would then see their friends leave and feel the pressure of being left behind. Jeremiah's words resonate here in a gloomy warning. "The harvest is past, the summer is ended, and we are not saved" (Jer. 8:20). This was to be a rhythm and a reminder to those who had fallen in shame, a time to be called to repentance, a sounding of a warrior's cry for fallen soldiers, a celebration of those who come to the Lord, and it was to push into the Day of Atonement (Yom Kippur) which was instated to remember all the sins of the people from the past year. As the blood was poured out on the mercy seat of the Ark of the Covenant, it was a bittersweet day. This day was given to help the people remember their salvation, but also to remain conscious and soberly consider all they'd been saved from.

The last piece of this systematic and scheduled rhythm into days, weeks, months, years, and special moments, was the Feast of Booths (October), which created a capstone to their liturgical and habitual year. Besides being a harvest festival where the fruits of their crop were picked, it was a joyful culmination of the divine provisions of the Atonement. Joy is prominent! The trumpets were blown each day, the water was ceremonially drawn from Siloam (celebrating the glorious provision of God's stream from the Rock at Meribah in Ex. 17:1-7), and the water pointed to all the blessings flowing from God down to Israel. There was a torch parade to remember God's pillar of fire by night, and everywhere, from homes to the square, booths were set up to remember God's shelters that were given to the people even while they wandered in the wilderness. Later Zechariah connected this feast not to the wilderness, for the tone of its joy did not match the context, but he connected it to the kingdom of God.

In essence, the schedule of God was to help the people remember God's story and to reawaken all their affections and joys at getting to be a part of it. Every action and detail was specifically manufactured and set up by God for the people to reenact the story—to relive it. The rhythm itself was to be a way to bring the joys of the past into the present, and it ignited a whole new set of affections as it was reenacted. Years had gone by, and so much had happened, and as the memories of the past collided with the happening of their current state, it kept them completely conscious and aware of how to interpret their reality.

God was doing much more within the people then they realized. He was setting up His home and His family. God was structuring the time within his walls, and fashioning the DNA of His family. He was aiming the arrow and trajectory of His people's journey at the target of His Name, fame, and grace. Their submission was developing as seen in following chapters, but it was not completed. Like any New Year's resolution, their resolve soon wore off in the wake of their familiar patterned behaviors. God needed to actively take time to craft new habitual practices their ways of seeing the world.

Whatever the case may be, patterns and habits are always set, and they are always forming. The bottom line question that all human kind must answer is, "who sets our rhythms—who is forming us." How this question is answered comes down to the issue of authority. God, with Israel, in so many words, posed this question to them many times, and throughout Israel's history their own habitual prioritizing landed them over and over again in bondage and idolatry—a testament to what humans do when left to themselves.

The natural posture of the human heart is to be bent! Bent toward things of lesser value and importance! God in daily, weekly, monthly, annually and yearly rhythms ensured that His people were aimed at the right story. This caused them to arrive at their intended destination. His destination isn't a wasteland, it is a Promised Land.

SCENE 7
COMMITMENT

Standing now on the verge of opportunity, the Israelites faced a whole new way of life. They were now in a position to really hope for something that they had long awaited. The expectancy of soul is something that we must realize had not been part of the Israelite outlook, at least for a very long time. The Promised Land had always been a glimmer in their eye, but due to their human and fleshly frailty in trusting God in His leadership, the people had never fully been able to arrive at a belief that they would actually get to go in. Their journey had been a battle ground of complaining and half-hearted attempts to go back to Egypt.

Now that they had arrived in some matter of speaking, God intentionally allowed them to pause to consider a few things upon entrance into the land that stood before them. Not only were their daily worship and habits going to be important, but most importantly the people were to realize that their primary purpose in the land was going to be to act as God's stewards and representatives. They were to steward and govern the land in the way that He would.

He was to be their God and they were to be His people. In being His people they were to first and foremost recognize and remember that their primary purpose as a people is to make much of who God is in all that they say and do. In the previous chapter God deals with the "do" of the Israelite nation. He wanted them to honor Him in their worship and so He initiated a system of sacrifice and respect by which they could approach Him in boldness, humility, and peace.

In Chapter 30, God's commands shift away from what the Israelites were to do, and moves toward what the Israelites were supposed to say. One of the primary attributes of God is that He's loyal, He's loving, He's wise, and He's trustworthy. To reflect such a nature as a human, is to follow suit not only in action but in word. The big idea of Chapter 30 in the book of Numbers concerns the idea of *vowing*.

Everything that proceeds out of any person's mouth is to reveal the image of something—words can either "image" the human condition or the divine character of God. As God's family, Israel was considered to be God's son and child, and this meant that the very likeness they portrayed of their Father in heaven was to be the very image that the nations surrounding the Promised Land would see and know of the Supreme God. In addressing the Israelites in their words, God assured them that to be His people, they were going to have to talk like Him.

God is discretionary, He's calculated, and every word that He speaks is sent to accomplish a divine action. Every word out of His mouth is sent with a purpose and it does not return void. So it is to be with the speech of God's people. They were to measure their words, they were to consider their words, and they were to know that every single word that proceeds from their mouths would be like a wrecking ball to the world or like a healing salve. Israel was to understand the power she had in speaking on God's behalf. In her vows and allegiances she was not to be a destructive force, but a healing remedy.

We know that one of the big ideas of Numbers 30 is the idea of *vowing*, first and foremost because the passage begins with Moses speaking to the tribes saying, "This is what *the Lord has commanded*. If a man vows a vow to the Lord, or swears an oath to bind himself by a pledge, he shall not break his word. He shall do according to all that proceeds out of his mouth." We must notice first and foremost that God required that all vows be done, and that they be done in a certain way. He affirmed allegiances unto His name, but He wanted to ensure that what a man or women said, so they also did. Again, what was most at stake here was the very nature of God. A man in approaching God, and committing himself to something, must do so on God's terms. When God speaks, He fulfills, so should man. We also know that vows were a big idea in this passage because there were three kinds of vows mentioned in the Bible, and all of them are mentioned in this chapter.

In the Hebrew language there are three different "weights" or "angles" to one's vowing. The first kind to be considered is that of the *neder*. The *neder* vow describes a pledging of one's property as an offering to God. Such a pledge is spoken in order for a person to obligate himself or herself to repay or pay a loan until it is fulfilled. In the Hebrew language, a person does not simply "repay" a *neder,* but they *Shalom* this vow. Shalom is a Hebraic reference to a holistic peace—it is total. Many weights accompany financial obligation. The lending, borrowing and exchanging of property is a terse business, and requires the full "us" of mental, social, emotional, and spiritual faculties as to ascertain when the property has been handled with the utmost integrity. The bottom line of this vow is that a person is to say something and then follow through with it. When a person vows a property they are to give it and when a promise is made it must be fulfilled.

The bottom line of such a command is the law of love. To come through on one's word is to value the human or the God on the receiving end. It is an act of respect for God to promise the land and follow through, and God is commanding that such integrity also be demanded of its inhabitants. The goal of such a desire in God's mind is not so much tied to the vow itself but to the character formation of the one uttering the vow. It must require a lot of someone to uphold their word. It requires sacrifice, diligence, courage, self-control, and faithfulness. The purpose then of such a vow such as the *neder* is God's command that His people be like Him in their very character.

God led them this far unto the Promised Land, and He is going to come through on His word. For them to live in the land, they were going to have to carry this ethic with them across the Jordan.

In Numbers 30 starting in verse 3, the Lord first addresses the women of households in their making of this type of vow;

 If a woman vows a vow to the Lord and binds herself by a pledge, while within her father's house in her youth, and her father hears of her vow and of her pledge by which she has bound herself and says nothing to her, then all her vows shall stand, and every pledge by which she has bound herself shall stand. But if her father opposes her on the day that he hears of it, no vow of hers, no pledge by which she has bound herself shall stand. And the Lord will forgive her, because her father opposed her.

If she marries a husband, while under her vows or any thoughtless utterance of her lips by which she has bound herself, and her husband hears of it and says nothing to her on the day that he hears, then her vows shall stand, and her pledges by which she has bound herself shall stand. But if, on the day that her husband comes to hear of it, he opposes her, then he makes void her vow that was on her, and the thoughtless utterance of her lips by which she bound herself. And the Lord will forgive her. (But any vow of a widow or of a divorced woman, anything by which she has bound herself, shall stand against her.) And if she vowed in her husband's house or bound herself by a pledge with an oath, and her husband heard of it and said nothing to her and did not oppose her, then all her vows shall stand, and every pledge by which she bound herself shall stand. But if her husband makes them null and void on the day that he hears them, then whatever proceeds out of her lips concerning her vows or concerning her pledge of herself shall not stand. Her husband has made them void, and the Lord will forgive her.

The idea here is that if a woman was to make a vow before her father or husband, and he did not void her statement with a disagreement to her words, then he, by his silent approval, gave his agreement to her commitment and she must fulfill it. If he stood to disagree or challenge her words, her vow was then undone.

Such a concept is hard to understand in light of *neder*, referring to the transfer of property and possessions. However, the daughter here was considered to be the father's possession in that he and his wife bore her and they were responsible for her well-being. For a father to love his daughter was for him to make sure that her actions and words were not a snare to her, but rather that everything she spoke would become a blessing to her and those around her. When a daughter was to marry, the father then *gave the daughter away* and transferred her as a possession to another man to be her husband. The husband was then to treat his wife as a possession, not as if he owned her, but in the sense that he would take the greatest care of her well-being and ensure that her words secured for her her best.

Proprietary promises such as this one were to be viewed in a place of highest value. Many might think of property as something to consume, but the Hebraic idea of property ownership and value is that of cherishing; as one cherishes the most beautiful find of jewels. This is the heart of the vow; not ownership but love.

This was to be a sign from God's heart to the people. It was not only to paint for them a picture of what loving and protective leadership and headship should look like in the family, but it was to illuminate the people's perspective to see how their Bridegroom, God Himself, acts toward them. God is deeply concerned with the vows and promises of His people. He affirms only those that will bring them blessing and He nulls and voids any rash words a human makes out of anger or spite; for this would not bring about good fruit for them.

In first addressing the women in their *neder* vowing before their fathers and husbands, God illustrates the primary way in which His people are also to relate to and worship Him. They are to submit themselves to Him as He is their loving husband and Father. The people are to see themselves as property, not in the consuming sense, but in the sense of highest honor, value, and cherishing. Thus, the use and transfer of any kind of property is to be vowed in this way. Things are not to be consumed, they are to be loved and taken care of with the greatest attention.

The second type of vow mentioned in Numbers 30 is that of an *eesar*, which means to *bind* in an oath (vs. 13). It speaks of a physical promise made between two people or entities to be tied together as if imprisoned to one another, etc. In Numbers 30 it is used to discuss a personal promise to "bind one's soul" to another as in marriage. It can be an active vow made to a husband in the present, or as one made by a single person waiting for their significant other in the future. This binding is to allow a person to enjoy the freedoms of their state and place in life. In the present, they may abstain and even "imprison" themselves voluntarily from something in order to hold out for the time and place of its proper and most pleasing use.

It can also traditionally imply that a person not only binds themselves to something, but vows not to touch something else. In securing one's self to one anchor, a person willingly binds themselves away from another. A person can temporarily make a vow to bind themselves *away* from food, sex, or other pleasures to better bind himself or herself *to* a greater focus on God, or for example, abstain from sex in singleness in order to focus on a greater satisfaction in marriage. A person who binds their soul, does so voluntarily, assuming a second kind of obligation (to abstain from pleasures) in order to reach a spiritual state of heightened innocence. Abraham once vowed to keep his hand free from greed (Gene. 14:22-23), and Boaz vowed not to give in to lust (Ruth 3:13). Deuteronomy 6:13 agrees this is the proper procedure for personal vows.

In the context of Numbers 30, the framework the text gives us is a vow in the context of abstaining in a marriage relationship. This was to heighten its effect and to give us a picture of God's intent for such a vow. When a woman willingly accepted a man she was binding two souls together and taking herself "off the market" to other offerings. This covenant commitment is an exact illustration of God's purposes, in that He wanted the other nations to see this portrayal before their very eyes in order to learn about a higher divine relationship that God Himself has with His kids. He wanted to ground His very image within the family and marriage. Any ensuing vow of abstinence on His people's part was only to be an extension of the paramount vow of commitment as illustrated in the marriage covenant.

The big idea here is that this vow was to be used if anything or anyone threatened to take the place of God in a person's life. Food, sex, and even a relationships can quickly move from being good things to deadly things if it they are used as objects of worship. This perversion is something God most severely wanted His people to avoid.

The third type of oath is mentioned in Numbers 30:13 is *shvooah*. This oath throughout Scripture is used as an "oath of completion." It is an interpersonal obligation. A *shvooah* is when a person swears (to another) that he/she will do something. In most cases this vow is not a spiritual issue, and an *eesar* vow can become a *shvooah* vow if a person binds their soul *publicly*. By publicly vowing an abstention, a person is committing before witnesses to complete their word. Jeremiah taught this is only good when it is declared regarding actions of truth, justice, and righteousness. Jeremiah answers as to how a vow can be truly just and truthful: it should beg the question "Where is God?" (2:6-8), it instructs us to pursue scripture as valuable (2:8), to fear God (2:19), to seek God in times of prosperity as well as times of trouble (2:27), and to be open to receiving correction (2:30). According to Jeremiah, doing these things in a practice of habit binds someone to truth, justice, and righteousness. In light of this, if a person is to put a public trust in God's authority, this is a pinnacle of such a vow. The *shvooah* ultimately is to point to the relationship that one has to their Maker. Only in finding this allegiance will one find true public truth, justice, and righteous living.

To delve into the idea of vowing further, it must be seen that underneath each vow is to always be a drive for love. Each vow's goal is always to be driven by love. Whether the vow causes a person to secure themselves to another, to vow to pay back a debt, or to publicly stand for a set of principles, the goal is always to preserve the greatest sense of value, dignity and worth for all the parties involved. For example, a Nazarite was to make a vow to abstain from wine. However, if a Nazarite was to attend a party where wine was being consumed, and it would be inconsiderate of a person not to partake in a self-controlled manner of the gift provided by the host, the Nazarite's Sage, or Mentor would override their vow for that moment. This is simply because the highest aim of the vow is what is most loving, not what is most rule abiding.

Fast-forwarding into the New Testament, it was the religious leaders in Jesus' day that had lost this understanding and heart behind vows. This is what led Jesus to say to the Pharisees, "You shall not swear falsely, but shall perform to the Lord what you have sworn. But I say to you, Do not take an oath at all, either by heaven, for it is the throne of God, or by the earth, for it is his footstool, or by Jerusalem, for it is the city of the great King. And do not take an oath by your head, for you cannot make one hair white or black. Let what you say be simply 'Yes' or 'No'; anything more than this comes from evil." In this teaching Jesus confronted the Pharisaic practice of using rule-formulas to create different levels of promises, oaths, and vows. The Pharisees created their own weight system to determine which of person's words was most and least binding. In this way, the Pharisees were able to excuse their own behavior. When they broke a vow they were able to lessen its importance, and they would excuse themselves from their obligation. They would use their vows to sound very religious and even pious, and they would justify themselves by their morality—using morals as their own law. Jesus therefore encouraged people not to swear in this way but to invest the simple words they did say into integral yes and no actions.

In light of this, the question remains as to whether the issuing of *vows* and the Lord's instruction to the Israelites in Numbers is pertinent to being under His authority and leadership. Are vows essential? Is a vow Godly? Jesus seems to hate wrongful vows, but even Jesus' half-brother James in James 5:12 seems emphatic about making rightful vows as a means to uphold one's honesty and integrity. James links righteous vows to a person of strong faith. It is not that vows make a person better than anyone else, but James does suggest that the power of the *tongue* is a mighty force. James knows the power of words that are said and not said. He knows the seriousness of how we are to reflect the image of God in our truthfulness and love, and He knows it only takes a great person of faith to take this seriously and to take captive their words in only speaking that which is most loving and true.

Consider Jeremiah 2-5 again. In these chapters, God chastised the people of Israel for no longer looking to Him. The people in Jeremiah's time did not bother to acknowledge God, and their vowing and careless use of words were but one aspect of how they were treating God as if He were dead. By speaking carelessly they acted as if God would not hear—as if He were gone. Vowing then, is simply a way of acknowledging that God is alive and is in our lives. To *neder*—dedicate our treasures, to *eesar*—bind our souls to righteous things and away from wicked things, and to *shvooah*—bear the responsibility publicly for our actions and mis-actions, is the sign of a Godly person. These vows instruct our hearts to live in a kingdom not our own. We bear responsibility to an authority greater than ourselves. Thus we do not own our words, God does.

This realization was the very thing that was meant to ensure Israel's long lasting hope in the Promised Land. If their possessions were seen and handled this way, it preserved marriages and homes. If they were to cling to goodness and hate evil it would preserve their safety and well-being. If they took on the responsibility of being God's spokesmen to the world, this would ensure their best.

SCENE 8
VENGEANCE

When vows are present and real commitment is present, then fortified walls of protection and allegiance are also erected. Without a certainty of loyalty and covenant, one can never have the assurance of safety. If a relationship is anemic in commitment it also perverts justice because either party involved is painstakingly linked to their own desires and ambitions, not to the good of another. Within the context of vows and steadfast love, there remained a dedication to justice. There remained trustworthiness to each other's word and well-being.

God's covenant authority to, through, and over His people demands His utmost attention, leadership, and truthful integrity. If the people are blessed in spirit, this too pleases God's spirit. If care is dispensed to the least of those in His kingdom, He too is honored. For a person to wrong and revile God's people is as if to spit into the face of that people's wedded confidant—a husband type figure. To do such an act is to aggravate and violate the Maker Himself. In regard to the covenant blessing that God made with His people—to bless those who bless, and curse those who curse—God made a promise to His people that an offense hurtful to them was equal to an offense toward His Holy Name.

Upon arriving in Numbers 31, God enacts such justice by ordering vengeance upon the Midianite tribe. The Midainites were a people once ruled by a man named Balak (mentioned earlier in this book), who when he saw the Israelite multitude coming into his land, he sought not to bless them but to put a curse on them. His fear and trepidation over this people and the God of Israel who encamped in their midst, drove him to solicit the helpful magic of a locally deemed "power-prophet" of sorcery and divination. Balaam, a crooked person, only interested in the manipulation of systems in order to fill his own pocketbook, was called upon by Balak, and after two or three attempts by Balak to get Balaam's attention, Balaam was persuaded to go to him and to curse the Israelites. We know, that as the story followed along, not only did God stand in the way of Balaam, but when Balaam finally reached a place to pronounce a curse on God's people, he could only mutter words of awe, astonishment, and submission unto the Israelite God. God's power had judged Balak's attempts at witchcraft by silencing his most vocal prophet.

The display in Midian is to highlight God's ability to thwart nations and enemies that come against his people, but nonetheless, Midian had ignited his anger. Not long after, the Israelites by their own sin and lustful thirst fell into the hands of the Midianite altar prostitutes. They began not only having sex with their people, but they began worshipping at the altars of their gods.

The purpose for rewinding, and remembering such a coquetry is to explain why God's reaction proceeds as it does in Numbers chapter 31:

> The Lord spoke to Moses, saying, 'Avenge the people of Israel on the Midianites. Afterward you shall be gathered to your people.' So Moses spoke to the people, saying, 'Arm men from among you for the war, that they may go against Midian to execute the Lord's vengeance on Midian. You shall send a thousand from each of the tribes of Israel to the war.' So there were provided, out of the thousands of Israel, a thousand from each tribe,

twelve thousand armed for war. And Moses sent them to the war, a thousand from each tribe, together with Phinehas the son of Eleazar the priest, with the vessels of the sanctuary and the trumpets for the alarm in his hand. They warred against Midian, as the Lord commanded Moses, and killed every male. They killed the kings of Midian with the rest of their slain, Evi, Rekem, Zur, Hur, and Reba, the five kings of Midian. And they also killed Balaam the son of Beor with the sword. And the people of Israel took captive the women of Midian and their little ones, and they took as plunder all their cattle, their flocks, and all their goods. All their cities in the places where they lived, and all their encampments, they burned with fire, and took all the spoil and all the plunder, both of man and of beast. Then they brought the captives and the plunder and the spoil to Moses, and to Eleazar the priest, and to the congregation of the people of Israel, at the camp on the plains of Moab by the Jordan at Jericho.

The Lord was distressed, angry, and overwhelmed with the injustice that was done to His people. Like an irate husband whose wife had been ravaged and raped on his own bed within his own house, the Lord's bride had been taken captive by lust and misled to willingly defile the sexual union between man and woman. The Midianites had raped His people and had stepped into His realm of authority and leadership, and as any good authority should be, the Lord was bound by His own terms, laws, and agreements. He voluntarily forced His own hand in the wake of His own vow to bring calamity on anyone who harmed His beloved. This war then was not merely an angry tantrum, but it was a just act on behalf of a God who is both angry and loving.

Moses and the leaders of Israel took it upon themselves to evoke this same amount of rage and indignation toward the people that had dared to suckle at the breast of Israel's purity without cause and love for her. So indignant was Moses, that when the men in verse 13-20 returned and had not killed the women who had been sexual partners to their men, thus bearing little boys of Midianite seed and cancerous disease, Moses ordered that all those who were not virgins, and all those boys who would grow up to be just like Balak, to be killed. It was an extermination of the multiplying power of the seed of sin that had planted itself in Israel's garden.

Only the little girls who had not known a man by lying with him were left to live. God did not allow for another legacy of death and injustice to promulgate and multiply itself, nor did he allow any more intruders to come into his home and steal what rightfully belonged to Him. His act of vengeance was an act of erecting a proverbial fence around Israel's home, and posting guard dogs out front to protect her barricaded and locked doors—all in an effort to secure and protect His own family.

God's war is holy and just. It is not like the warring spirit of selfish ambition and pride that enters the world through man. This type of war first attacked the lineage of men like Cain and Abel. It was not a venomous and murder-thirsty drive to get what one wants at the expense of someone else. God had already spoken openly about murder as being wrong throughout the Old Testament. This instance more greatly resembles the flood in Noah's day, or the rescue of lot by Abraham in the first "holy war" in Genesis 14. God's beloved had been stolen and taken into foreign hands. The evil had so permeated the fabric of Midian, that like the flood, God needed to rid their species in hopes that a rainbow could still shine. This crusade is consistent with Leviticus 19:16 where God says, "not to seek revenge, but to love your neighbor."

Here, and many times before, like in Deuteronomy 20, God gave the orders for war, but the truth of its justice lay in its motivation. God's motives were pure and most holy. His judgments were most sound, and His forbearance most patient. He never acted rashly, nor did He ever act blindly. He saw the facts, He knew the depths, and His wisdom stretched before and beyond when time and life on earth begins and ends.

This reality makes God the only one worthy and able to make such a distinction between killing and murder here in Numbers. The motive for murder is human; the motive for God's order in killing is divine. It is to enact justice. His justice does not demand more than it is given by evil, but God's seeks only to reclaim the exact spoil that was stolen from Him. This is a warranted response, a response taken by a God who controls the victory and defeat of nations.

The purity of the authority of God, as used here to take the lives of Midian, is proven in its purity later in the story of Scripture when God does not hesitate to give His own Son Jesus as a ransom for the many prisoners that evil has so malignantly taken. Even God does not expect that He will remain indifferent to killing, as He orders it upon Himself. This God, so brutally committed to His own word and commitment to His people, shed His blood in His people's place as a defense against their enemies. This is to enact what Isaiah and Micah spoke of as a day when nations would beat their swords into plowshares (Isaiah 2:4; Micah 4:3). Nations are not to lift up sword against nation, and no one will study war anymore. That day will be a day of God completing His kingdom in coming; though it is seemingly far off, in the last days, when God rules the earth with a rod of iron, God himself will go to war against his enemies; crushing all opposition (Zechariah 14:3-16). God, the great warrior, will be victorious.

And ultimately that what is at stake here. This passage reveals the true nature in which authority is tied to a subordinate. An attack on the subordinate is one in the same with the authority's image as well. Israel is God's people! It is His sheer act of grace to wrap up His own reputation into hers, and to defend her as if He is defending Himself. For Midian to sexually pollute God's people and to transmit their spiritually transmitted disease of hatred, condition, and careless abuse into the worldview of God's people, is to distract and derail them into desiring another image altogether. To sleep with the enemy means that Israel is to lose her ability to show forth the Triune God.

All of heaven is stirred to action because God's glory has been challenged by diversion. God's family has been pillaged, and His beloved people's pleasures have been manipulated. God's war on His enemies has developed, been instigated by, and resulted from a rebellious people that at some point decided that their desires were to be placed before their Maker's. God orders war for such a choice!

Ever so benevolently, this war foreshadows a war that He even orders on His own Son. Unless some medication is prescribed to such a cancer, the disease continues its warring rampage. Unless Jesus dies at the hands of those fighting to preserve perversity, and seeking to overtake His purity, Jesus can have no lasting victory. The only way to win such a battle is to let it seemingly win, and to rise above it—revealing that God's authority can rule over every trick that the enemy can come up with in an attempt to steer God's world off course.

Because true justice is activated, God demonstrates many striking things about Himself. Firstly, He takes matters into His own hands so that His people will not have to. God acts upon perfect decree and operates on the clearest intel that is available. He can see everything without error. If Israel were to have taken such matters into their own hands, they would have found their pursuit to be incomplete and lacking many valuable perspective choices that could ensure their victory. Secondly, He proves Himself not a liar, in that He defends His covenant promises, and He anchors His people's hopes in the fact that they truly and really do have nothing to fear! Thirdly, the war, as incited by God against His enemies is also more complete than that of any human effort. The motives of humans in enacting violence are to obtain what their own hearts want. The human heart only sees what it can do for itself. God on the other hand sees a much greater battle that's waging. His war is not merely enacted on flesh and blood, but on principalities and demonic empires that masquerade as human rulers. He does not enact a war to shore up physical security, but to release all that He loves from spiritual and eternal torment, rule and control. His victory is to be total in that it is to purchase for His people a victory in the full and complete realms of the mind, the body, and the spirit.

Lastly, God's war is to publicly shame rulers and prophets like

Balaam and Balak. A human attempt at revenge and vengeance can only bring so much shame to the offending party. A human attempt can bruise the enemy, but cannot soundly defeat it. Even if an army publicly humiliates another culture, that culture will still rise up again. In the hearts of those a people is a poison that cannot be conquered by a human sword. God lays down a judgment that is far more total! His war is not only to cripple the spreading disease, but to annihilate its germ and its source. The human therefore is like a Kleenex, wiping at the problem, but never stopping the evil from running. God's justice is like the narcotic that targets the bacteria, kills its root and sets up camp in the human body to make sure that the worm never squirms again!

SCENE 9
BELIEF

The people of Israel certainly benefited from God's hand as it went before them. They benefited from their loving family "Head of household" as He made decisions on their behalf and for their betterment. Perhaps a question should be asked nonetheless amidst all that had happened. God's intentions and motives have been made painstakingly clear, but not much has been said recently of the people's viewpoint as to whether or not they were observing all of this. Did the people believe that God really had their best interests in mind? Did they respond much like people in our day do to God's justice, wisdom, and perfect attempts at victory, with confusion, bitterness, and doubt? Were they obeying and believing God's protection in and over them? If they were, were their motives pure?

One must admit that from a human perspective, God's actions seem a bit ethically questionable. Many of those in Israel most likely suffered with wandering questions and thoughts about the actual nature of God. The safety felt under God's hand was reassuring, but it came with a weight of fear and trembling. What if God were to turn on them in this way? What if they were to reach into a treasure chest to steal God's forbidden riches only to find themselves on the business end of His whooping stick?

The tension of resting in God's goodness and trembling at His justice is precisely the balance that He asks His people to live within. The Proverbs tend to couple together this attitude of fear with a sense of trust and goodness, and it calls it *wisdom*. This is the place from which all good decision making emanates from; a place of deep ceded trust in the safety of God's hands, but a shaking of the knees at the thought of ever leaving His fingers for what might be on the outside of that hand.

Numbers answers this question in chapter 32 as the camera lens zooms in on the particular requests and actions of the tribe of Reuben and Gad. From all outward appearances, Reuben and Gad rested and resided under God's leadership and did quite well for themselves. The first verses of Numbers 32 tell us that they had many livestock. God's smile shone upon them and made them a great people group. With all their prosperity and the hope of God at their back, the request that Reuben and Gad made to Moses and Eleazar in Numbers 32 makes sense:

> And they saw the land of Jazer and the land of Gilead, and behold, the place was a place for livestock. So the people of Gad and the people of Reuben came and said to Moses and to Eleazar the priest and to the chiefs of the congregation, 'Ataroth, Dibon, Jazer, Nimrah, Heshbon, Elealeh, Sebam, Nebo, and Beon, the land that the Lord struck down before the congregation of Israel, is a land for livestock, and your servants have livestock.' And they said, 'If we have found favor in your sight, let this land be given to your servants for a possession. Do not take us across the Jordan.'

This is an honest appeal from a people that had tasted God's goodness. Nothing prohibited them from coming to Moses and all the leadership that God had provided in order to enable them to request whatever their heart wanted. Reuben and Gad surely expected an answer in the positive. They saw God as good, and when it came to their livestock there was no reason to believe that God wanted anything less than their best.

But a question looms in the mind of the reader, "Why did Reuben and Gad not want to go into the Promised Land." I mean they believed God right? They loved God, right? Who couldn't love a God who is for you and not against you? Who couldn't trust a powerhouse God that was willing to risk His own reputation to save yours? And yet, even in the wake of all that had happened, in God over and over again showing His covenant blessings to Israel's people, the request still came, "Do not take us across the Jordan."

From a human standpoint, this is a legitimate request, a bold request, and an even seemingly faith-filled request. God does not give unless we ask, right? From God's perspective unfortunately, something else was operating. God knew the hearts of men, and in this moment, a sounding echo resonated with something Jesus encountered with the disciples in the book of John chapter 2 verses 23-25. Here's the account:

> Now when he was in Jerusalem at the Passover Feast, many *believed* in his name when they saw the signs that he was doing. But Jesus on his part *did not entrust himself to them*, because he knew all people and needed no one to bear witness about man, for he himself *knew what was in man*.

Later in John 12 it went on to say, "nevertheless, many even of the authorities believed in him, but for fear of the Pharisees they did not confess it, so that they would not be put out of the synagogue; for *they loved the glory that comes from man* more than the glory that comes from God."

Somewhat of a stench wafts up from the motives of Reuben's requests. It caused the tribes to fall short of fully desiring the full weight of glory that God had prepared. The Promised Land was a representation of God's glory. It was a place of God's rule and reign on earth. Gilead, at least how it's used in this instance, represented an inheritance, yes, but one that was clearly compromised and not fully loaded with all of God's intentions. Reuben and Gad began to show the tale-tell signs that false belief and trust had taken root in their souls. On the outside, their demands looked pious, bold, and almost admirable. Nevertheless, to God they were a stink in his nose, for Reuben and Gad believed and trust God only as far as He led them unto their own advantage. As soon as God appeared to be fighting for someone else as a priority, the Reubenites and Gadites began to dismiss this God as being controlled by His own selfish and petty wants.

Reuben and Gad fell into the pride of life and the lust of the eye (1 Jn. 2:16), a sin that is common and plaguing to humanity. Their pride led them to do several things in particular. Firstly they began thinking of themselves more highly than they ought. Their thinking was motivated by an ingrown security. Reuben was the firstborn of Israel who had lost his birthright. He had been eclipsed by Judah, and Gad was born to Zilpah and a bunch of Reuben impersonators. Manasseh who had also liked their appeal was the first-born and was eclipsed by his younger brother Ephraim.

A similar makeup existed in all these personalities. People who believe they deserve certain treatment, at some point always rise up to demand what they feel they deserve. The question must be posed then, "What develops in a person when all that they hold to is a sense of entitlement?" Reuben and their followers silently and tightly had held to a conviction ever so subtle. Their hidden belief was that they were better than everyone. They were entitled to the "firsts" and they were not about to have that opportunity ripped from them again. In their minds, the Promised Land was not so much a grace and a gift to them, but it was something owed to them.

Little did they know that in falling into the first trap of pride and lust of the eyes, they were about to be devoured by the real lion within the trap. Secondly, they began to weigh their "good" against "God's great satisfaction." Gilead was a prosperous land, yes, but they had never seen anything different. All they knew was this is as good as it will get. They operated out of their slave and poverty mentality of getting it while the getting was hot, and they jumped on a small opportunity that lost them the greater one.

Reuben and Gad were near-sighted. They could only see close up. They were motivated by short cuts, instant gratification, and lust which drove them toward satisfying their selfish greed.

Thirdly, this landed them right in the war zone of their own self-annihilating self-centeredness. The Reuben wannabes were looking out for themselves, and in doing so they were overtaken by individual convenience rather than the public and common good. They could no longer act righteously because true righteousness is to do justly and to love mercy. These attributes are others-focused. Once Reuben and his gang became centered on self, they lost the whole purpose of what God was trying to do in the journey in the first place. They no longer could do right for others because they no longer saw others.

Finally, the logical end to such a trajectory of self-centeredness was a culmination of fear and doubt. Their self-care of themselves led them to protect their own. The thought of losing their own good only seemed to paralyze them with fear and doubt. If God was to reason with them, they would not have been able to follow even if they wanted to.

Fear and doubt is crippling. The Promised Land was a better sell, but the here and now for Reuben and Gad is all they wanted. They wanted instant gratification and the feeling of security, even if it cost them everything. What they got is a false wall of fear and doubt to make them feel safe, but what they lost is the real safety of God.

Moses, being a wise leader, interpreted their request and pinpointed its true intention:

> But Moses said to the people of Gad and to the people of Reuben, 'Shall your brothers go to the war while you sit here? Why will you discourage the heart of the people of Israel from going over into the land that the Lord has given them? Your fathers did this, when I sent

them from Kadesh-barnea to see the land. For when they went up to the Valley of Eshcol and saw the land, they discouraged the heart of the people of Israel from going into the land that the Lord had given them.' And the Lord's anger was kindled on that day, and he swore, saying, 'Surely none of the men who came up out of Egypt, from twenty years old and upward, shall see the land that I swore to give to Abraham, to Isaac, and to Jacob, because they have not wholly followed me, none except Caleb the son of Jephunneh the Kenizzite and Joshua the son of Nun, for they have wholly followed the Lord.' And the Lord's anger was kindled against Israel, and he made them wander in the wilderness forty years, until all the generation that had done evil in the sight of the Lord was gone. 'And behold, you have risen in your fathers' place, a brood of sinful men, to increase still more the fierce anger of the Lord against Israel! For if you turn away from following him, he will again abandon them in the wilderness, and you will destroy all this people.'

Moses saw right through their pitiful attempts at piety and called their bluff. They were a stiff-necked people uncircumcised in heart and ears, and were resistant to the Holy Spirit (Acts 7:51). Their bold attempt to claim what was theirs only exposed their lack of faith.

The fight was not over however because Reuben and Gad still wanted to play their little charade, and they responded to Moses by telling him that they would fight for Israel. Just to make sure that Moses did not misinterpret them, they reframed his supposedly false understanding of what they'd asked (sarcasm pretty thick) into this pithy statement:

Then they came near to him and said, 'We will build sheepfolds here for our livestock, and cities for our little ones, but we will take up arms, ready to go before the

> people of Israel, until we have brought them to their place. And our little ones shall live in the fortified cities because of the inhabitants of the land. We will not return to our homes until each of the people of Israel has gained his inheritance. For we will not inherit with them on the other side of the Jordan and beyond, because our inheritance has come to us on this side of the Jordan to the east.'

Oh, mighty Reuben and their faith! They did not intend to fend for themselves. They were attempting to be part of the family after all. Right? Wrong! First off, if this gesture of nobility was truly motivated by courage, unity focus, and the families' betterment, why did they not suggest this to begin with? The overflow of their heart spoke in the first request they had made. This attempt was merely to save face. If this was not convincing enough, a verse found in 2 Kings 15:29, tells us that in the Assyrian exile enslavement, these tribes east of the Jordan were carried off some years before the other tribes. This remained consistent with Moses' warnings to the selfish tribes in Numbers 32:23 when he said, "But if you will not do so, behold, you have sinned against the Lord, and be sure your sin will find you out." These tribes were found out in their sin because their belief and allegiance to their King Yahweh was only motivated by sinful motives. Yes, it is true that these tribes lived in prosperity albeit seemingly for a while, but the joyride did not last long, and God demonstrated in the Assyrian exile that His justice is perfect and unavoidable.

However, these tribes wanted to keep up the false charade and in cowardice utter to Moses in vs. 25 "your servants will do as my lord commands." They did so at the price of their awarded inheritance. Yet in verse 38 their true motivations still rang clear in that upon conquering the cities in that region, they changed and renamed the cities.

This might appear insignificant but the motives for doing so can only be two-fold. Either they changed the names of them (v. 38) to show their authority in the land, or the change of the names might have signified a change of owner. This was a necessary change because the previous names of the cities were idolatrous. Nebo and Baal were names of the current gods, which they were forbidden to make mention of (Ex. 23:13), and which, by changing the names of these cities, they endeavored to bury these gods in oblivion.

Due to Reuben and Gad's previous sequence of approach, and judging the evidence that follows in the rest of Scripture, my guess is that they renamed the cities to reflect their own names, kingdoms, riches, and authority. They erected kingdoms of prominence, but the real shade and shelter of the Lord's rule left them as it crossed the Jordan and onto the other side. These tribes became masked criminals—they laid false claim to what they did not own, and they did it all under the guise of a belief that they claimed to honor.

In what way then did these Reuben wannabes follow and obey the Lord? Out of what motives? These are tough questions to answer, but they pertain to Numbers' overarching theme of journey and authority. Upon entering the Promised Land, God shored the people up by reminding them of the nature of covenant vows. He secured them in His commitment to His people and His promises to them even against their enemies.

In these passages, their true guts and glory were revealed and challenged for what they really were. God was a means to an end in their minds. He was a boat on which they had sailed to get across the sea into a land of their own individual convenience. Their slave heart and perspective remained, for to them freedom was still defined by getting what one deserves. They were hardwired to protect what they thought was their own entitlement, and they would not release even to the Lord of Hosts. To them, His authority carried the stench of control, and they just could not stomach that anymore.

In an attempt to alleviate their fear of being under God for the rest of their days, they fell right into the hands of their own worst fears, and were left exposed and without a shield. Their own impatient greed, pride, and lust procured for them only death. Their self-seeking revelry only served to consume them and eat them up from the inside out. These tribes revoked their right to value the family of

God, they collapsed under fear, they fell into doubt and pain, and lost the greatest hope of their soul.

So the question remains, "is this true belief?" Should believing in something cause a person to forsake and distrust it? I think not! Belief should embrace the mantle, the covering, the hedge, and the banner of authority. His banner over us is love! (Song of Songs 2:4).

28

SCENE 10

STAGES OF A SLAVE

The journey and storyline of the book of Numbers allows its readers to be led to an inevitable conclusion. The current state of the book has led to yet another climax in highlighting Reuben and Gad and their selfish and false belief in the living God. In a sense, they provide a grand parable that epitomizes all that Israel has been throughout the journey. Numbers 33 recounts Israel's journey, not as a walk of fame to be remembered, but as a walk of shame attributed to their own self-promotion. The only thing worth highlighting is that of the covenant love of God. The concluding chapters of this saga provide the sobering edge needed to humble Israel as they entered the Promised Land.

It is very curious to me that Moses' writing likens the journey of the Israelites to "stages." Numbers 33:1-4 says,

> These are the *stages* of the people of Israel, when they went out of the land of Egypt by their companies under the leadership of Moses and Aaron. Moses wrote down their *starting places, stage by stage,* by command of the Lord, and these are *their stages* according to *their starting places.* They set out from Rameses in the first month, on

> the fifteenth day of the first month. On the day after the Passover, the people of Israel went out triumphantly in the sight of all the Egyptians, while the Egyptians were burying all their firstborn, whom the Lord had struck down among them. On their gods also the Lord executed judgments.

The following verses of the chapter then proceed into naming all the different locations and stopping places that the Israelites made along the course of their travels.

In the first part of Moses' *travel log* and *journal*, verses 5-10, he records the beginning stages of Israel as a child as she traversed out from underneath slavery at the hands of the Egyptians. Israel's travels took her to Succoth which means "to block," as she was shut off from the influence of the Egyptians. Then to Etham where the Lord "shut them in" and even required them to retrace a few of their steps in going back to Migdol—a place right under Egyptian noses. Though Israel in proximity had been freed, their freedom of spirit was still on the horizon. At Marah, which means bitter, God led Moses to a bitter and salty spring in order to give the Israelites a picture of their bitter soul; a soul that was only to turn sweet under the Lord's leadership. Then, in progressing toward the Red Sea, the people landed at Elim where there were 12 springs and 70 trees—a symbol of a new people divided into new tribes under new human leadership. Then, as we know, they were ultimately delivered from the pursuit of their enemies for the last time in the spectacle and miracle of the Red Sea deluge.

The children of slavery coming out of Egypt were a people of great immaturity. Upon leaving the Egyptian empire they were fatherless and homeless. Their way of thinking had been changed due to being freed, and they no longer knew on whom to depend. The maturity of a baby is to suckle at its mother's breast and not to ask why. The baby does not ask the mother why they are being fed. The baby does not make decisions based on its own welfare. The baby is simply led blindly and is at the mercy of a parent much bigger and stronger than themselves. The Israelites had nursed the Egyptian rule for too long. Its system was perverted, but this was the system that Israel knew—it had formed them. When God gathered them to Himself, he called out the child in them. He was calling them to grow up under His rule. His deliverance of them was not merely an exile, but an adoption.

God, in His infinite mercy and wisdom, began to hedge His children in by giving them protective boundaries, and even isolating them. He made them travel under His whim and directions in an effort to recalibrate their ability to hear, respond, and obey. As their Father, Israel became a people of sonship. They were trained by His loving hand, and as an infant steps out on its own, it is liable to touch things it cannot touch simply because its ingrown slavery has taught it to do so. Hence, the tactic of God was taken to shut His people in, to place them under new leadership, and to address their deep-rooted motivations.

Below the surface their motivation was bitterness. They had nursed at the bosom of Egyptian provision but had grown all the more bitter for it. The lack of emotional connection to their mother nation, and the usury they experienced at the mercy of their bad parent's hand had left them with a bad taste in their mouth. These enslaved people were driven by bitterness against anything entitled "master." The idea of following a "Lord" was not all that appealing. God knew such things, and prophesied His leadership as sweet and satisfying, and punctuated His promise with a sweet release of His people from the Egyptians in the parting of the Red Sea.

It was almost as if the Israeli disciples were growing up. They'd moved from *infancy* and *total dependence*, to the place of a *toddler* and a place where they needed *guidance* and *utter protection*. In Numbers 33:11-15, their journey again progressed as God moved them into a time of *young childhood* in learning *character* and *understanding*; into understanding the "why" behind everything they did.

God had them on a journey in their young childhood. The people went wandering in the wilderness of Sin. The terrain was difficult and it was an uphill climb, but for the Israelite child to grow, they needed to come in contact with their real human form. At their basest nature, they were idolaters and sinners—delivered by the King of the Cosmos nonetheless. They were to understand what they would become if left to themselves in order to ready them for a surrendered dependence on a God who could remedy and heal their condition.

Verses 17-37 in this Chapter records for us everything that took place up until the time of Aaron's death. The Israelites were led to Hezeroth where Miriam was afflicted, to Rithmah, Libnah, Rissah, Kehelatha, and Mount Shepher known as "brightness"—a mountain in the desert. They were led through Haradah—meaning fear—Makeheloth, Tahath, Terah—meaning wanderer—to Mithkah, a land of sweetness, to Hashmonah, a land of fatness, to Moseroth, Ben-jaakan, and to the caves of Hor-Haggidgad; then to Jotbathah, Abronah, Ezion-geber, Kadesh and finally into the land of Edom and Mount Hor where Aaron died. All of these locations spoke louder than merely their names. God's planned traverse throughout the duration of Israel's childhood was to usher them into a process, a way, and a path along which they were to relearn their way of looking at life. God was rehabilitating their sin and slavery mindset by keeping them off balance.

As a young child learns and grows in mental functions through mobility, Israel grew through her mobility. Each location was to be a painting of what God was doing. He was casting off her fear, He was assembling her and dealing with her affliction, He was making her wander but only unto the destination of greater sweetness, fatness, protection and joy.

The goal of such a movement was to prepare Israel for *young childhood* and *pre-adolescence* when she would come before the base of Mt. Sinai and be given God's law. They were to be given God's moral ethic, His statutes, and they were to talk through what it meant to live for Him and before Him. This was to be a catapult into their *adult years* where they were about to walk this stuff out in a very real journey of trial and error.

Our journey in this book through Numbers clearly reveals to us what a journey of failing and redemption is. This story traces Israel's journey, but hidden in it is all of humanity's reality.

God systematically addresses Israel's poverty mentality by giving them a regimen of bread. They were to get what they could when they could in order to prepare for their next day, but they were subject to walking in daily provisions. God dealt with their "owe me mentality" by bringing them face to face with their sin as revealed by His law. God also clearly dealt with all the bitterness that had formed in them in the wake of their sin. Their bitterness was poisonous, for it stirred up anger (Prv. 15:1), stirred up strife (Prv. 10:12), and it made them quick to want vengeance and not to wait on the Lord (Prv. 20:22). Their flesh was allowed to rule (Col. 3:5-10), and this caused self-centeredness, judgmental attitudes, and distrust toward anything human or divine.

Israel slowly grew in *stages*. As a baby she needed a parent to provide her with coddled affection, attention, care, and benevolence. As a toddler she needed better boundaries and to be led by a God who expected of her to follow without question, and as a young child she needed to be led and taught in the way that she should go and to have her sin dealt with as it surfaced. As she progressed into young adolescence and adulthood she needed discipline, daily, weekly, monthly, and yearly rhythms and habits, and daily provision. She needed leadership that taught her the art of trusting the hand of a loving God. All of this was to grow her up to a place where she would not only love her God and her people, but that she would be ready to inhabit a land—to inherit a kingdom of her own!

PART IV

ACT 4

SCENE 1

THERE BUT NOT YET, THE PROMISED LAND

Every good story holds its tension. Every good novel has its sequel. Every good drama ends with a cliff-hanger—something that's unresolved that leaves the reader wanting more. Every tension seems to engage us a little more. It makes us investigate to see if we missed something. When we're left in wondering it makes us retrace our steps in order to re-evaluate, and in doing so, we rediscover the story in new ways and with very real nuance that we missed the first time. In a sense, this investigation back into the story causes us to enter the story ourselves and to attempt to figure things out as if it meant something to us. Numbers is written in this way. If one is to isolate Numbers from the rest of the Bible, its book leaves us wanting more, and it leaves us hoping for a sequel.

As the last three chapters commence, God prepares His people for entrance into their Promised victory. The people of Israel did not know the specifics of all that was in front of them but they could glimpse it as if it was a shadow or a pale image reflected off a glassy sea. God had described the Promised Land to them and yet the full imagery of a land flowing with milk and honey was not full and easy to process to them. Was it a land of literal milk and honey? Was God merely painting a picture of what it is like by likening it to things that are familiar to Israel?

The only reference point that Israel had to go back to is their own lineage and history. Their history is a romantic tragedy at best. It is a story that began in a lush and supple Garden in Eden. This was a land flowing with all things sweet and all things nourishing and enriching to life. The Garden, God's domain, and the place where Adam and Eve walked with their God and were His people, was the only picture hoped for. This was their Paradise Lost.

Humanity once had a *land*, and had once seen the fruit of the *seed*, and were themselves a part of the *blessing* in God's Garden. Eden was a place where humanity had not only been *around* God's presence, but they were *in* God's presence. The original idea of blessing in the Jewish mind was that to be where God is, is to be where good is. For an Israelite to assess and reinvestigate their roots, they would only find this expectation lying ahead of them.

This land, Canaan, bordered on the West by the Mediterranean, stopped on the East by Kadesh-Barnea, shortened in the South up from the River of Egypt, and stretching North to Mt. Hor to Hamath, was their promise. It was the original campground of Adam and Eve, and it had been ripped away from them as a result of their own sin. They had forsaken God's rule, they had wanted something altogether different, and the very thing that got them kicked out of the Garden is the very thing that led them back in—God's authority. At one time they had chosen their own way, and in the process they had lost God's best. Now, at the hope of a better promise, Israel was again going to be God's people and He was to be there God. God intended this from the beginning and in Numbers 34:1-15, as He roped off the boundaries of this land in an effort to show them all that He was still about. He did this to communicate to them very clearly what He was not allowing to come in.

Later in their anthology, the land of promise is compared to Eden, where saints have the access to the tree of life and the promise of immortality (Ezekiel 36:35; Joel 2:3). In Jeremiah 31:8-10 it says,

> Behold, I will bring them from the north country, and gather them from the coasts of the earth, and with them the blind and the lame, the woman with child and her that travails with child together: a great company shall return thither. They shall come with weeping, and with supplications will I lead them: I will cause them to walk by the rivers of waters in a straight way, wherein they shall not stumble: for I am a father to Israel, and Ephraim is my firstborn. Hear the word of the Lord, O ye nations, and declare it in the isles afar off, and say, He that scattered Israel will gather him, and keep him, as a shepherd doth his flock.

Linked to such a picture was a promise of an even greater covenant in Jeremiah 31:31-34;

> Behold, the days come, says the Lord, that I will make a new covenant with the house of Israel, and with the house of Judah: Not according to the covenant that I made with their fathers in the day that I took them by the hand to bring them out of the land of Egypt; which my covenant they break, although I was a husband unto them, says the Lord: But this shall be the covenant that I will make with the house of Israel; After those days, saith the Lord, I will put my law in their inward parts, and write it in their hearts; and will be their God, and they shall be my people. And they shall teach no more every man his neighbor, and every man his brother, saying, Know the Lord: for they shall all know me, from the least of them unto the greatest of them, saith the Lord: for I will forgive their iniquity, and I will remember their sin no more.

Jeremiah uses exilic language, in that he looked back to the moment of Israel's freedom from Egyptian rule, and he even acknowledged that their deliverance was to *point* to a greater covenant ... a new one! Israel's entire trek is a typified journey of a new covenant that was to become fleshed out in full in the future.

Currently however, Israel stood at a new place of Genesis—a do over. This was their only expectation, and yet so far short of what God actually intended to give them. God initiated a brand new way of thinking in their midst. Like the seed and source that God used to plant His Garden in Genesis 1, God seeded this Promised Land and filled it with all of His abundance, and now re-awakened His vision from before.

Like a seed planted in the ground however, there is a sense in which even after a plant is fully in bloom it can never be fully separate from its seed—its source. Israelite ears heard throughout their entire history that God was going to lead them to a land, through a seed to give them a blessing. In their minds they expected a place where the land was the end in itself. Needless to say, a land cannot be in existence without its originating seed.

For this reason, Israel had a very incomplete expectation about what actually lay in front of them. God was not merely leading Israel back to a land. The land was yet another symbol and *diorama*—a *result* of a greater *cause*. For Israel to find the true land, it was not for them to simply inhabit a geographical region, but it was to enjoy God and God alone—the source and seed.

This made sense, because in Genesis 17 God promised to Abraham a land that he would enjoy as an everlasting possession—Canaan. However, Abraham died before he obtained this promise. If the land was to be the end in itself then God had failed in His promise. If God had fully intended to bring His people into a physical land, then God had already failed the patriarch Abraham.

When we consider the fact that all of the land of Canaan was promised to Abraham, a land that is far greater than he or they would actually need, and yet he received none of it, we must assume that what lay before Israel had some other meaning then a literal view allows. We are either left with this or we must admit that God had lied.

Rather, instead of it being an end of itself, it served as yet another symbol—*a diorama*—for the reality to which it points. To build and preserve tension in our look at these ideas, and not to give resolve to quickly, let's leave this idea for now and continue on to chapter 34:16-29 where God again ordered Moses to divide up the chiefs, households and tribes in order to receive their inheritance. God systematically sifted through the men to instate leadership. Again, God was not making an effort to get rid of authority and unleash anarchy as a sign of true promise. His promise included the electing of good and gracious leaders.

If this was not to be just a physical reality in a tangible land, but a spiritual reality pointing beyond the land to God Himself, we must interpret it as so. Here God took His people out from under Egyptian slave authority and brought His people to the precipice of the Promised Land. He chose to administer authority that was grounded in the family and was divided up amongst human men, chiefs and leaders of tribes (this echoes the system of Revelation where we see twenty-four elders sitting on thrones, ruling God's final kingdom. The kingdom was and is not to be a removal of authority, but the instating of true leadership; leadership absent from human ambition and any desire to seek its own control). Human leadership was only to be instated to carry out the most loving and perfect command of God—meaning the best for God's people. These men were to be as Paul says in 2 Thessalonians 3:7-10, *imitable.*

God went even further in Numbers 35:6-34 in not only setting up a boundary land and a leadership structure, but also a judicial system.

> The cities that you give to the Levites shall be the six cities of refuge, where you shall permit the manslayer to flee, and in addition to them you shall give forty-two cities. All the cities that you give to the Levites shall be forty-eight, with their pasturelands. And as for the cities that you shall give from the possession of the people of Israel, from the larger tribes you shall take many, and from the smaller tribes you shall take few; each, in

proportion to the inheritance that it inherits, shall give of its cities to the Levites.

And the Lord spoke to Moses, saying, 'Speak to the people of Israel and say to them, When you cross the Jordan into the land of Canaan, then you shall select cities to be cities of refuge for you, that the manslayer who kills any person without intent may flee there. The cities shall be for you a refuge from the avenger that the manslayer may not die until he stands before the congregation for judgment. And the cities that you give shall be your six cities of refuge. You shall give three cities beyond the Jordan and three cities in the land of Canaan, to be cities of refuge. These six cities shall be for refuge for the people of Israel, and for the stranger and for the sojourner among them, that anyone who kills any person without intent may flee there.

'But if he struck him down with an iron object, so that he died, he is a murderer. The murderer shall be put to death. And if he struck him down with a stone tool that could cause death, and he died, he is a murderer. The murderer shall be put to death. Or if he struck him down with a wooden tool that could cause death, and he died, he is a murderer. The murderer shall be put to death. The avenger of blood shall himself put the murderer to death; when he meets him, he shall put him to death. And if he pushed him out of hatred or hurled something at him, lying in wait, so that he died, or in enmity struck him down with his hand, so that he died, then he who struck the blow shall be put to death. He is a murderer. The avenger of blood shall put the murderer to death when he meets him.

'But if he pushed him suddenly without enmity, or hurled anything on him without lying in wait or used a stone that could cause death, and without seeing him dropped it on him, so that he died, though he was not his enemy and did not seek his harm, then the congregation shall judge between the manslayer and the avenger of blood, in accordance with these rules. And the congregation shall rescue the manslayer from the hand of the avenger of blood, and the congregation shall restore him to his city of refuge to which he had fled, and he shall live in it until the death of the high priest who was anointed with the holy oil. But if the manslayer shall at any time go beyond the boundaries of his city of refuge, to which he fled, and the avenger of blood finds him outside the boundaries of his city of refuge, and the avenger of blood kills the manslayer, he shall not be guilty of blood. For he must remain in his city of refuge until the death of the high priest, but after the death of the high priest the manslayer may return to the land of his possession. And these things shall be for a statute and rule for you throughout your generations in all your dwelling places.

'If anyone kills a person, the murderer shall be put to death on the evidence of witnesses. But no person shall be put to death on the testimony of one witness. Moreover, you shall accept no ransom for the life of a murderer, who is guilty of death, but he shall be put to death. And you shall accept no ransom for him who has fled to his city of refuge that he may return to dwell in the land before the death of the high priest. You shall not pollute the land in which you live, for blood pollutes the land, and no atonement can be made for the land for the blood that is shed in it, except by the blood of the one who shed it. You shall not defile the land in which you live, in the midst of which I dwell, for I the Lord dwell in the midst of the people of Israel.

'The lands that are given to the Levites, the firstborn of Israel, are to be filled with cities of refuge where the wrongfully accused can settle in justice, and where the guilty can settle to await a fair trial and avoid citizens taking things into their own hands.'

There were distinctions made between a murderer and a killer and assignments of justice made in differentiating avengers of blood and their ability to right the wrong from that of judges who were to decide and govern lawful justice. Following, and once again was a system of justice for crime but also for assimilating inheritance to families. God kept His promise to the daughters of Zelophehad (vs. 2). He alloted their inheritance, and also made provisions for those that would try and abuse this system. Those who married others within other tribes were declined their inheritance (vs. 3). God even defined what is and is not marriage. This definition would qualify and disqualify the receiving of such estates. Marriages between mother and son (Lev. 18:7-8) father and daughter (Lev. 18:6; 21:2-3), stepchildren (Lev. 18:8,17), aunts (Lev. 18:12-14), sister and half-sisters (Lev. 18:9; Deut. 27:22), and daughters-in-law (Lev. 18:15), etc. were prohibited. Real laws were defined to protect the way God designs things. God even made sure that a system of pay-back and account reckoning was in place with the rule of Jubilee.

In the final chapters of Numbers God affirms that His land would be a place of newness, but in the same breath He allowed for the injustice and sin that would continue to take place by erecting continual forms of judicial governance. We can see that a continual theme of *incompletion* rings between the lines of the final moments of Numbers. There's something not fully realized here, there's a tension that remains. In some sense Israel was about to tread upon her promise, and even in the land she was to expect that everything would not be perfect. Israel was to admit that she herself was far from perfect, and even awful at best. In Israel stepping into what was promised, she's not admitting that she's arrived, but rather that God had arrived. She was still broken yet slowly being reassembled, but the cloud of God's Lordship was ever complete.

There's something spiritual and eternal that lay ahead of Israel. Israel herself is a symbol, a diorama, and a masterpiece of something far greater. Fast forwarding on into the New Testament allows us to see a glimpse into what this means in Hebrews 10:16-17; "'This is the covenant that I will make with them after those days, declares the Lord I will put my laws on their hearts, and write them on their minds,' then he adds, 'I will remember their sins and their lawless deeds no more.' Where there is forgiveness of these, there is no longer any offering for sin." What's shared in this passage is the completion of the *incomplete* symbol of the Promised Land. God did not want people to merely obey His laws, He wanted them to embody them on their hearts. He did not just want to send wrongdoers to the Levitical first-born cites of refuge, God wanted to send a final priest in the line of the Levites as the firstborn over all creation. All of this was in order that He might become in Himself the city and the tower of refuge that all would run to in order to find safety.

This is why Hebrews continues by saying; "Therefore, brothers, since we have confidence to enter the holy places *by the blood of Jesus* ..." etc. Jesus is both physical fullness and heavenly fullness. He combines all of physical being and spiritual being into one man as the new Israel and the Promised Land. The land and the people were symbols filled with the meaning of Jesus.

Jesus as spoken of in John 1:1, is the word and *seed* that germinated, breathed, inspired, and created the world. The Promised Land is to point to a land in Christ. The leadership structure in Numbers is to allude to a coming kingdom on earth. The cities of refuge were provided to isolate and keep death away from God's territory and allow people to live free of death and receive correct justice; ultimately pointing to the death-free world of God's heavenly country. This heaven-on-earth is to be a place of perfect economy and justice, both where true murders are excluded, but where those who are repentant or who have been falsely accused are allowed in on the merits of grace and forgiveness in the work of Christ. The kingdom is to be a place where all of marriage is culminated into a beautiful union with God.

The Promised Land points to a very real place for the establishing of the household and family of God. A place where heaven meets earth—a Kingdom. This is the tension in the story of Israel. Hebrews 11:39-40 says, "And all these, though commended through their faith, did not receive what was promised, since God had provided something better for us, that apart from us they should not be made perfect." Israel's story is held in tension, and so is all of humanity's story. The tension is found in the shadows. Every single event and providence is a mere shadow of dull gray that tells the story of something very colorful to come. God forms a people and leads them along a journey. We are in this journey. You are in this journey. We sojourn in a land that we long to take control of, and it longs to take control of us. We suffer under the weight of our own miserable leadership and slavery mentality, and God ever-so-benevolently leads and rehabilitates us in stages.

God is growing up His people in the knowledge of His truth, and most times our thinking resembles the same half-hearted, self-entitled, enslaved, whiny, anarchical, idolatrous, and perverted thinking as that of Israel. Israel, and we, are the reason that God had to enter our story. Israel is spoken of as God's son, and they failed. Jesus did not! Christians are spoken of as God's children, only the basis of what Jesus finished on our behalf. Where Israel and we fail to trust God's provision, Jesus trusted even through 40 days in the desert. Where Israel and we fail at the hands of our enemies, and where we are beaten by a culture that listens to prophets that talk like donkeys, Jesus rode triumphantly as King on a donkey to wage war on a cross to defeat all such enemies and prophecies of death.

Jesus is the land, Jesus is Israel, Jesus is the seed, Jesus is the blessing for Israel and all nations, and the reason for Israel's journey. Jesus is the better Moses who leads us into the Promised Land where Moses fell short (Yeshua—meaning God saves), and He now rules and reigns in the hearts of His church. We are His people and He is our God. Jesus' kingdom future, is one that we now await in paradise, while in the meantime we sojourn in the desert as Jesus slowly grows us into people who, in Him, are soon be able to fully serve in His kingdom alongside of Him.

. . .

Conclusion to the Story:

The big idea is that JESUS is LORD! His Lordship is over all, in all, and through all. There is nowhere we can go that is not subject to Christ's control and leadership, even though we may not think it so. Every pain in the world is caused by a rejection of this authority. Every broken home is at some point caused by someone who thinks they know better than Jesus. Without this Jesus, we operate with a slave mentality. We only give into what brings advantage to us, and in the process we feast on dried up shadows, dioramas, and imitations of the real thing. We miss the colors. To come under Christ's leadership is to live life in color as slaves to righteousness not to sin. It's not a life of abstinence and rules, it's a life of freedom, enjoyment, and a kingdom created where we can revel in all that our Creator has made, and do so with the intended purpose for which it is designed. It's a life led in rhythm and relationship, where God gives real boundaries and forms, and allows us to interact with Him as Moses did in prayer. It's a life woven improvisationally through this narrative work of art that God is working in us to paint. Whatever our hand may find, it can be wielded for kingdom causes if we are subject to the King who commands us in how to proceed.

This book started with what appeared to be an oxymoron of a thesis. How can one think that for one to be free, they need to come out of slavery and immediately come underneath authority? It seems preposterous! Unless however, one finds a perfect authority under whom to submit—whose Lordship puts our enjoyment in His glory as a first priority. A King like this we can trust! This is Israel's story! It's the journey of a people brought out of slavery and into a new kingdom of freedom. Now it's your turn.

ENDNOTES

[1] Image taken from http://oneclimbs.com/2011/03/06/sanctuary-vesture-a-brief-overview-and-comparison-via-temple-study/

[2] Taken from http://biblelight.net/KeyofDavid.htm

[3] 1. The turning of water into wine (John 2:1-12), 2. The healing of the royal official's son (John 4:46-54), 3. The healing of the paralytic at the Bethesda pool (John 5:1-17), 4. The feeding of the five thousand (John 6:1-14), 5. The walking on water (John 6:15-25), 6. The healing of the man born blind (John 9:1-41), 7. The raising of Lazarus (John 11:1-46)

[4] Mike Cosper, *Rhythms of Grace* (Wheaton, IL: Crossway, 2013).

[5] See also how the Israelites observed important Feasts and Celebrations, and how they reflected the coming of Christ: In the Spring was Passover (Pesach) Lev. 23:5, in which the Unleavened Bread (*Chang Ha Motzi*) was prepared the morning after (Lev. 23:6). Look at the matzah (unleavened bread) and see that it is striped: "By His stripes we are healed"; pierced: "They shall look upon me whom they've pierced," and pure, without any leaven, as His body was without any sin. And the Passover custom of burying, hiding and then resurrecting the second of three pieces of matzot (the middle

piece), presents the Gospel *(Afikomen)*. There was then the Feast of the First Fruits *(Reshit Katzir)* in Lev. 23:11—representing the fertility of the land—Christ's resurrection—Easter. The Feast of Pentacost *(Shavu'ot)* in Lev. 23:16—marked summer harvest—bread baked with leaven—church comprised of both Jew and Gentile. The Fall Feasts like the Feast of Trumpets *(Yom Teru'ah)*—blowing trumpets—sign of victory. There was Atonement *(Yom Kippur)* in Lev. 23:27 where the blood was poured on the mercy seat—Jesus is our mercy seat (Rom. 3:25—propitiation). And the Feast of Tabernacles (Sukkot) in Lev. 23:34—Where God's shelter and protection of Israel in the Desert was remembered.

www.ingramcontent.com/pod-product-compliance
Lightning Source LLC
Chambersburg PA
CBHW070138100426
42743CB00013B/2752